Successful Business Intelligence

Second Edition

Unlock the Value of BI & Big Data

About the Author

Cindi Howson is the founder of BI Scorecard (www.biscorecard.com), a resource for in-depth BI product reviews, and has more than 20 years of BI and management reporting experience. She advises clients on BI strategy, best practices, and tool selections; writes and blogs for *Information Week*; and is an instructor for The Data Warehousing Institute (TDWI). Prior to founding BI Scorecard, Cindi was a manager at Deloitte & Touche and a BI standards leader for a Fortune 500 company. She has an MBA from Rice University. Contact Cindi at cindihowson@biscorecard.com.

About the Technical Editor

Mark Hammond is a technology writer working in the IT field since 1998 with a focus on business intelligence and data integration. An award-winning journalist, Hammond serves as a contributing analyst to The Data Warehousing Institute and provides services to leading enterprise software companies. He can be reached at mfhammond@comcast.net.

Successful Business Intelligence

Second Edition

Unlock the Value of BI & Big Data

Cindi Howson

New York   Chicago   San Francisco
Athens   London   Madrid   Mexico City
Milan   New Delhi   Singapore   Sydney   Toronto

Cataloging-in-Publication Data is on file with the Library of Congress

McGraw-Hill Education books are available at special quantity discounts to use as premiums and sales promotions, or for use in corporate training programs. To contact a representative, please visit the Contact Us pages at www.mhprofessional.com.

Successful Business Intelligence: Unlock the Value of BI & Big Data, Second Edition

1 2 3 4 5 6 7 8 9 0   DOC DOC   1 0 9 8 7 6 5 4 3

ISBN: 9781265943042
MHID: 1265943042

Sponsoring Editor Wendy Rinaldi	**Copy Editor** Lisa McCoy	**Composition** Fortuitous Publishing Services
Editorial Supervisor Jody McKenzie	**Proofreader** Richard Camp	**Illustration** Fortuitous Publishing Services
Project Manager Howie Severson, Fortuitous Publishing Services	**Indexer** Karin Arrigoni **Production Supervisor** Jean Bodeaux	**Art Director, Cover** Jeff Weeks
Technical Editor Mark Hammond	**Graphic Design** Stephen Space, Space Studios	**Cover Designer** Jeff Weeks
Researcher Meg Johnson		

For Keith

Contents

Preface

Business intelligence consistently rates at the top of companies' investment priorities. Despite its priority, businesspeople routinely complain about information overload on the one hand and the inability to get to relevant data on the other. BI professionals complain organizational issues and limited time and resources prevent them from unleashing the full potential of BI. As a technology, BI usage remains modest, with significant untapped potential.

The first edition of this book was published in late 2007, and there were a couple of "aha" moments that led to the first book. After I spoke at a user conference on the need for a better business–IT partnership, an IT person stopped me to say how inspired he was, that he felt motivated to talk more to the business users and was less intimidated by them. In truth, I hadn't thought anything I said was all that inspirational, and it certainly wasn't new. And yet, I had forgotten how challenging the IT–business relationship can be, particularly for BI, which lies at the crossroads between business and technology. Shortly after, I read Jim Collins's book *Good to Great* (HarperBusiness, 2001) and heard the author speak at a conference. In reading his book about what leads some companies to outperform others, it got me thinking about why some companies succeed with business intelligence and others fail. At the same time, I was judging the TDWI Best Practices awards—offering me previews of some who have delivered big impact—while consulting with companies who were struggling with basic information needs. I continue to see a big disparity in companies who are exploiting BI and big data, and others who are floundering.

While some of the same challenges remain, in 2013, the influences of big data, cloud, mobile, and visual data discovery have had a profound influence on business intelligence. Leading organizations are doing more with less, finding insights faster, and working in a culture where everyone works as a team. I wanted to understand the role that some of these new innovations played in their successes and whether, as the headlines suggested, "big data is the new oil" or just a passing fancy.

My hope for this book, then, is that it is a resource for both business users and the technical experts that implement BI solutions. In order for businesspeople to exploit the value of BI, they must understand its potential. The customer stories in this book are meant as much to inspire as to offer valuable lessons on both the successes and the pitfalls to avoid. These customers illustrate just how much value BI and big data can bring. When BI is left only for the IT experts to champion, it can provide only limited value. The real success comes when people take action on the insights BI provides, whether to improve financial performance, provide best-in-class customer service, increase efficiencies, or make the world a better place.

About Product References

Customers in this book and throughout the industry use a variety of products and technologies in their business intelligence deployments. In describing BI components, I occasionally reference specific vendors and products as a way of providing concrete examples. Such references are not meant to be an exhaustive list of all the products available on the marketplace or an endorsement of specific solutions.

Recommended Audience

This book is recommended reading for

- People who feel their organization is not making the most optimal decisions or who recognize the data they have amassed is not being exploited to its potential
- Executives who sponsor BI initiatives
- BI directors, program managers, and project managers
- Technology experts who are asked to design and implement any aspect of the BI solution
- Anyone involved with a BI project that is struggling to deliver value

This book is intended to provide practical advice on what business intelligence and big data are, what drives the adoption of BI by leading companies, what its components are, and what the technical and organizational issues are that most affect BI's success. This book is not a technical reference on how to architect a solution or implement the software. For suggestions on more technical books, see Appendix B.

Chapter 1 defines business intelligence, its history, the business and technical drivers, and the approach to researching this book. Chapters

2 and 3 define the components of a business intelligence solution, with the data warehouse and an analytic ecosystem on the back end and the BI tools on the front end. Chapters 4 to 13 describe the factors that most contribute to a company's successful use of BI from both a technical and organizational perspective. Chapter 14 offers a glimpse of BI's future, with words of wisdom from leading companies. If you are looking to understand ways BI can help your business, Chapter 1, Chapter 4, Chapter 5, and Chapter 9 should be on your must-read list.

I hope this book will turn your BI and big data initiative into a wild success with big impact!

—Cindi Howson

Acknowledgments

First and foremost, I want to thank the customers who willingly shared their stories and devoted their time so that others embarking on a business intelligence journey can benefit from their insights and avoid the pitfalls. While more and more companies have adopted BI and been successful, the number of companies who are either allowed to talk about their experiences or have the time to share their opinions has gotten smaller. Competition for talent is tight, and in a fierce business environment, secrets to BI success are a competitive advantage. The successful BI companies walk a fine line in sharing their stories to improve the industry, motivate their teams, and attract top talent, while not giving away their competitive advantage. So I thank all of them for their commitment to the industry and to this book. In particular, thank you to Roger Groening, Andrew Dempsey, Mark Carter, Jonathan Rothman, Jim Hill, Jeff Kennedy, and Ed McClellan, who also spearheaded the efforts at each of their companies to allow me to talk to the right people and who have shared their insights and enthusiasm for BI with me for years. Thank you to each of the vendors who have enabled me to meet so many exceptional customers over more than a decade.

Survey data helped support trends and insights, so I thank everyone who participated in the survey and those who helped promote the survey. There seems to be a deluge of industry surveys, and with time a precious and limited resource, I am grateful for each response and tailored comment.

Thank you to Meg Johnson for juggling so many hats, helping me narrow the list of case studies, and researching all my obscure questions.

A number of industry experts have allowed me to include references to their work within this book, all voices who have shaped my thinking and who share a similar goal to help companies make sense of all this stuff: Mike Ferguson, particularly on cloud and big data; Ralph Hughes on agile development; Curt Monash on SMP and MPP; Mark Madsen on the merits of columnar and a strong dose of big data reality; Jonathon Geiger on data governance; Richard Hackathorn on time to value; Jill

Dyche and Phillip Russom on master data; and Colin White, whose talk in Rome on big data years ago was the first time I remotely understood it. Thank you as well to Stephen Few for weaning me off my use of pie charts and first encouraging me to use visual data discovery software years ago to better analyze survey results. I owe my beginnings as an independent analyst to Wayne Eckerson, now of Tech Target, and to TDWI, who has provided me with so many opportunities to teach, to learn, to inspire, and to be inspired. Paul Kautza helps ensure my materials and knowledge stay fresh, and Brenda Williams provides glimpses into the most successful companies, while the faculty and crew provide expertise and camaraderie in what could otherwise be a lonely endeavor.

The journey from concept to book is a long one. To anyone who read my article "Seven Pillars of BI Success," back in 2006, you provided encouragement that the industry needed more insight on how to succeed with BI beyond the technology. Thank you to David Stodder, then the editor at *Intelligent Enterprise* and now director of research at TDWI, for helping me craft a glimpse of what would become this book. The role of a technical editor seems a thankless one, and yet, I am fortunate that Mark Hammond was willing to work with me on this book, challenging me to dig deeper and explain more, when time was short and deadlines passed. I knew Mark by name as the co-author of the book *E-Business Intelligence* (McGraw-Hill, 2000), but never realized he also authored so many fabulous research reports. It was truly a commitment, and I thank him for helping make this book better than I could do on my own! Thank you to my editor, Wendy Rinaldi, for encouraging me now through two books; Howie Severson and Jody McKenzie for making a beautiful and quality finished product; and to Mark Trosino for making sure it reaches more readers! Thank you to Stephen Space, designer extraordinaire, for transforming my stick figures into beautiful artwork and clearer concepts.

Thank you to Keith, ironically one of my first business users who helped me stay focused on the business value, not the technology, and who has been my partner in work and life. Thank you, Megan and Sam, for reminding me that in order to tell people's stories and inspire others, you have to laugh along the way and dream big dreams. Thank you to my father, who taught me a strong work ethic, the importance of entertaining while informing, and always doing my best. May he rest in peace.

BI and Big Data from the Business Side

Just as the eyes are the windows to the soul, business intelligence is a window to the dynamics of a business. It reveals the performance, operational efficiencies, and untapped opportunities. *Business intelligence* (BI) is a set of technologies and processes that allow people at all levels of an organization to access and analyze data. Without people to interpret the information and act on it, business intelligence achieves nothing. For this reason, business intelligence is less about technology than about culture, creativity, and whether people view data as a critical asset. Technology enables business intelligence and analytics, but sometimes, too great a focus on technology can sabotage business intelligence initiatives. It is the people who will most make your BI efforts a wild success or an utter failure.

Business Intelligence by Other Names

Business intelligence means different things to different people. To one businessperson, business intelligence means market research, something I would call "competitive intelligence." To another person, "reporting" may be a better term, even though business intelligence goes well beyond accessing a static report. "Reporting" and "analysis" are terms frequently used to describe business intelligence. Others will use terms such as "business analytics" or "decision support," both with varying degrees of appropriateness. In talking to a leader in the public sector, she said most of her stakeholders shy away from the term "business intelligence" because with the global financial crisis largely precipitated by Wall Street, "business" has become a tainted word. Instead, she prefers to refer to initiatives in this area simply as "data."

How these terms differ matters very little unless you are trying to compare market shares for different technologies. What matters more is to use the terminology that is most familiar to intended users and that has a positive connotation. No matter which terminology you use, keep the ultimate value of business intelligence in mind:

> Business intelligence allows people at all levels of an organization to access, interact with, and analyze data to manage the business, improve performance, discover opportunities, and operate efficiently.

BI

The acronym for business intelligence is BI, and as information technology (IT) people like to use a plethora of acronyms, BI is one more that can sometimes cause confusion. BI as in "business intelligence" is not to be confused with "business investments" (although BI is something the business may invest in), "business insight" (although it is something BI may provide), or "bodily injury" (if you are using BI in the context of insurance). Even within the BI industry, confusion abounds as some people use BI to refer to the whole technical architecture (including the data warehouse, described in Chapter 2) as well as the user front-end tools (described in Chapter 3). Others think of BI as referring only to the front-end tools.

Business Analytics

Business analytics as a terminology has gained in popularity in recent years, perhaps because analytics sounds so much more exciting than simply intelligence. In fact, a few vendors and consultants (usually who are trying to sell you something new), will try to pigeon-hole BI as being only historical and simplistic reporting. It's not. Most people will differentiate BI with "advanced analytics" to refer to statistical analysis and predictive modeling. But here, too, some general BI solutions and consultants will use the term "business analytics," regardless if it includes predictive analytics or not.

I confess, I was willing to jump on this bandwagon too, suggesting to the publisher that we rename the book *Successful Business Analytics,* but it seems designating a book a second edition prohibits changing the main title, and having a second edition anything is more important in reaching the right readers. Let's hope so!

Big Data

Some have referred to data as the new oil in the 21st century. Those who mine it well will hit pay dirt, and those who don't will be sitting on wells of untapped potential, data wastelands. Others are a bit more wary, thinking the whole concept of big data is like the gold rush of the 1840s in which people invested and lost fortunes. I've heard one pundit decry the comparison of big data to oil, as oil has gotten us into trouble on multiple fronts, whether global warming or wars in the Middle East or disaster in the Gulf Coast. Big data, like oil, can provide enormous benefit, yet there will be risks to privacy and security, as well as dangers not yet identified.

The term "big data" was first used by a computer scientist at Silicon Graphics in the mid-1990s.[1] A few tech industry magazines began using the term in 2008 to refer to larger data volumes, generally in the petabyte range, but it was really 2012 when "big data" hit the mainstream. Stories on big data were front and center in everyday news outlets, including the *New York Times,* the *Washington Post,* the *Economist, Forbes,* and the *World Economic Forum.* I am seeing the term big data increasingly being used for anything data related, even when it's small. I suspect that with its appearance in mainstream media, big data as a term will eventually replace BI and business analytics in the general lexicon. However, within the technology profession, big data is distinct and has three main characteristics that differentiate it from general BI: volume, velocity, and variety.

- **Volume**   While many traditional BI deployments have gigabytes and terabytes of data, big data runs in the petabytes.
- **Velocity**   Early data warehouses may have been updated weekly and evolved to daily updates. With big data, both the velocity of new incoming data and the pace of decision-making have led to new technologies to handle the speed of incoming data. Machine-generated data from smart meters, RFID (radio frequency identification) devices, web logs on e-commerce sites, and social data, for example, show the velocity of new data.
- **Variety**   Much of BI's early days related to analyzing data from transaction systems. As new types of data have been digitized, there is a greater variety of content to analyze, such as textual data in the form of tweets, social comments, blogs, medical record notes, photos and images, and video.

Gartner research analyst Doug Laney first laid out the 3Vs of big data in the late 1990s (then at Meta Group) that are now part of the big data lexicon.[2] With these characteristics in mind, it's not surprising that some of the initial big data applications were developed in and used by startup companies such as Yahoo!, Google, and Facebook. Early adopters of big data technologies included the gaming industry and electronic commerce. However, we are also seeing uses in the medical community to find cures for diseases. Terror and crime prevention also use big data, which played a role in identifying the Boston Marathon terrorists as the FBI sifted through millions of photos, pressure cooker purchases, and digitized clues.

Just as "business analytics" has become a popular term, with "big data" becoming a mainstream term, it is sometimes used more broadly than it should be. As one BI director lamented about the recent hype, "Big data is not our challenge. It's still the complexity of the data." There also have been some "big data" implementations on Hadoop I've reviewed that measure only in the gigabytes.

What Business Intelligence Is Not

A data warehouse may or may not be a component of your business intelligence architecture (see Chapter 2), but a data warehouse is not synonymous with business intelligence. In fact, even if you have a data warehouse, you can only say your company is using business intelligence once you put some tools in the hands of the users to transform data into useful information.

How Business Intelligence Provides Value

Business intelligence cuts across all functions and all industries. BI touches everyone in a company and beyond to customers, suppliers, and with public data, to citizens. As stated earlier, though, business intelligence can only provide value when it is used effectively by people. There is a correlation between the *effective* use of business intelligence and company performance.[3,4] However, simply having better *access* to data does not improve performance;[5] the difference is in what companies *do* with the data.

BI for Management and Control

In its most basic sense, business intelligence provides managers information to know what's going on in the business. Without business intelligence, managers may talk about how they are "flying blind" with no insight until quarterly financial numbers are published. With business intelligence, information is accessible on a timelier and more flexible basis to provide a view of

- Sales in various regions and by various product lines
- Expenses compared to budget
- Warehouse inventory for a particular product or raw materials
- Sales pipeline versus forecast

When any particular metric is not where it should be, business intelligence allows users to explore the underlying details to determine why metrics are off target and to take action to improve the situation. In the past, if managers monitored the business via paper-based reports or a fixed screen in a transaction system, they had no flexibility to explore *why* the business was operating a certain way. For example, many companies use BI to monitor expenses to ensure costs do not exceed budgets. Rather than waiting until the close of the quarter to discover that excessive expenses have reduced profitability, timely access to expense data allows managers first to identify which business unit is over budget and then to take immediate steps to reduce overtime pay or travel expenses, or to defer purchases, for example.

BI for Improving Performance

Used effectively, business intelligence allows organizations to improve performance. Business performance is measured by a number of financial indicators, such as revenue, margin, profitability, cost to serve, and so on. In marketing, performance gains may be achieved by improving response rates for particular campaigns by identifying characteristics of more responsive customers. Eliminating ineffective campaigns saves companies millions of dollars each year. Business intelligence allows companies to boost revenues by cross-selling products to existing customers. Accounting personnel may use BI to reduce the aging of accounts receivable by identifying late-paying customers. In manufacturing, BI can facilitate a gap analysis to understand why certain plants operate more efficiently than others.

In all these instances, accessing data is a necessary first step. However, improving performance also requires people's interaction to analyze the data and to determine the actions that will bring about improvement. Taking action on findings should not be assumed. People have political, cultural, and financial reasons for not taking the next step. To leverage business intelligence to improve performance, you need to consider all these issues. A company may implement a BI solution that provides intuitive access to data. If this data access is not leveraged for decision-making and acted upon, then BI has done nothing to improve performance. The reverse is also true—when BI is used in a company without a sound business strategy, performance will not improve. Incorrect alignment of incentives can also sabotage desired performance improvement.

> A key sign of successful business intelligence is the degree to which it impacts business performance, linking insight to action.

Measuring the business impact of business intelligence can be difficult, as improvements in performance are attributable to factors beyond business intelligence. How to measure business intelligence and big data success is discussed in Chapter 4.

Operational BI

While early business intelligence deployments focused more on strategic decisions and performance, BI increasingly plays a critical role in the daily operations of a company. In this regard, accessing detailed data and reviewing information may be necessary to complete an operational task. For example, as part of accepting a new order, a customer service representative may first check available inventory. Such an inventory report may be a standard report developed within an order entry system, or it may come from a BI solution, whether stand-alone or embedded in the order entry application. Other examples of operational BI include the following:

- Travel agents and airlines use operational BI to monitor flight delays so they can proactively reaccommodate passengers with connections.
- Hospitals and emergency rooms use business intelligence to determine optimum staffing levels during peak periods.
- Restaurants use BI to estimate the wait time for a table based on the number of current patrons and average length to dine.
- Walt Disney World's Magic Kingdom uses business intelligence for its service that issues park visitors FastPass tickets to avoid standing in long lines for rides.[6] The business intelligence tools monitor waiting

times at the most popular rides to balance the number of tickets issued in given periods throughout the day.

- Call centers use BI to monitor call volume and hold times.
- Distributors and supply chain personnel use BI to find the most optimal delivery route and methods. For example, FreshDirect, a supermarket chain in the New York metro area, uses dashboards to track truck routes and determine aging of produce and alternate routes in severe traffic situations, such as when the president is in town.[7]

Operational business intelligence most differs from BI for management and control purposes in both the level of detail required and in the timeliness of the data. Operational BI may involve accessing a transaction system directly or through a data warehouse (see Chapter 2) that is updated in near real time multiple times throughout the day. Business intelligence for management and control purposes may also be in near real time, but can also be based on weekly or monthly data. The role that operational BI plays in decision-making and how successful BI companies are using it is discussed further in the section "Right-Time Data" in Chapter 8.

BI for Process Improvement

The operations of a business are made up of dozens of individual processes. BI may support the decisions individuals make in every step of a process. It also may be used to help streamline a process by measuring how long subprocesses take and identifying areas for improvement. For example, manufacturing-to-shipment is one process. In the absence of business intelligence, a company may only realize there is a problem when a customer complains: "My order is late" or "I can get that product faster from your competitor." By analyzing the inputs, the time, and the outputs for each step of the process, BI can help identify the process bottlenecks.

- Mail-order companies monitor the number of packages prepared by hour and day. Any changes in these metrics may lead to a process review to see how the workflow can be optimized.
- At an oil and gas company, cash flow was problematic. A review of the process showed that gas was being delivered to customers on time, but an invoice was only sent a week later. Reducing the time in the delivery-to-invoice process helped the company solve cash-flow problems. Business intelligence tools allowed the company to identify the

problem and then to ensure compliance with a new rule of invoicing within one day of delivery.

- Boeing uses near-real-time dashboards to track assembly of its 787 Dreamliners. The dashboards are visual representations of key assembly, shop order instance, status and critical production constraints, emergent process documents, and part shortages of each production aircraft.[8]

BI to Improve Customer Service

The quality of customer service eventually manifests itself in the financials of a company. Business intelligence can help companies deliver high customer service levels by providing timely order processing, loan approvals, problem handling, and so on. For example:

- Whirlpool uses business intelligence to monitor its warranty program to understand root causes for warranty problems and improve customer satisfaction with its products.[9]
- United Airlines uses business intelligence to monitor how full business-class cabins are and to ensure its most valued customers receive complimentary upgrades when space permits.[10]
- FlightStats provides real-time travel information on delays so that if a passenger is en route and might miss a connecting flight, the travel agent can automatically rebook them.
- Netflix tracks how often a customer gets their first-choice DVD.[11]

BI to Make the World Better

Business intelligence for management and control and performance improvement gets a fair amount of media attention. An increasingly important value in business intelligence, though, is in empowering people to improve the world.

- Police departments in Richmond, Virginia,[12] Charlotte, North Carolina,[13] and Humberside, England,[14] for example, have used business intelligence to help police officers respond better to call-outs and to reduce crime rates.
- School systems use business intelligence to understand the effects and trends in student test results and grades based on gender, attendance rates, and teaching methods.
- A number of hospitals, including Cleveland Clinic,[15] Barnes-Jewish Hospital in Missouri,[16] Seattle Children's Hospital, and many in

Northern New Jersey operated by Emergency Medical Associates, use business intelligence to reduce patient wait times, improve care, and manage costs.[17]

- The Austin, Texas, fire department uses dashboards to balance budget constraints while ensuring safety of its firefighters and citizens by monitoring response times to emergency calls.[18]
- Second Harvest Food Bank of Florida uses BI to track food donations, pantry levels, and community needs.[19]
- Medtronic, maker of medical devices such as pacemakers, uses BI to measure and monitor how its devices are improving the lives of its customers. Currently, every three seconds a person's life is saved or improved by a Medtronic device.[20]
- At the University of Ontario Institute of Technology, greater collection of streaming data in neonatal intensive care units allows real-time data on vital signs to save lives and to understand the interaction of infection, medication, and conditions like sleep apnea or irregular heartbeats.[21]

BI in Sports, Politics, and Everyday Life

The book and subsequent movie *Moneyball* put a face to the concept of using data to gain a competitive advantage. At its heart is the idea of doing more with less. Without the same budget for salaries as the New York Yankees and Boston Red Sox, Oakland A's General Manager Billy Beane turned to deep data analysis to evaluate players and assemble the best possible team. Beane's approach, based on a statistical baseball practice known as sabremetrics, strives to assess talent by a number of metrics more complex than the high-level measures such as batting average, home runs, and earned run average. This pioneering approach challenged old-school thinking in which baseball executives and coaches relied on gut feel and surface metrics to put together a team by free-agent signings, trades, and call-ups of minor leaguers. As depicted in the film *Moneyball,* when the new approach seems to have the team continue on its losing streak, Beane's statistical colleague replies, "We don't have enough data... the sample size is too small." Frankly, as a BI practitioner, I would have caved at that point, no matter the sample size. It's a great scene that reflects the importance of staying the course, learning from mistakes, and trusting facts. Beane and the statistician proved they were right, statistically speaking. Beane was an early adopter of mining the rich troves of statistical data that's collected in major league baseball data to put together the best possible team, but such data analysis is increasingly common in all forms of sports.

For example, the NFL team the San Francisco 49ers announced it would be using iPads to collect and compare player data in real-time while scouters evaluate players at college visits. In European soccer, Chelsea Football club is using player data and statistics in its recruiting process.[22]

The value of big data is in its analysis, but it starts with the ability to collect more data, more rapidly. To that end, many runners now track their pacing and run data with an iPod armband and specialized wristwatches. Both Nike and Under Armour, for example, are developing clothing that captures athlete performance data.

Nate Silver, meanwhile, has become a kind of oracle for politics, sports, and gambling. He initially developed and sold a forecasting model to Baseball Prospectus to analyze and predict player performance.[23] In the 2008 presidential race, he correctly predicted the outcome for 49 out of 50 states, giving him mainstream recognition. In the 2012 presidential race, he correctly predicted the presidential race for all 50 states. ESPN acquired Silver's blog, FiveThirtyEight, from the *New York Times*.[24]

The Open Government Initiative set out by President Obama in 2008 required that the chief technology officer (CTO) and chief information officer (CIO) of the United States publish a dashboard that showed citizens the progress toward openness by each major federal agency. As part of that effort, more and more public data has been made directly accessible to citizens. While the raw data is often now available, I would argue that still so much more can be done to make it *useful*. Media outlets have been the first line in presenting public data in a more consumable form. A number of states in the United States have open data initiatives, allowing citizens to track everything from education progress to health patterns, crime rates, and economic issues.

BI for Discovering New Business Opportunities

Business intelligence helps businesses assess and uncover new business opportunities by exploring data and testing theories. For example:

- Companies use data to understand the value proposition of pursuing joint ventures and mergers and acquisitions.
- A hospitality company uses business intelligence to explore hotel capacity rates as a way of developing the time-share business.

The Business Intelligence Market

With business intelligence providing significant benefits across so many industries and all business functions, it's not surprising that BI has bubbled to the top of many companies' IT investment priorities. Many analyst firms and surveys cite BI as the number one or number two IT investment priority. From a market perspective, the business intelligence market (which includes the data warehouse platforms discussed in Chapter 2 and the front-end tools discussed in Chapter 3) is a $34.9 billion market, according to analyst firm IDC.[25] Its growth rate for 2012 was 8.7 percent, a slowing down from 15% growth in 2011 and what had been double digits for many years. Even so, considering the global economic downturn and other information technology markets whose growth has been anemic, BI remains a hot software segment.

As a set of technologies, business intelligence emerged in the early 1990s. Of course, decision-making processes existed long before the information technology to support them. Historically, businesses could rely more on gut-feel decisions because they may have been closer to their customers and the products. The cost to support decisions with facts was high and usually involved gathering data manually. More recently, business and technology forces have converged to make business intelligence mission-critical and an essential part of doing business.

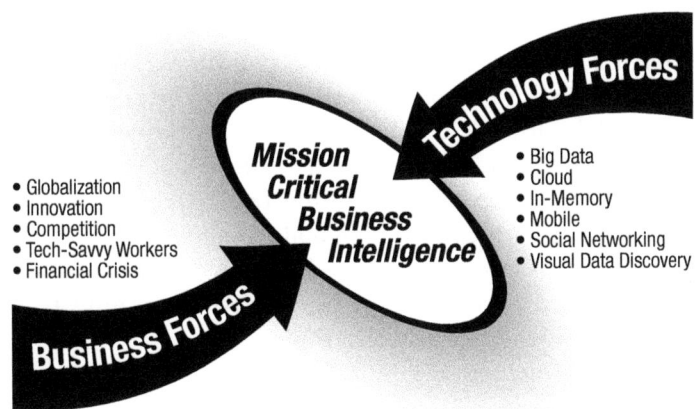

Business Forces Driving BI

The business landscape has changed dramatically in the last 20 years. Many businesses now operate and compete on a global basis with 24/7 operations. The wealth of information at consumers' and businesses' fingertips puts greater pressure on pricing and makes customer churn a constant threat across industries. The pace of change is rapid. Companies compete on time-to-market and product innovations at a frenetic pace. With mobile phone apps, customers can be served up loyalty coupons the moment they enter a store. And if your store fails to have the best price or the right product on hand, comparison shopping is done in real time on the same device.

With the global financial crisis and numerous accounting scandals, shareholders demanded more transparency and accountability. The Sarbanes-Oxley Act of 2002 makes inaccurate financial reporting a criminal offense.

> Businesses can't afford not to know what's going on, internally and externally, and in levels of detail never before imagined or required.

Shift Within the Workforce

Changing workforce demographics also play a role in the growing use of business intelligence. A sizeable portion of senior managers did not grow up with computers. Technology for these people was once viewed with a wary eye. Giving workers too much access to information was often perceived as a threat to power. Data was something to be hoarded. Contrast that with schoolchildren today who learn the value of data analysis early by graphing demographics and sales data in spreadsheets to identify trends. College graduates newly entering the workforce grew up in a time when the Internet was becoming mainstream. They have never not had immediate access to data. Data analysis and business intelligence is increasingly standard curriculum in many MBA programs. Technology literacy is assumed, whether at work or play.

Social networking, initially embraced by generation Y, has raised people's expectations for self-assembled work teams and collaboration. Send someone a picture? Click! Share an article? Click. Contrast the immediacy of Facebook and Twitter with access to corporate data that usually involves applying for security, getting permission from the data owner, and so on. The next generation of workers is not accustomed to barriers to knowledge. This rise of social networking in the consumer

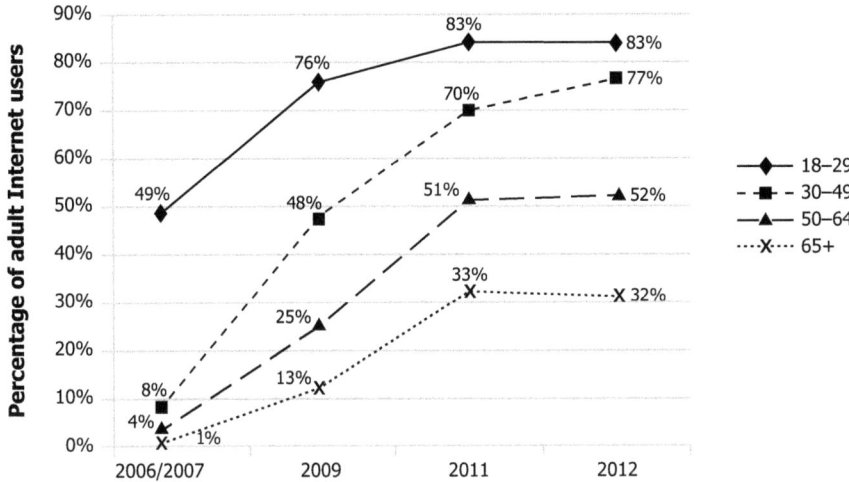

Figure 1-1   Use of social networking by generation

world is influencing the enterprise with a range of new applications geared toward the social enterprise.

Figure 1-1 shows the growing usage of social networking by age group, according to the Pew Research Center.[26] Notice that for workers under the age of 29, adoption is highest. More than 77 percent of workers under the age of 50 use social networking.

Technology Changes Enabling BI

Rapid change in technology has been one driver of this frenetic pace of business change; it also has enabled business intelligence for everyone—all employees in a company, as well as external stakeholders—not just information technology experts, programmers, and power users. Figure 1-2 shows how technology and BI tools have changed over time to extend the reach of business intelligence.

There is one crucial aspect of extending the reach of business intelligence that has nothing to do with technology, and that is relevance. Understanding what information someone needs to do a job or to complete a task is what makes business intelligence *relevant* to that person. Much of business intelligence thus far has been relevant to power users and senior managers but not to frontline workers, customers, and suppliers.

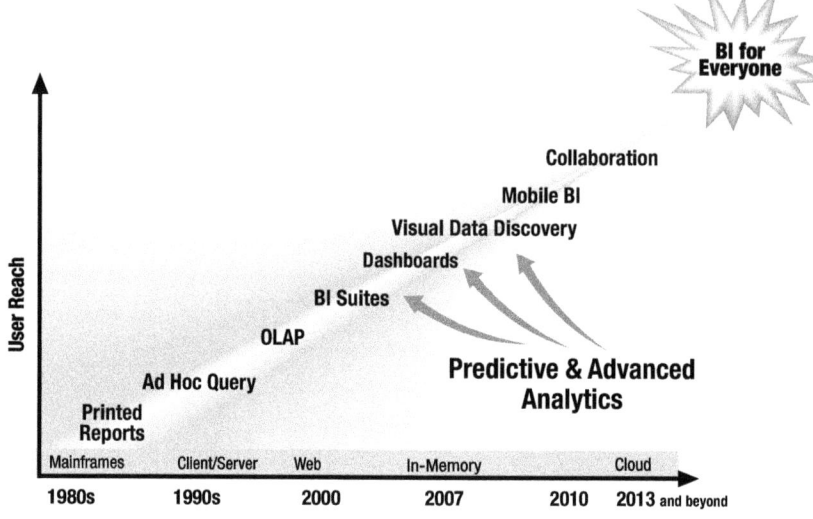

Figure 1-2   Evolution of BI technology

Data Explosion Contributes to Information Overload   The volume of digital data has exploded. What once was handwritten or typed onto a piece of paper to process an order is now entered into a system with increasing detail. In 1990, only 1,000 terabytes (TB) of disk storage was sold worldwide. In 2012, an estimated 2.8 zettabytes (ZB) of digital information was created . . . the equivalent of 2.7 trillion GB (for the zero-challenged like myself, that's 12 zeros), according to IDC estimates.[27,28] Digitizing text, images, and video is not enough. That information also needs to be tagged and structured in a way that it can be used in analysis. Although we are capturing and storing vast volumes of information, only a small portion of data is ready for analysis.

The average manager spends two hours a day simply looking for data, and half of the information found is later determined to be useless.[29]

> If you feel like you are drowning in information, it's because you are. You have to manage the data deluge and focus on a fast time to insight for optimum business value.

While data has gotten bigger, ensuring a fast time to insight has gotten harder. Researchers at one university have noted that when decision-makers are presented with more data, decision-making is slowed.[30] We want to make a perfect decision and to be sure we have assessed every relevant input.

When business intelligence is deployed effectively, all that data becomes a strategic asset to be exploited. The proverbial needle in the haystack may be the single insight about a customer that locks in their loyalty. Or it may be the secret to lowering production costs.

At the Speed of Thought   It might seem that with the explosion of data, accessing more data would get slower. Yet computer processing power and addressable memory have increased to the point that accessing large volumes of data can now be done at the speed of thought. Twenty years ago, you might have waited a month for a complex, printed report that ran on a mainframe computer for days. Ten years ago, that same report might have taken hours, a marginal improvement. Today, the same report may run in subseconds on a purpose-built business intelligence appliance and be delivered to a smartphone. The rise of in-memory computing as an analytic platform is discussed in Chapter 2.

Cloud and Web-Based BI   Web-based business intelligence allows tools to be deployed across corporate intranets and extranets to thousands of employees and external customers in a matter of hours. With the client/server computing of the early 1990s, it took days to install and configure PCs for just a handful of users. The Web has simultaneously broadened the reach of BI while allowing IT to lower the cost of ownership of BI. The cloud has further allowed BI teams to spin up new data centers and application servers in a matter of hours. The cloud as an infrastructure and approach for applications such as Salesforce.com has shown that not all enterprise software needs to be installed on-premise. In the BI world, cloud is still in its infancy, but showing signs of momentum.

BI Industry Consolidation   In 2007, Oracle acquired Hyperion, best known at the time for its performance management software and Essbase online analytical processing (OLAP) technology (defined in Chapter 3). This marked the beginning of a period of fierce industry consolidation, later followed by SAP's acquisition of Business Objects and IBM's of Cognos, both completed in early 2008. Industry consolidation raised both the level of awareness and conversations about business intelligence. What once may have been treated as optional and departmental was now viewed as part of the overall company infrastructure and as much more strategic. With larger-scale deployments and increasing data volumes, the analytic appliance market segment also went through a period of consolidation in 2010 with EMC acquiring Greenplum, IBM acquiring Netezza, Teradata acquiring AsterData, and HP acquiring Vertica.

Evolution of BI Platforms and Tools   BI platforms include multiple front-end components, such as business query tools, dashboards, and visual data discovery (discussed in Chapter 3). These components are optimized for different users' needs and usage scenarios. Previously, companies had to buy these multiple modules from separate vendors. Interoperability was nonexistent, and the cost to deploy was high. As a single vendor now offers a full platform or suite—either from innovation or acquisition—the components are integrated from an infrastructure point of view. With broader capabilities on an integrated platform, business intelligence can reach more users based on their unique requirements. As BI platforms have gotten broader in their scope and capabilities, they are more often managed and owned by a central IT or a central BI team. This has sometimes made BI enhancements and improvements slow.

Somewhat in response to slow BI deliverables, visual data discovery tools have rapidly become synonymous with self-service BI and business agility. Their rapid growth has also been in part due to greater scalability of in-memory computing. This market segment is expected to grow at three times the pace of the overall BI market as illustrated by specialty vendors such as QlikTech and Tableau Software. In 2012, most BI platform vendors added visual data discovery to their tool portfolios.

Visual data discovery tools have reinvigorated and reengaged disillusioned business users who were frustrated by slow and monolithic solutions, but I can't help but think this is simply the BI pendulum swinging between line-of-business–led BI versus centralized, corporate BI. In the mid-1990s, much of the excitement about OLAP technologies, particularly Essbase (now Oracle) and Cognos PowerPlay (now IBM) was about that business unit autonomy. Users didn't have to go to IT to create a report; instead, they could load all that data into a cube and explore the information via a graphical user interface. When success grew like wildfire, IT was asked to support these OLAP deployments, which were forced to evolve to become more enterprise grade. That enterprise grade led to greater complexity and slower delivery times. Will the same happen with visual data discovery tools? Time will tell, but for now, I am hoping this generation of technology will strike that happy medium: for users to be agile and autonomous, with just enough control.

Mobile BI   The wild success of the Apple iPad should serve as an important lesson for all BI evangelists: Nobody asked for a tablet computer. Instead, Apple identified some latent needs and an opportunity to bridge the portability and utility gap between a laptop and a smartphone. Some of the most successful BI applications have not been from a strict requirements document. Instead, they've been inspired from someone who believed in the value of data and saw a problem that BI could solve.

The Apple iPad was first released in June 2010. The iPad 3 was released in March 2012, selling three million units in three days, one of the most successful technology launches in the industry. It's being blamed for threatening the likes of such established companies as Dell, HP, and even Microsoft, as global PC shipments have declined. By 2014, analysts estimate that sales of tablet computers will be only 14 percent lower than that of personal computers.[31]

The iPad's influence in the BI space was initially with managers and executives. Portable dashboards, touch-enabled and simply beautiful on this new device, have re-engaged executives who have long sought an easier, more engaging BI interface. Vendors have scrambled to improve support for tablets, and the industry is once again debating the best technology approach: native applications or HTML5. Anyone who bet on Adobe Flash or BlackBerry has suffered the consequences of changing technology and leadership. As the adoption of tablets has expanded beyond early adopters, it's enabled new classes of BI users who are mobile workers, particularly field sellers, technicians, and delivery personnel.

Extending BI and information to mobile workers and traveling executives has only further accelerated the pace of business as people are always connected, 24 hours a day, seven days a week.

Open Source Open-source software is software whose source code is made publicly available for others to extend and distribute.[32] The use of open-source software can both lower a company's cost of software, because a company is not paying a vendor for a license, and at the same time can speed innovation as the public enhances the software. Open source in the BI world has given rise to new companies such as Jaspersoft, Pentaho, and Talend, but it has also permeated many BI platforms. For example, the open-source database MySQL is now used as a BI repository for several vendors. The open-source search technology Lucene is leveraged in many BI vendors' search engines. And in the big data software segment, Hadoop is the leading open-source big data project.

Social Networking The data generated by social networking tools, whether Facebook, Twitter, or YouTube, has brought new data sources to be analyzed and contributed to the growth of big data. Furthermore, it's changed the expectations for how people want to work in a collaborative way. BI user interfaces have been influenced by social networking, bringing collaboration features into the BI platform.

Battle Scars

Business intelligence is a catalyst for change. Anyone with a vested interest in preserving the status quo may not welcome a business intelligence initiative. Expect some battle scars. One CIO described his company's business intelligence initiative as an emotional process to get through, but necessary to execute the business's vision. Those who keep the value of business intelligence and the greater good of the company always in their vision will ultimately succeed.

Some of the BI battle scars include the following:

- Power struggles between IT and the business when either loses areas of control or disagrees on the scope and approach

- Jobs eliminated when custom report developers were no longer needed
- A marketing manager fired when a company realized just how badly the manager was performing campaign management
- Software and technology that does not always work as expected, and vendors who merge, get acquired, or change strategy in ways that affect your BI deployment

The Research

As a consultant and industry analyst, I did not want only my own experiences, opinions, and customers to be the primary influence on identifying those aspects that most enable organizations to unleash the full potential of BI and big data. Instead, I wanted these lessons to come from a larger sample of visionary companies and survey respondents. The research for this book then had four main components: a survey, in-depth case studies, a review of literature on award winners and early adopters of big data, and my own insights. In addition to consulting on this topic, I have judged The Data Warehousing Institute (TDWI) Best Practices awards for multiple years and teach a course on the topic at their conferences.

The Successful BI Survey

The Successful BI survey was conducted in June through September 2012, with 634 qualified respondents. Survey demographics are included in Appendix A. The survey was promoted through TDWI newsletters and articles, *Information Week* newsletters, BI Scorecard newsletters, and social media.

Survey Demographics   There were 634 qualified responses, from a mixture of large companies (36 percent of respondents) with annual revenues greater than $1 billion, medium-sized companies (27 percent), and small businesses (26 percent).

The majority of survey responses were from the United States (67 percent), followed by Europe (14 percent), Asia/Pacific (10 percent), and Canada (3 percent).

In terms of functional area, the largest percentage of survey respondents came from corporate IT (43 percent), with responses from a mixture of other functional areas. When asked to describe their role within the company, 24 percent described themselves as a hybrid business/IT person, and another 13 percent were business users.

Survey respondents came from a mix of industries.

The Successful BI Case Studies

Surveys are an ideal method for providing statistical information on trends and insights for explicit questions. However, if the survey fails to pose a question or provide a ranking option as to something that contributed to a success or failure, such omissions can mask the true drivers of success. As a way of unearthing these drivers, I scanned the market for companies consistently recognized for their business intelligence initiatives and honored by magazines, industry analysts, and software vendors. Such industry recognition, though, is often a self-selecting process: If a company does not submit an application or call for presentation, analyst firms and magazines are not aware of their achievements. As a way of addressing this limitation, I looked through years of notes from the dozens of industry conferences I attend each year for companies who had wowed me with their stories. I also investigated companies who were recognized for their sustained business value in books and lists such as *Good to Great* and *Fortune*'s fastest-growing companies to understand what role business intelligence played in their company's success. As big data is a theme to the second edition of this book, I looked for companies that were investigating and deploying new technologies in this area.

For in-depth case studies, I pruned the list to a cross-section of industries, company sizes, BI applications, and technology used. The final list of companies highlighted in depth in this book are leaders in business intelligence whose BI initiative has had a significant impact on business performance and who could speak officially about their experiences. Throughout the book, I refer collectively to this final group as the "Successful BI Case Studies." It is a term that some are uncomfortable with; they argue they have not achieved all that is possible. Several, in fact, purposely elect not to apply for any industry awards for this reason. Some of the case studies may not be award winners, but I have included them because of their unique stories and the profound impact BI has had on their companies.

- **1-800 CONTACTS** The company won TDWI's Best Practices Award for BI on a Limited Budget, demonstrating that BI does not have to be expensive. While many companies start with BI in finance and marketing, 1-800 CONTACTS began their BI efforts with front-line workers in their call centers. 1-800 CONTACTS was profiled in the first edition of the book and was since acquired by WellPoint, a health benefits company.

- **Constant Contact**   As a small business owner, I have been using Constant Contact for email marketing for ten years. The company has experienced rapid growth and now handles email marketing for more than 500,000 businesses. Their initial product of email marketing has expanded to any tool that facilitates customer engagement including social networking, event management, and digital storefronts. Their use of BI has evolved too to include self service, an analytic appliance, and Hadoop with the goal of improving the time to insight.
- **The Dow Chemical Company**   While Dow has received some vendor recognition awards, they are quite humble and quiet about their BI achievements. It's rare to hear them speak at an industry conference. I began my career in business intelligence at Dow, and while I have been privileged to work with a number of visionary customers throughout my consulting career, I continue to refer back to some of the best practices garnered from Dow's business intelligence project. Dow was profiled in the first edition of the book, and since that time has gone through another major acquisition of Rohm & Haas and is on its next-generation BI architecture.
- **Emergency Medicine BI (EMBI)**   Emergency Medicine BI is an evolution from a project that started at Emergency Medical Associates (EMA). This company provides dashboards to emergency room physicians, nurses, and administrators to improve patient care, manage wait times, and control costs.
- **FlightStats**   This company was profiled in the first edition of the book when it was in its early stages of its business intelligence journey. Having demonstrated success with internal customers, they now have a large scale solution for consumers leveraging big data, open source, and mobile. FlightStats is a unique company whose entire business model is based on business intelligence.
- **Learning Circle**   Learning Circle helps school districts and communities analyze data to improve student outcomes. I heard representatives from Nationwide Insurance, who sponsored the initiative that evolved to an independent nonprofit organization, speak at an Information Builders conference several years ago, with a lofty vision of improving inner-city high school graduation rates, then at 50 percent. As a parent and believer in the value of education, their vision and journey inspired me. The initial project has expanded to other school districts and communities and is a clear case of BI making the world a better place.

- **Macy's** I confess, I don't like to shop. Oh, I love gorgeous clothes all right, but the process of shopping is not my idea of fun. Call me a female anomaly or just plain busy! This retailer caught my attention at a Tableau user conference, with some innovative analysis of big data and social data. This company also most reflects that investments in BI and, in particular big data, sometimes require a leap of faith.
- **Medtronic** Medtronic is the world's largest medical device manufacturer. I first met BI team members back in 2008 when they were evaluating visual data discovery tools to complement their BI platform. Then in 2012, during an SAP Sapphire keynote, Medtronic's early adoption of in-memory and text analytics was mentioned as a way of mining data that previously had been inaccessible. Few companies are able to access and analyze what some refer to as "dark data," data that is collected but not structured in a way that allows for analysis. Medtronic is ahead of the industry in its efforts to do so.
- **Netflix** Movie watching has never been more cutthroat, with more choices for DVD viewing and streaming of movies, TV shows, and now Netflix-original content. I first met Netflix at a TDWI chapter meeting and at several MicroStrategy conferences. As content viewing has moved from disc to streaming, their use of the cloud to deliver content is bleeding edge.
- **Norway Post** I was honored to meet Norway Post at Hyperion's 2005 user conference. The story of their transformation from a public entity, with both terrible financial performance and poor customer service, to a private postal service with stellar performance is at times equally painful and inspiring. Just how bad it was and how far it has come serves as a lesson that no matter how conservative a company or the industry in which you operate, having a solid business intelligence platform and performance oriented culture can lead to incredible success. This case study was in the book's first edition. As many of the original BI team members have moved on, I have made only minor updates to this case study.

    To gather these stories, I relied on open-ended questions as to how successful they considered their business intelligence initiative, how much it contributed to business performance, and to what they attributed their ultimate success and interim failures. In studying these companies, I asked to speak to the usual suspects—BI program managers, sponsors, and users—but in addition, I asked to speak to the skeptics who did not believe in the value of business intelligence or who resisted using the solution internally. What would it take for them to use business intelligence? Finally, while all the companies could cite measurable business benefits from the use of business intelligence, we analyzed how and if these business benefits were reflected in various performance measures such as financial reports, or in the case of Learning Circle, state published school report cards.

Without the time and insights these companies willingly shared, this book would not have been possible. I, and no doubt, the business intelligence community, thank them for letting us learn from their lessons!

Where Are They Now?   If you read the first edition of this book, you might be wondering what happened to some of those initial case study companies.

- **Corporate Express**   Corporate Express was acquired by Staples in 2008, and most of my contacts for the original case study have moved onto other companies.
- **Continental Airlines**   Continental Airlines was acquired by United Airlines in 2010. Since that time, their customer service measures have gone from first to worst. In talking to some members of the original BI team, they lamented the culture clash of United's waterfall approach to development versus Continental's agile approach. A number of those key members eventually left the company. United is clearly mid-journey in its integration, but is not at a point that reflects an effective use of data.

Then and Now

When I looked back at the 2007 edition of this book, at the time, many BI practitioners were frustrated by business stakeholders who didn't understand the real value of business intelligence. Others cited the greatest challenge as being not in the data warehouse or in BI tools, but rather, in the 100+ source systems and the frequency with which source systems change.

Fast forward six years to 2013, and the challenges have shifted. Today, most BI projects have strong executive sponsorship (see Chapter 6), but the influence of culture seems to be playing a bigger role between moderate and wild success. The pace of change and users' voracious appetite for new data and new capabilities is outpacing the bandwidth of many BI teams. As a fallout of the great recession, cost as a concern has displaced the notions of control and integration. More visionary, nimble BI teams are looking to new technologies, such as the cloud, open source, in-memory computing, and solutions from startups, to help them respond faster and cheaper.

Best Practices for Successful Business Intelligence

Based on this research, following are the top ten secrets to successful business intelligence and unlocking the full value of BI and big data. Some of these items are not secrets at all. In fact, they are such well-known drivers of BI success that some practitioners will walk away from projects that do not, for example, have executive-level sponsorship. The secret then is not always in the what, but rather, in the *how*—how to get and keep executive-level sponsorship, how to foster an analytic culture, or how to organize BI teams for better business alignment.

- Measure success in multiple ways, using objective measures when available and recognizing the importance of benefits that cannot be readily quantified.
- Understand the effect of Luck, Opportunity, Frustration, and Threat (LOFT) to catapult your BI initiative from moderate success to wild success. Use the LOFT effect to identify BI applications that address your organizations biggest pain points, biggest opportunities, or biggest threats.
- Garner executive support to ensure BI infiltrates all corners of an organization to provide competitive advantage and business value. Use the executive support to foster an analytic culture. Openly sharing data about poor performance takes a strong executive who needs to support those who so bravely share bad news and second guess decisions not based on facts.
- Align the BI strategy with the goals of the business by ensuring IT and business personnel work more as partners and less as adversaries.
- Start with a solid data foundation and add to it incrementally and continuously to improve the quality, breadth, and timeliness of data. Recognize that data does not have to be perfect to be useful.
- Evangelize the use of BI and find the relevance for BI for every worker in the company, as well as for customers and suppliers.
- Use agile development processes to deliver BI capabilities and improvements at a pace commensurate with the pace of business change.
- Organize BI teams and experts for success and build a solution that balances departmental needs while maximizing economies of scale of an enterprise solution.
- Choose appropriate BI tools that meet the user and business needs and that work within the technology standards that IT can effectively support.

- There are several other secrets, such as embracing innovation, promoting your successes and the applications, and investing in training.
- Deal with the present and be pragmatic in your approach, but keep an eye to the future of where you want to take your BI and big data analytic capabilities. Monitor your evolution and maturity across the various factors for impact.

Chapter 2

Technobabble: Components of a Business Intelligence Architecture

Every BI deployment has an underlying architecture. The BI architecture is much like the engine of a car—a necessary component, often powerful, but one that users, like drivers, don't always want to or need to understand. For some companies new to BI, the BI architecture may primarily be the operational systems and the BI front-end tools. For more mature BI deployments, and particularly for enterprise customers, it will involve ETL (extract, transform, and load) tools, a data warehouse, data marts, BI front-end tools, and other such components. This environment may include multiple databases and platforms for different levels of detailed data, cleansed data, and analytic complexity. With the advent of big data, some BI environments also include Hadoop clusters in addition to a traditional data warehouse platform. With the rise of in-memory processing, some companies with smaller data volumes may bypass a data warehouse entirely and use their in-memory layer as an alternative.

When IT discusses BI with users, we readily fall into technobabble, and sometimes inscrutable acronyms abound. Most car drivers know that cars have a battery, a transmission, and a fuel tank—an adequate level of knowledge for having a conversation with a mechanic or salesperson, but arguably not so much expertise to begin rebuilding an engine. In this chapter, then, I'll present the major technical components that make up an analytic architecture and that business users should have at least a high-level understanding of. If you are a technical expert, you might find this chapter to be overly simplified. If you are looking for a reference on any one of these components, consult the list of resources in Appendix B.

Chapter 3 explores the sleek "chassis" of this BI architecture, the BI tools.

Operational and Source Systems

Operational systems are the starting point for most quantitative data in a company. Operational systems may also be referred to as "transaction processing systems," "source systems," and "enterprise resource planning" (ERP) systems. As Figure 2-1 illustrates:

- **Manufacturing system**   When a product is produced, the production order is entered in the manufacturing system. The quantity of raw material used and the finished product produced are recorded.
- **Sales system**   When a customer places an order, the order details are entered in an order entry system.
- **Supply chain system**   When the product is available, the product is shipped and order fulfillment details are entered.
- **Accounting system**   Accounting then invoices the customer and collects payment. The invoices and payments may be recorded in an operational system that is different from the order entry system.

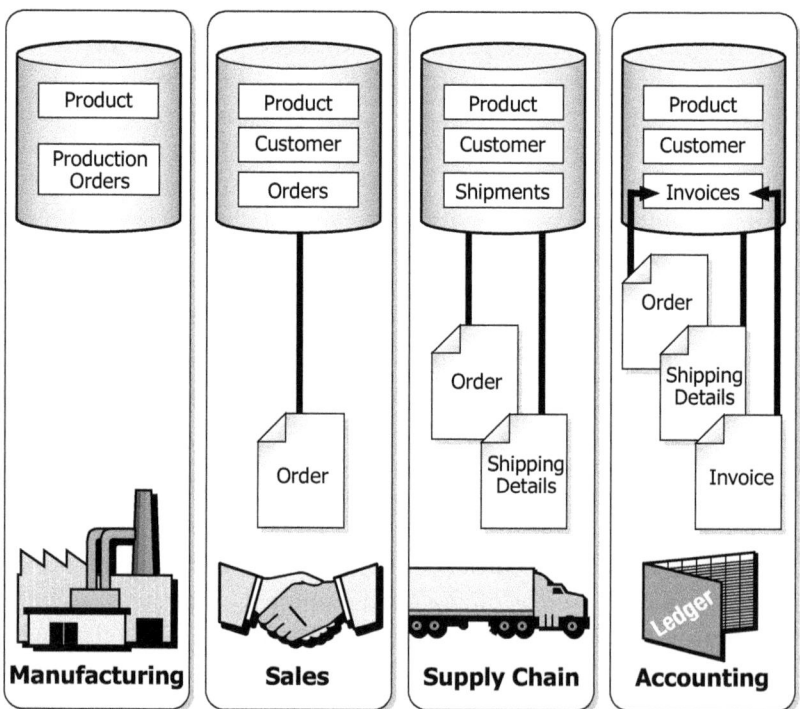

Figure 2-1   Operational systems record data from operational tasks.

In each step in this process, users are creating data that can eventually be used for business intelligence. In addition, to complete a task, operational users may need business intelligence. Perhaps in order to accept an order, the product must be available in inventory. As is the case with many online retailers, customers cannot place an order for a product combination (color, size) that is not available; a report immediately appears with a list of alternative sizes or colors, usually referred to as *embedded BI*.

When business intelligence is integrated with an operational system or supports an operational task, it is referred to as operational business intelligence, and the supporting report or nugget of information is called embedded BI.

The operational systems shown in Figure 2-1 may be custom-developed transaction systems or a purchased package from companies such as Oracle (Oracle E-Business Suite, PeopleSoft, J.D. Edwards, Siebel), SAP, or Microsoft (Dynamics GP). With custom-developed operational systems or with modules coming from different vendors, data may be manually entered into each system. A better approach is to systematically transfer data between the systems or modules. However, even when data is systematically transferred, the Customer ID entered in the order system may not, for example, be the same Customer ID entered in the accounting system—even though both IDs refer to the same customer!

Ideally, consistent information flows through the process seamlessly, as shown in Figure 2-2. ERP systems ensure adherence to standard processes and are broader in scope than custom operational systems of the past. From a data perspective, ERPs reduce duplicate data entry and thus improve data quality (see Chapter 8). With an integrated ERP, a common set of reference tables with consistent customer IDs, product codes, and chart of accounts are shared across the modules or applications, collectively referred to as *master data*.

Within the business intelligence life cycle, the operational systems are the starting point for data you will later want to analyze. If you do not capture the data in the operational system, you can't analyze it. If the operational system contains errors, those errors will only get compounded when you later aggregate and combine them with other data.

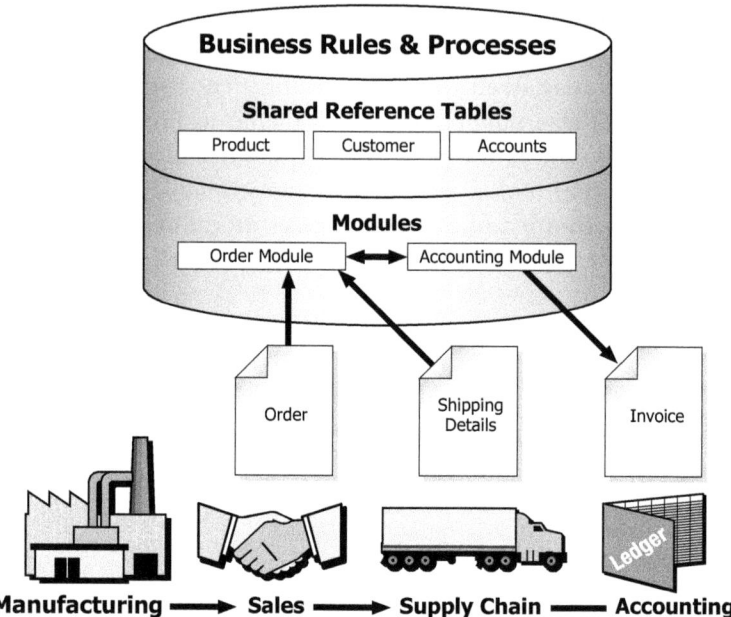

Figure 2-2 ERP systems reduce duplicate data entry and ensure adherence to standard processes.

Additional Source Systems

While much of the data warehouse (described in the next section) is populated by internal operational systems, data may also come from additional data sources, such as

- Distributors who supply sales and inventory information
- Advertisers who supply rates, readership, and advertising events
- Click-stream data from web logs that show the most frequently viewed products or online shopping cart analysis for partially completed orders
- Market prices from external research firms
- Social data from Twitter and Facebook where customers may be talking about your products
- Machine-generated data, sensors, and radio frequency identification (RFID) that may communicate, for example, which product is on which rail car and where the rail car is on the track

Whether this additional data gets loaded into a central data warehouse will depend on how consistently it can be merged with corporate data, how common is the need for the data, the business value in analyzing it, and politics. If the data is not physically stored in the data warehouse, it may be integrated with corporate data in a specific data mart or analytic sandbox. Disparate data sources may, in some cases, also be accessed or combined within the BI front-end tool, a key feature of many dashboard and visual data discovery products.

Data Transfer: From Operational to Data Warehouse

BI often involves analyzing summary data and combining data from multiple operational systems. To facilitate this, data will be extracted from the operational systems and loaded into a data warehouse, as shown in Figure 2-3.

This process is referred to as *extract, transform, and load* (ETL). More recently, some data warehouse teams have changed the order in which they do certain things and call it ELT (extract, load, transform).

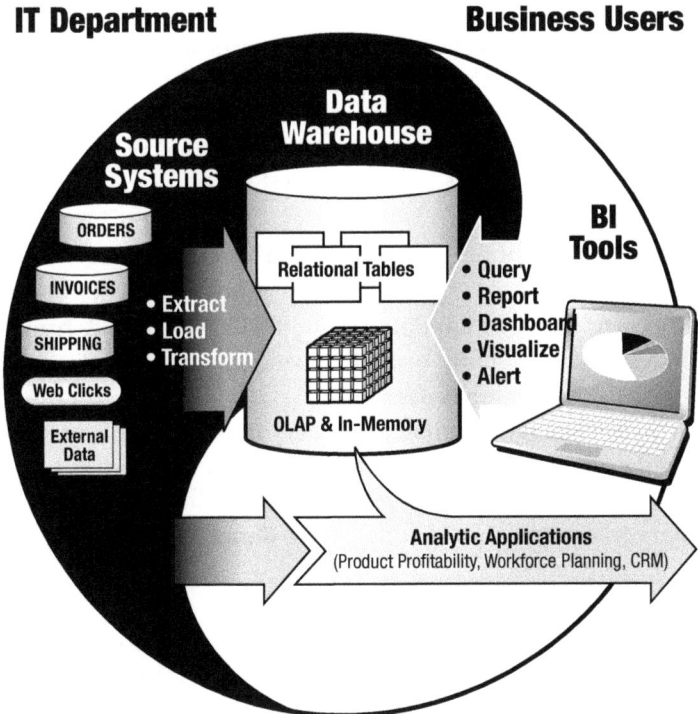

Figure 2-3   Major components in the business intelligence life cycle

The "transform" process of ETL is often the most time-consuming, particularly when multiple disparate systems are involved. Inconsistent codes (product ID, customer ID), handling of incomplete data, and changing codes to meaningful terms (1 = not shipped, 2 = shipped) are all part of the transform process.

Early data warehouse efforts usually relied on custom-coded ETL, and many still do. As packaged ETL solutions have come on the market, custom-coded ETL processes have been replaced with purchased ETL solutions. Popular solutions for ETL include Informatica PowerCenter, IBM Infosphere DataStage, Oracle Data Integrator, and Microsoft Integration Services (a component of SQL Server), as well as open-source Talend.

NOTE Throughout this book, I will mention specific vendor products as a way of providing you with concrete examples. These listings are not exhaustive, and exact product names frequently change amid vendor acquisition and product releases and rebranding.

Why Not Extract Everything?

In designing a data warehouse, requirements analysts will ask users what they need so that the ETL specialists can figure out what should be extracted from the source systems. Because much of BI is unpredictable in nature and users often don't know what they want until they see it, you might ask "why not extract everything?" in the event that you might one day need that data.

There are a number of reasons why all the data may not be extracted:

- The time window in which data can be ETL'd (extracted, transformed, and loaded) may be small, especially since many companies and data warehouses serve a global user base.
- There can be a negative impact on query performance when too much detailed data is stored in the data warehouse.
- Limited time, money, and human resources force a prioritization of what data to extract and include in the data warehouse.

Historically, there was also a high cost associated with replicating too much data. However, with lower storage costs and the growing adoption of the Hadoop Distributed File System (HDFS), this reason is less valid.

Enterprise Information Management

As the data warehouse industry has matured and ETL tools have evolved, this market segment is increasingly referred to as *enterprise information management* (EIM). EIM includes ETL tools, but also will include data modeling tools, data quality, data profiling, metadata management, and master data management (MDM).

Metadata   IT professionals talk a lot about metadata and go to great pains to make the business understand its importance. So with a chuckle, I will give you the classic definition: Metadata is data about the data. Helpful, isn't it?

Metadata is similar to an old card file in a library or book details on Amazon.com. A digital card file in a library (or the book details on Amazon) tells you which category a book belongs to, when it was published, and so on. Metadata may describe such things as

- When the data was extracted from the source system
- When the data was loaded into the data warehouse
- From which source system an item originated
- From which physical table and field in the source system it was extracted
- Transformation rules and logic
- How something was calculated—for example, *revenue* = (*price* × *quantity sold*) − *discounts*
- What the item means in a business context (revenue is based on the amount invoiced and does not include returns or bad debts)

The first few bullets in this list may not be all that interesting to many business users, but they are critical in the design and functioning of a data warehouse. These items are also important in knowing how timely the information you are analyzing is. If, for example, the data warehouse did not fully load due to a processing error, you need to be aware of this and consider this incomplete data in your reports.

As you move down the list, the items become much more important to all business users. A salesperson, for example, may have a different definition of revenue than a finance person does. As more people use BI, metadata is critical in ensuring a common business terminology and in ensuring users really know what the data means. Where the data is extracted from and stored is referred to as *technical metadata,* whereas business definitions and calculations are referred to as *business metadata.*

Master Data Management   Phillip Russom, director of research at
The Data Warehousing Institute (TDWI), defines master data management (MDM) as follows:

> Master data management is the practice of defining and
> maintaining consistent definitions of business entities (e.g.,
> customer or product) and data about them across multiple
> IT systems and possibly beyond the enterprise to partnering
> businesses.[1]

Master data includes the code and descriptions for customer, patient,
student, product, charts of accounts, regions, and so on. *Master data
management* is what ensures that the product ID from the product table
shown in Figure 2-2 is ideally the same ID across all the applications.
This product ID is stored and maintained in one common place so that
the relevant operational and business intelligence systems can access and
share it. In practice, rarely is there a single product ID, for a variety of
technical and organizational reasons. In this case, master data will include
the mappings of the different product IDs that really are the same product
represented in different systems. Master data also includes hierarchies of
how individual products, customers, and accounts aggregate and form the
dimensions by which you analyze various facts (see the "Data Warehouse
Tables" section later). If this all sounds a little boring and unimportant to
you, read the story of how pivotal a role master data has played in Dow
Chemical's business intelligence success in Chapter 8.

The Data Warehouse

A data warehouse is the collection of data *extracted* from various operational systems, *loaded* into an operational data store or staging area, then
transformed to make the data consistent and optimized for analysis. With
some business users, "data warehouse" has become a dirty word, associated with "expensive," "monolithic," and of no business value. Other terms,
such as *reporting database* and *data mart,* are also used and may sound less
monolithic to some business stakeholders. In reality, they both serve similar purposes but might have different scope and technical architecture.

Do I Need a Data Warehouse?

Many ERP implementations were sold on the promise of delivering
business insight, but this is not their main purpose, and ERP alone
does not deliver business insight. Having a single operational system

that ensures consistent business processes and that uses consistent reference data (customer, product codes) will make business analysis significantly easier. But there are a number of fundamental differences between operational systems and an analytic environment highlighted in Table 2-1. This analytic environment may be based on an in-memory engine, data warehouse, or data marts.

It is because of these myriad differences that I would argue all companies need an analytic environment, regardless of the size of the company. The technical architecture may vary, and whether that includes a data warehouse may vary, but its necessity does not. I have worked with customers with fewer than 20 employees and less than $1 million in revenues who needed a "reporting database," and I have worked with customers with greater than $20 billion in revenues who needed a "data warehouse."

Why Bother with a Data Warehouse at All?

Many customers new to BI want to skip the data warehouse and deploy a BI tool directly against the operational system. This may seem like a faster approach to business intelligence. In some instances, it may be an acceptable way to start with BI, and this approach addresses operational BI needs. However, for most companies, you will want a data warehouse separate from the transaction system when

- You need to perform cross-subject or cross-functional analysis, such as products ordered versus inventory on hand. Such information may exist in two different systems or different modules within an ERP system and are thus combined into the data warehouse.
- You want to perform analysis on summary information, aggregated by time (month, quarter) or by some other hierarchy (product groupings). These hierarchies often don't exist in transaction systems, and even when they do, running such voluminous queries within a transaction system can slow it to the point of interfering with data entry.
- You need consistently fast reporting and analysis times. Because of their different purposes and design, data warehouses allow for faster queries than operational systems.

Data Marts

A data mart can be a subset of the data coming from a central data warehouse, or a data mart may also be a single subject area populated directly from multiple source systems. Whereas a data warehouse is

Difference	Operational System	Analytic Environment
Purpose	Primary function is to process orders, post journal entries, complete an operational task.	Primary purpose is to provide access to information to manage the business by providing insight that leads to improved revenues, reduced costs, quality customer service, and alignment of strategic goals.
History	Current information with very little history; data may periodically be purged from the transaction system to ensure fast inputs.	Larger amounts of history allow multiyear trend analysis, this year versus last year comparisons.
Timeliness	Real-time information.	Information extracted on a periodic basis (hourly, daily, weekly). Operational data warehouses may extract information in real time or several times throughout the day.
Level of detail	Detailed data down to the line item or level of data entry.	Aggregated data with varying degrees of granularity.
Response time	Fast inputs, but slow queries.	Read-only; tuned for fast queries.
Table structure	Normalized tables in the thousands.	Parts of the data warehouse may be normalized, but the parts business users query are normally denormalized in star or snowflake schemas. The data warehouse will have fewer tables than the source systems have.
Dimensions	Rarely hierarchical groupings	Hierarchical groups give level of time, chart of accounts, product groupings, customer groups, and so on.
Reporting and analysis	Fixed reports by one detailed dimension (cost center, plant, order number, customer ID, patient ID, student ID).	Fixed or ad hoc reporting and analysis by multiple dimensions across all business functions.

Table 2-1   Comparison of Operational Systems with an Analytic Environment

designed to serve the needs of the enterprise, a data mart may serve the needs of a particular business unit, function, process, or application. Because a data mart is aligned with a particular business requirement, some businesses may want to skip the data warehouse and build an independent data mart. According to industry research, compared to when data warehousing first emerged in the 1990s, fewer companies use this as the primary approach,[2] as independent data marts have been met with limited success and over time have a higher implementation cost. A number of solutions can be used to create a data mart, including relational databases, OLAP cubes, or in-memory solutions.

Data Warehouse Tables

Within the data warehouse, data is physically stored in individual *tables* within a relational database. Your company may use the same relational database software for your ERP system as for your data warehouse (for example, Oracle, Microsoft SQL Server, IBM DB2) or a relational database specifically designed for business intelligence (Teradata, Netezza, Greenplum, Actian ParAccel).

Experts will deploy a number of different table design approaches to support the diverse business needs, performance requirements, and storage constraints. Most data warehouses have two types of tables: (1) a *fact table* that contains keys into the dimension tables and numeric information to analyze, such as sales, inventory, or calls (such facts are often referred to as *measures*) and (2) *dimension tables* that allow analysis of measures from different perspectives, such as product, time, or geography.

A fact table can have millions of detailed rows of data, commonly referred to as having a "finer granularity," or can be significantly smaller, containing mainly summary numbers. To improve the performance of queries, database designers may choose to create *aggregate or summary tables* around a fact table such that there may be a DAILY_SALES_FACT table, MONTHLY_SALES_FACT table, and YEARLY_SALES_FACT table. One fact table together with its associated dimension tables is referred to as a *star schema,* as shown in Figure 2-4.

Dimension tables are also referred to as *lookup tables* or *reference tables.* The dimension tables can be broken into more than one table; for example, detailed material IDs may reside in a MATERIAL_ID table. The groupings and product hierarchy for the material IDs may reside in a separate table, such as PRODUCT_GROUPING, as shown in Figure 2-5. This type of structure is referred to as a *snowflake design* and is

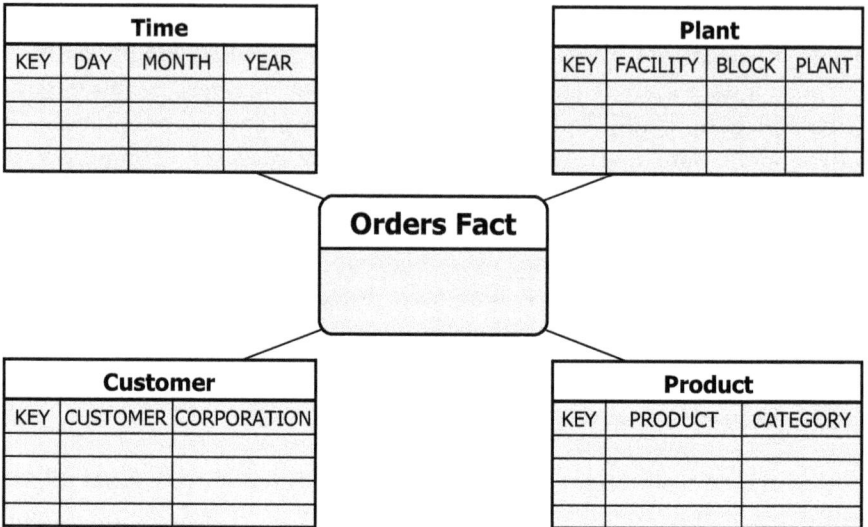

Figure 2-4   Star schema

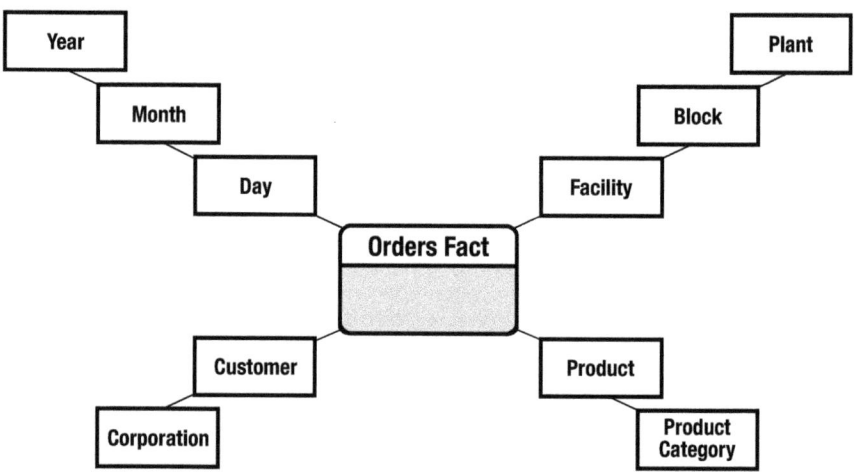

Figure 2-5   Snowflake design

used in data warehouses that have extremely large dimensions. You can think of dimensions as the ways by which you want to analyze facts—for example, sales *by geography* or sales *by product*.

In a transaction system, data is stored in a way that allows for fast data entry with minimal amounts of data duplicated across the physical tables. Data is said to be stored in *normalized* tables in a transaction system when a minimal amount of data is replicated in each table and a data element needs to be updated in only one place. This type of data model may also be used in an operational data store (ODS), a part of the data warehouse that contains a granular level of detail, rarely used directly for reporting and analysis but often a building block for summary tables. For example, the same customer name does not appear in multiple rows in a table. In a data warehouse or data mart, the emphasis is on storing data in ways that facilitate analysis and that speed query performance. Data redundancy is less of a concern, and as the data warehouse is a read-only environment, there is less concern about having to change multiple instances of the same value in thousands of tables and rows. Normalization in an operational system means the facts and the dimensions will be spread across many tables. For example, order information may exist in both an ORDER_HEADER table and an ORDER_LINES table, as shown in Figure 2-6. Trying to report on which customers bought which products means joining multiple tables and aggregating information from multiple tables, which will produce incorrect query results. Earlier, in Figure 2-4, all of the order information was extracted into a single ORDERS_FACT table, making it easier to query.

Dimensions and hierarchies often do not exist in the transaction system. For example, the transaction system may store a plant ID for the individual facility that produces a product, but it may not contain information about where the plants are located and to which business units they belong. This hierarchical information is often only stored in a data warehouse or in a separate master data management system.

In some respects, business users may not care about how the data is physically stored, whether in the data warehouse or in the transaction system. A business view in the BI tool (see Chapter 3) will often

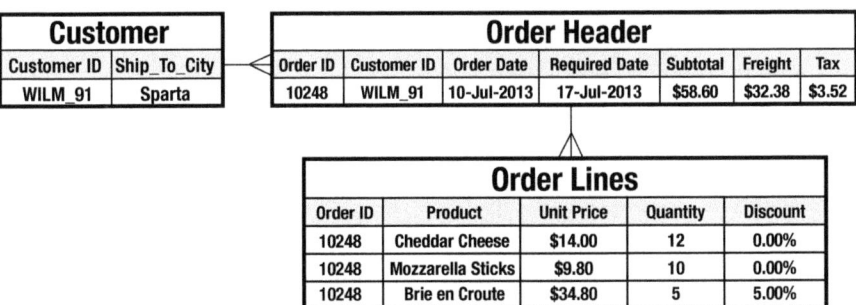

Figure 2-6 Normalized tables in a transaction system or operational data store

hide such technical issues. However, the better that business users can define requirements in advance, the better that data modelers might be able to store data in a way that facilitates the analysis. For example, if a user wants to analyze something like staffing levels versus sales performance and these two subjects exist in different fact tables and data marts, such analysis can be a challenge with certain BI tools. If users want to routinely analyze these two different subject areas together, then the data modeler may ultimately decide to store them in one common fact table.

The Data Warehouse Technology Platform

To drive a car, you need roads, highways, and a transportation infrastructure. Similarly, just as in a BI environment, a number of servers and networks may be involved:

- The server(s) on which the relational database management system (RDBMS) is running
- The server(s) that run the ETL software and processes
- The web server(s) that provide the entry point into the BI environment
- The BI server(s) that process queries, dashboards, and reports (see Chapter 3)

As part of this technical infrastructure, multiple servers may mirror each other for performance, load balancing, failover support, and so on. The network between the servers and the end users (whether internal business users or external customers) are also critical pinch points in the BI environment. Much of the time, this infrastructure gets taken for granted unless there are performance or reliability issues. Historically, the BI infrastructure has been implemented on premise. However, as companies have outsourced their data centers and as BI platforms have evolved to leverage cloud-based technology, part of the BI infrastructure also may be housed in the cloud.

Analytic Appliances

Data warehouse appliances combine the server, the database, and the data storage into one system.[3] Leading data warehouse appliance vendors include IBM Netezza, EMC Greenplum, Teradata, HP Vertica, Oracle Exadata, SAP Sybase IQ, and 1010data. SAP Hana is an in-memory database that runs on hardware manufactured by a number of hardware vendors. The promise of an appliance is a complete, optimized solution that delivers better performance at a lower cost of ownership than if a company were to purchase and install these individual components.

Most data warehouses are currently built on relational databases that are also used for transaction systems. Relational databases were designed for fast transaction processing, but not specifically for fast or robust analytics. Some of the concepts discussed in the earlier sections of storing data in star schemas help improve performance and analysis. A DBA will apply a number of performance-enhancing techniques, such as adding indexes, partitions, summary tables, and so on, to improve performance.

Analytic appliances, on the other hand, are purpose-built for fast query and analysis. Some of the differences in design approaches over relational databases *may* include use of columnar storage and parallel processing (Oracle Exadata uses relational storage).[4] In Figure 2-7, the individual rows in a traditional relational database are now stored in individual columns. With row-based storage, if you want to analyze total sales by customer, three rows of data must be read, and all columns are accessed.

In Figure 2-8, the columns of data that are not relevant to calculating total sales are ignored, so only two columns of data are accessed. This type of storage may allow for a fast read, but not a fast write required for a transaction processing system or real-time data.

For an analytic-type query, columnar storage may be more efficient when exploring aggregate data. Columnar database engines also use compression techniques and may require less disk space than row-based counterparts.

Beyond the columnar storage, the concept of massively parallel processing (MPP) uses the power of multiple distributed CPUs for better performance and scalability. A single system will manage the distributed nodes. Memory is not shared across the CPUs, and disk storage is usually not shared. Symmetric multi processing (SMP), on the other hand, uses multiple CPUs but on a single server; the memory and disk storage can be shared across CPUs. As the server demands increase, you can add CPUs to the server for increased scalability. With these architectural differences, MPP is often referred to as "scale out" and SMP as "scale up.[5]" Database and hardware vendors with differing approaches will naturally argue their architecture is best, but the notion of best varies widely on a number of factors.

If analytic appliances are so ideal for BI, then why bother using a traditional server and relational database? Cost is one of the biggest

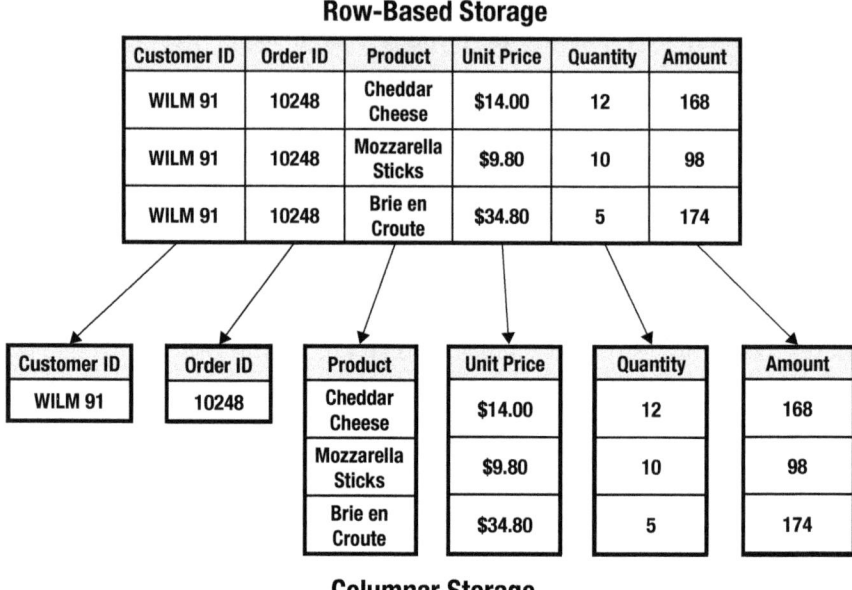

Figure 2-7   Relational databases store data in rows; columnar databases store data in columns.

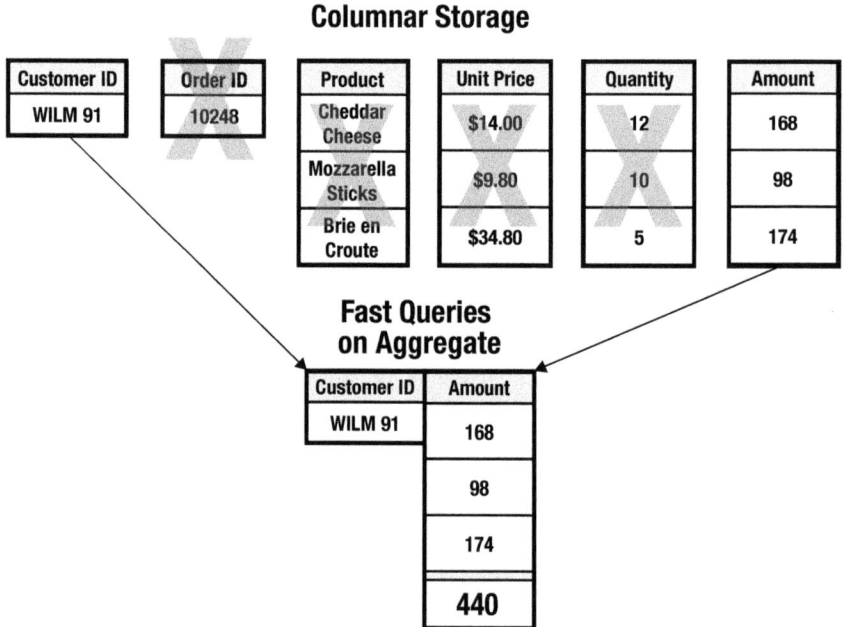

Figure 2-8   Columnar storage allows for fast analytic queries.

reasons. Also, if you are just starting out with a BI initiative, it may make sense to use the relational database platforms you already own and have expertise in. Over time, as your BI requirements evolve and mature, an analytic appliance may complement or replace a traditional data warehouse. For example, when Dow Chemical began its data warehouse project in the early 1990s, analytic appliances did not exist. As the number of users and analytic requirements grew, Dow began using SAP BW Accelerator, one of the first appliances to use in-memory processing and a precursor to its latest technology, Hana. According to Mark Carter, a systems architect at Dow, the use of an appliance has improved query performance dramatically and reduced the amount of time DBAs spent manually tuning the Oracle databases.[6] Likewise, Constant Contact began their BI deployment on a traditional relational technology. As the number of users, data volumes, and analytic complexity grew, they added the IBM appliance, Netezza. They have had performance gains ranging from 24 to 206 times faster, with less effort to manually tune the database.[7]

See Figure 2-11 later for a broad architecture based on the right technology for the right analytic workload that also includes big data technologies.

Cloud BI

The widespread use of the cloud in major software segments, such as sales force automation, payroll processing, and workforce management, has influenced the use of the cloud in BI environments. Initially, cloud BI was restricted to Software as a Service (SaaS) solutions. With an SaaS model, customers simply subscribe to a solution and typically upload their data to the cloud. A third-party vendor hosts the technical infrastructure that customers then access via the Web. As the cloud has matured, there are a number of variations in how it can be used for a BI implementation:[8]

- **Infrastructure-as-a-Service (IaaS)** is when a third-party provisions virtualized servers, storage, and network resources to run databases and applications. IaaS provider examples include GoGrid, Savis, Rackspace, and Amazon Web Services. With IaaS, you pay as you go for the hardware, storage, or computing power and will then buy and deploy your own software to build a data warehouse and BI solution.
- **Platform-as-a-Service (PaaS)** is when a third party provides optimized software on top of IaaS that can be used to build applications.

The preconfigured software may include application servers and database software, as well as the BI software. Amazon Redshift includes the Actian ParAccel analytic database as part of its PaaS. Microsoft Windows Azure, for example, provides the hardware, along with SQL Server, and currently sharing of reports developed in Reporting Services. Google BigQuery includes cloud-based storage and a SQL-like query interface. MicroStrategy Cloud runs its own data centers offering MicroStrategy, as well as data integration via Informatica and a number of database partners, including Teradata and Actian ParAccel.

- **Software-as-a-Service (SaaS)** includes the infrastructure and applications that can be directly consumed by business users. Some SaaS vendors will use IaaS providers. Most often, the data is replicated from an on-premise environment and loaded in the BI SaaS database, but a few allow a reachthrough to on-premise data.

While many broad BI platform vendors are beginning to offer BI in the cloud, a number of smaller firms differentiate themselves based on their cloud architecture. Early innovators in this space include Gooddata, 1010data, and Birst.

Figure 2-9 shows a conceptual architecture of a cloud deployment. PaaS and SaaS solutions have been gaining traction mostly in companies whose business operates in the cloud, small to mid-sized companies, and individual business units. For example, the Netflix streaming business unit uses Amazon Web Services for delivering content to viewers, so it makes sense that the data warehouse is also housed in the cloud using Amazon's Storage Center (S3).[9] The DVD business unit's data warehouse, meanwhile, is on premise, where most of that data originates. FlightStats, meanwhile, has to serve up flight updates to 5 million users a month, so it uses Amazon for its infrastructure.[10]

In the financial services industry, Huntington Bank chose to use MicroStrategy Cloud for a new commercial loan dashboard. The bank already had an on-premise BI solution, but because this was a new set of data for a new application and new dashboard capabilities, the IT team recommended deploying in the cloud. Deployment in the cloud enabled a faster implementation time and lower cost of ownership than installing the hardware and software on premise. The cloud is used to support the MicroStrategy BI application and dashboards, but the loan data is left in the on-premise data warehouse.[11]

Learning Circle, meanwhile, uses Information Builders WebFOCUS for its student dashboards. Information Builders does not provide an out-of-the-box SaaS solution. However, school districts often have

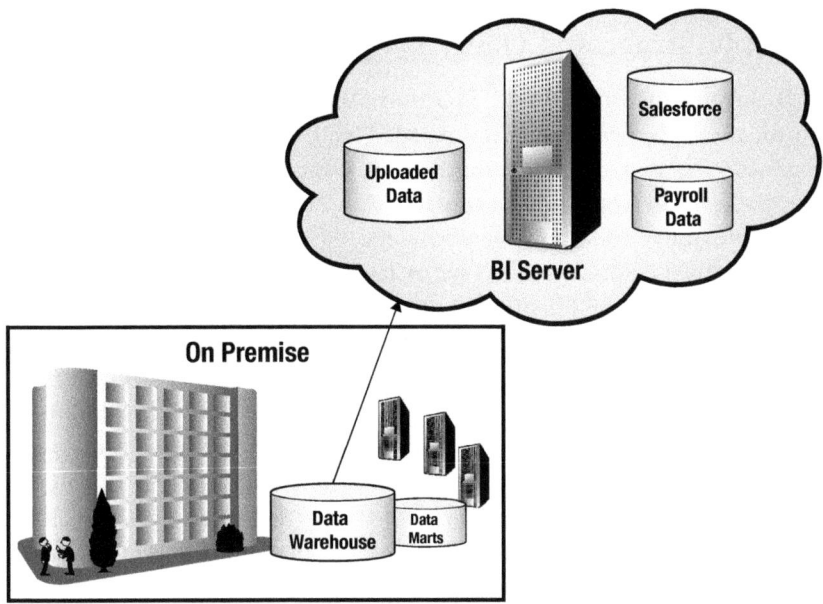

Figure 2-9   BI in the cloud leverages cloud-based servers. Data can either be loaded in the cloud or left on-premise.

limited resources to invest in their own BI infrastructure. For these reasons, Learning Circle uses a cloud infrastructure within the Ohio Education Computer Network (OHECN), a trusted data center for student data and compliant with federal privacy laws. OHECN hosts the school data and BI applications in their data center, enabling data to be shared across school districts (within privacy and security constraints), without requiring separate on-premise servers.[12]

Big Data Technologies

In certain circles, big data has become synonymous with Hadoop. In reality, though, a number of technologies come into play with big data, including traditional data warehouses, analytic appliances, and in-memory platforms, as well as Hadoop and a number of NoSQL databases. If you consider the generally accepted characteristics of big data as described in the previous chapter as including volume, velocity, and variety, some relational data warehouses certainly scale by volume to terabytes and petabytes. The difference with Hadoop and NoSQL databases is that they also handle a variety of information, such as web

What Is Structured Query Language (SQL)?

SQL, pronounced "sequel," is a computer language used to communicate with a relational database.[13] SQL is a common language, regardless if you use a database from Oracle, IBM, Microsoft, or Teradata. Querying a database with SQL can be fairly complicated. Business query tools will generate the SQL behind the scenes so business users don't need to learn how to write SQL code. While there is a common set of SQL commands, such as SELECT and SUM, each database vendor may have its own SQL extensions or dialect. RANK, for example, is a popular SQL expression among business users, but it is an expression that not all relational databases support. Sometimes when trying to develop a complex business query, you may run into limitations inherent in the SQL language. For example, a query about sales for this quarter would generate simple SQL. Asking a query about which products were cross-sold to the same customers this year versus last year would require very complex SQL and may be better answered either in an analytic database or OLAP database.

click-stream, social data, images, or video. In addition, they can better handle the velocity of updates such as from machine-generated data, RFID devices, or web clicks. The pace of these inputs is exponentially greater than, for example, office workers entering orders in a transaction system.

A NoSQL database, now referred to as "not only SQL," is defined as nonrelational, distributed, open-source, and horizontally scalable.[14] Most of the data warehouse and analytic platforms discussed thus far have been relational, or columnar, and involved proprietary technologies. There are a number of NoSQL databases using a variety of approaches to store data.

Hadoop is one of the most widely used big data solutions gaining momentum in the BI space. Hadoop is an open-source project originally started within Google in 2003, then adopted by Yahoo!. One of the project's originators, Doug Cutting, adopted the Hadoop name from his son's toy elephant. Hadoop collectively refers to a number of open-source subprojects, and as with open-source projects, there are different implementations of Hadoop, including Cloudera, MapR, and HortonWorks. While initial entrants into the Hadoop world were from startup companies, the likes of IBM, Microsoft, and Oracle have all announced or released Hadoop-based solutions.

Because Hadoop itself is free software and customers don't have to buy a specialized system, it also can have a lower upfront cost than a traditional database. Whereas in a traditional relational data warehouse or mart, information is organized into tables and fields within those tables, Hadoop only requires files and pointers to those files. The Hadoop Distributed File System (HDFS) accounts for the data storage layer that can be distributed on any hardware (see Figure 2-10). In a relational world, before data can be captured, it needs to be strictly modeled into tables and fields. In a NoSQL world, a table does not have to be created first, and the data only needs to be loosely described.

MapReduce is the framework that sits above the Hadoop Distributed File System to process tasks (see Figure 2-10). A Hadoop cluster could reside on one physical box, but it is the ability to distribute work across multiple computers that lends itself to scalability. The MapReduce layer will take a request for data or a computation, break the task into smaller pieces, and distribute it to the various nodes in the cluster. MapReduce is batch oriented, in contrast to real-time SQL queries against a data warehouse or in-memory exploration in new BI tools.

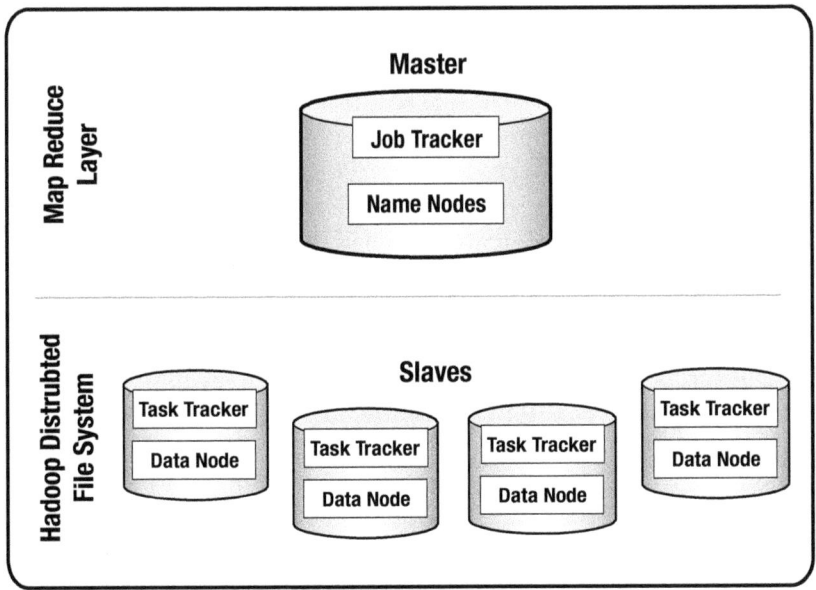

Figure 2-10   Hadoop conceptual framework

Hive is a virtual data warehouse on top of Hadoop that provides a SQL-like interface, called HiveQL. HiveQL is then converted to MapReduce jobs that execute on the Hadoop cluster. A challenge, though, is that it is not true SQL so users may receive unexpected results when trying to use a traditional BI tool with Hive. Also, because MapReduce is batch oriented and Hadoop is distributed, it can handle vast data volumes but is not optimized for analytic queries. This market segment is innovating rapidly, with new solutions announced each quarter to address query performance. In the fall of 2012, Cloudera announced Impala, a real-time query engine for Hadoop that it plans to release to the open-source community. In 2013, EMC announced Greenplum Pivotal HD, which provides native integration with Apache Hadoop to Greenplum's MPP database. Because it goes through the Greenplum relational database, it provides true SQL support. A flurry of SQL on Hadoop announcements have since followed from other vendors, including IBM BigSQL, Microsoft Polybase, and Teradata SQL-H.

HBase is another important subproject within Hadoop. HBase is a NoSQL, columnar database that uses HDFS for its storage layer.[15]

Hadoop deployments have been touted for the large, cost-effective data scale. As of June 2012, for example, Facebook's Hadoop deployment was at 100 PB, across 2,000 nodes. eBay cited 16 PB of data, over 4,200 processors.[16] FlightStats, on the other hand, does not have large data volumes but requires a cost-effective and flexible database to serve millions of traveling customers each month. The company has a traditional SQL database for historical flight data, and in addition, uses a NoSQL database, MongoDB, for real-time flight data.[17]

With the rise of Hadoop and other NoSQL solutions, some NoSQL pundits have proclaimed the death of the traditional data warehouse. Yet most analytic experts and vendors disagree with this notion, and instead, expect that NoSQL databases will become just another piece of an evolving analytic architecture. A TDWI survey in April 2013 found only 10 percent of companies had a production deployment of Hadoop, but another 63 percent expect to adopt this technology in the next three years.[18] It's important to note, though, that the survey base is heavily BI oriented, while many initial Hadoop deployments are not managed by central IT or BI teams. Figure 2-11 shows a next-generation analytic environment with big data, sometimes referred to as an analytic ecosystem. Because Hadoop was not originally designed for analytics, data scientists may execute jobs and computations in Hadoop, and once satisfied with a particular result set, may bring a subset of data into the traditional data warehouse or in-memory engine for broader consumption.

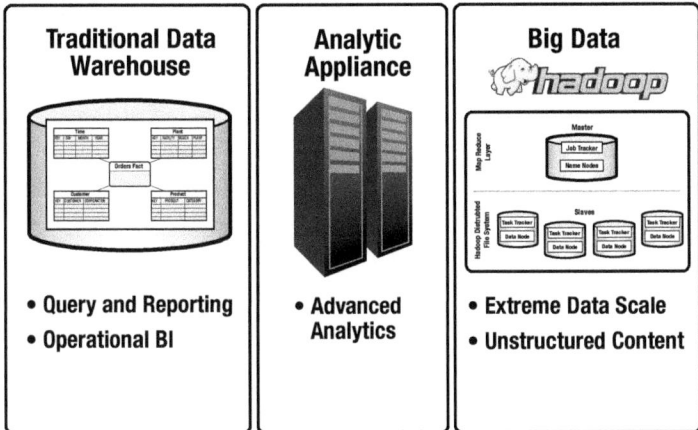

Figure 2-11 Next-generation analytic architecture with big data

Conceptually, Macy's uses such an analytic ecosystem. Within the Macy's brick-and-mortar retail stores division, Oracle and Teradata are used for the data warehouse. Within the dot-com division, IBM DB2 is used for the data warehouse. Marketing analytics needs to pull data from both outlets, and in addition, combine click-stream and social data such as Facebook comments and Twitter tweets to monitor shopping trends and campaign effectiveness.[19] Given both the data volumes and unstructured content, Hadoop is used for this type of application. Tableau Software allows experts to explore data in Hadoop and publish the findings as dashboards.

Best Practices for Successful Business Intelligence

The BI architecture consists of the ETL tools and processes, the data warehouse, the technical infrastructure, and the BI user tools. The operational systems provide the basic data that feeds the data warehouse either in real time or on a periodic basis. External data sources from partners, suppliers, web log files, social data, and public data may feed into the data warehouse. The underlying foundation of a BI architecture is complex. The implementation can either facilitate business intelligence or become so monolithic and inflexible that it becomes a technical data wasteland. Business requirements and technology continue to evolve to bring greater flexibility and analytic power with greater data volumes to more classes of users. To ensure the BI architecture meets the business requirements:

- Business users should have a working understanding of the technical issues, components, and terminology that affect their requirements and ability to access data.
- IT personnel should minimize technobabble and avoid overemphasizing the technical architecture for technology's sake.
- An analytic ecosystem might include traditional relational databases, analytic appliances, and NoSQL solutions that balance cost, complexity, and analytic capabilities with data and user scalability.

The Business Intelligence Front-End: More Than a Pretty Face

If the business intelligence *architecture* is like the engine of the car, then the BI *front-end tools* are like the body: sporty, sleek, fast, and where the razzle-dazzle of color, handling, and chrome finish all matter. You can have a perfectly architected data warehouse, and yet if you don't have the right BI front-end tools, you won't achieve business intelligence success. Technical capabilities matter here, but so do subtle differences such as look-and-feel and ease of use. Conversely, while you can have a powerful, intuitive BI front-end, if you have not paid attention to the underlying technical components discussed in the last chapter, users will blame the tool for any underlying problems, whether bad data or poor performance. You need to get both aspects right, even if it's only the tools that are visible.

This chapter describes the various BI front-end tools that are highly visible to business users. Chapter 12 discusses the importance of matching the tools with the right user segment and the role such tools have played in successful companies. As discussed in Chapter 1, vendors offer an increasing breadth of capabilities within one BI platform, or suite of tools. Throughout this chapter, I will mention specific vendor modules to provide concrete examples. This list is not exhaustive, and as vendors acquire each other and/or introduce new modules, specific names may change. For updated product names and modules, consult the BI Scorecard web site.

Utopia: Self-Service BI

Offering users self-service BI is a top priority for many BI teams. The vision is that if users have easy-to-use BI tools, they can service themselves, asking tough business questions that yield the most value, without any assistance from IT. There would be no more IT backlog of requests, and users could act at the fast pace business demands. That's the vision for BI utopia. Reality is a bit different, and there are a number of variables, including staffing, complexity, and tech savviness.

Figure 3-1 presents a spectrum of self-service BI scenarios. There are significant differences in the degree of user sophistication, required IT involvement, and how much a user can accomplish. For example, if a user is able to write their own SQL queries and is intimately familiar with the data models and nuances, they don't need IT to get to their data. They may merge and explore data from different data sources using an Excel spreadsheet. At the other end of the spectrum is a casual user, perhaps a front-line worker such as a salesperson, call center operator, or truck driver. They only access a fixed report or dashboard to see a list of customer visits, sales order volume, and so on. At most, they will want to tweak the report to filter it for certain regions or to re-sort it by last order data or order size. These report consumers are not data analysts, so they don't know SQL, nor should they. IT has been involved up front in defining the report requirements and programming the report.

The gray area comprises the middle two boxes, business query and visual data discovery, in which users want to author their own queries, but they don't know SQL. With a business query tool, IT must first define a metadata layer or business view of all the physical tables in a data warehouse. Users only have access to data sources, tables, and fields that IT has exposed in the business view, so less flexibility than

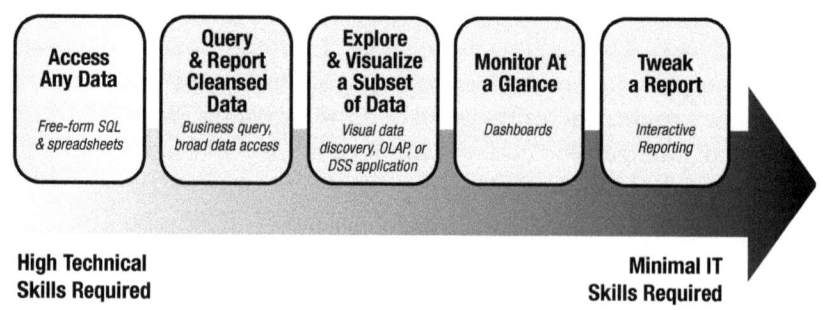

Figure 3-1   Self-service BI continuum

in the freeform SQL, but they have broader access and more flexibility than the next category, visual data discovery. Visual data discovery tools are considered easier to use than business query tools and require less initial IT involvement, often because a subset of the data has been loaded into an in-memory engine. For this reason, this new category of visual data discovery tools is becoming synonymous with self-service BI, but clearly, it is not a complete picture. So as you think about your vision for self-service BI, consider the use case, sophistication of the users, degree of IT involvement, and breadth of data sources.

Business Query and Reporting

Business query and reporting tools are often referred to as "ad hoc query tools." This terminology is a little misleading, as in fact the queries are not always ad hoc (as in spontaneously crafted) but rather are often fixed reports. The difference is that a business user, usually a power user, may have built the report, rather than an IT person. The business environment changes at a rapid pace, and, unable to wait weeks or months for IT to develop a new report, business users often demand the ability to create queries and reports themselves. Business query and reporting tools allow for this and are most often used for decision-making and management purposes. The business query and reporting tool is a key module to provide users with self-service information access. When business intelligence first emerged as a category in the early 1990s, it was based on the advent of business query tools that allowed users to create queries without knowing SQL. For the first time, data locked up in relational databases was now accessible to those other than SQL programmers.

In some cases, a report is truly ad hoc; it's a one-off business question that will never be posed again. Ad hoc queries may be exploratory in nature as users try to find the root cause of a problem, test a theory, or consider changing a business model. Table 3-1 lists some sample fixed reports that may lead to an ad hoc query. As users explore the data, what started as an ad hoc query or one-time question may later become a fixed report. It's important to recognize the iterative nature of business intelligence and ensure you have flexible business intelligence tools.

Getting to the data is just one capability of business query tools; the other aspect is presenting and formatting the data in a meaningful way, loosely referred to as *reporting*. The terms "query" and "reporting" are sometimes used interchangeably because a business query and reporting tool will have both capabilities—getting to the data and formatting it to create a report.

Functional Area	Fixed Report	Purpose	Related Ad Hoc Query
Supply Chain	Inventory by Product	To determine if an order can be fulfilled today by the primary warehouse	If I'm short at my main warehouse, can I supply the product from elsewhere?
Marketing	Top 10 Customers by Quarter and Product	To understand which customers generate the most revenue	Which customers fell off this quarter's list? Are there certain products we can cross-sell?
Supply Chain	Raw Material Receipts and Delivery Times	To determine how long it takes to acquire raw materials and which supplier can fulfill purchase orders fastest	Are there other suppliers who can respond faster?
Management	Patients per Hour	To understand busy periods and wait times	Do staffing levels correspond to busy times?
Accounting	Accounts Receivable Aging	To identify the number of days particular invoices have been open; which customers are greater than 60 days?	Have these customers paid late before? Has a reminder notice been sent?
Human Resources	Average Salary by Job Level	Monitor compensation	Are there differences in pay by tenure, age, or gender?

Table 3-1   Sample Fixed and Ad Hoc Reports

Business query and reporting tools vary widely in their formatting capabilities. The most basic of formatting capabilities allows for changing the font of column headings and making them bold and centered. Conditional formatting will, for example, display numeric values in red when negative or below target and in green when positive or above target. Simple report styles include displaying information in a cross-tab report, a chart, or a master-detail report with groupings and subtotals.

Tools may provide a set of templates to create nicely formatted reports that use a consistent corporate look and feel. More complex formatting capabilities include the ability to present multiple charts on a page, perhaps coming from different data sources.

Examples of business query tools include SAP BusinessObjects Web Intelligence, IBM Cognos Workspace, and MicroStrategy Web.

A Business View of the Data

Business query tools allow business users to access a data source via business terms without having to write any SQL. The data source could be a data warehouse, as described in Chapter 2, or it might be direct access to an operational system. A key feature of a business query tool is that it has a business view or metadata layer that hides the complexity of the physical database structure from the business user by

- Using business terminology rather than physical field names. For example, a user may select a dimension such as Customer Name rather than a cryptic field such as CUST.L33_NAME (the physical table and field name in the relational database management system [RDBMS]).
- Automatically connecting related tables via joins.
- Providing metrics that may calculate and aggregate facts such as revenue, number of customers, number of orders, number of incidents, and average selling price.

Figure 3-2 shows an example of building a query with the SAP BusinessObjects universe, one of the first products to introduce the concept of a business view.

This business view is the most important piece of your BI front-end tools, and one in which the business and IT must work together to model. This can be both a blessing and a curse because there is some upfront work (the curse), but this investment helps ensure consistency and ease overtime (the blessing part!). For integrated BI platforms, the business view is common to all the BI tool modules: business query, reporting, analysis, and dashboards. When the business view looks too much like the data warehouse or source system with confusing table and field names, business users are overwhelmed and can too easily build incorrect queries. Poor business view design also forces users to put too much logic and too many calculations inside individual reports and dashboards. For these reasons, in some organizations, the power users within a business unit, function, or department are responsible for

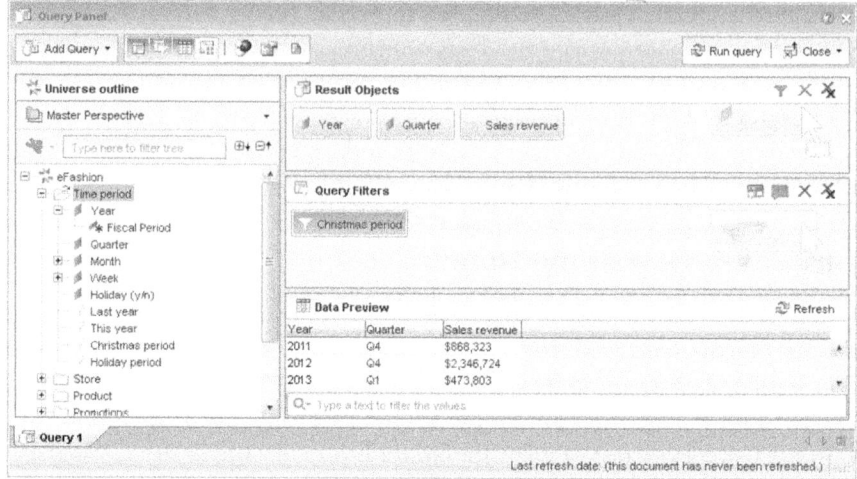

Figure 3-2   The SAP BusinessObjects universe presents users with a business view of the data.

building the business view or metadata layer; in others, it is the central BI group or data warehouse team that will build and maintain the business view.

Visual Data Discovery

As a BI software segment, visual data discovery tools are one of the most rapidly growing modules. The analyst firm Gartner estimates that this segment will grow at three times the pace of the overall BI market. Whenever there is a new category of software, there is confusion about what characterizes the software and what capabilities set it apart. An appropriate analogy would be that of the Apple iPad tablet. If you compare an iPad to a traditional laptop computer, it would not compare well: The first iPad lacked a keyboard, printing feature, and a universal serial bus (USB) port. This doesn't make it a bad product, but it warranted a separate category of devices and an evolution in understanding how to evaluate it and when to use it. A similar challenge exists in the visual data discovery market segment, so when Gartner first published its research report "The Rise of Data Discovery Tools" in 2009, it specifically omitted one of the leading vendors in this space, Tableau Software, because at that time, Tableau lacked an in-memory engine. It could be fast, a key characteristic of visual data discovery tools, but it did not initially use in-memory processing to accomplish that performance, a criterion that Gartner used to characterize players in this market.

> I define visual data discovery as a tool that speeds the time to insight through the use of visualizations, best practices in visual perception, and easy exploration. Such tools support business agility and self-service BI through a variety of innovations that may include in-memory processing and mashing of multiple data sources.

Visual data discovery moves the focus of BI from the "what" to exploring "why," "where," and "when." Users may not know precisely what information they are looking for and instead will navigate and drill within a data set to uncover particular details and patterns. So in a business query tool, the question is "What are my sales this month?" In a visual data discovery tool, the question may be "What are the characteristics of those customers with higher sales?" Perhaps it's age, income, gender, or location. The results of the query may be rendered on a geographic map or scatter plot showing the relationship between sales, income, and age.

A business query module that simply allows you to create a visualization is not a visual data discovery tool; currently, business query tools force you to start with a tabular data set and then manually pick a chart style. The business query tool requires a business metadata layer; a visual data discovery tool may lack one. However, because these tool categories both have a role in self-service BI, business users and IT teams will argue about the need for both tools. Table 3-2 compares these two modules that deliver self-service BI.

A conversation around visual data discovery tools typically goes like this:

IT: We already have a BI tool, why do we need another one?

User: Yes, but this one lets me create my own queries.

IT: So does our current business query tool.

User: But you make me take two days of training before I can figure out what to do. (Silently in the user's head: *And it takes months to add new data elements!*)

IT: That's to be sure you get the right data. It's for your own good; trust us, we know how messy our data is.

User: I know my data. You're the ones who overcomplicate things. Besides, this tool is easier, and prettier, and faster!

… at which point there is a stalemate or the business user gives up and buys their own solution. The bottom line is that this segment is still relatively new, evolving, and not well understood. At the same time, because of the agility and ease with which users can get to their data and unearth insights, visual data discovery should be part of every company's BI tool portfolio.

Characteristic	Business Query	Visual Data Discovery
Maturity	Mature, released in the early 1990s	Emerging
Business view	Required	Optional
IT involvement for initial setup	Yes to build business view metadata layer	Minimal, perhaps to create a query extract
Where authoring is done	Web	Mainly desktop, but some support Web
Initial data display	Tabular	Chart or tabular
Personal and multiple data sources	Rare but expanding	Common
Performance	Variable, depends on how well tuned the underlying database is	Fast, using in-memory processing, caching, or analytic database
Types of visualizations	Common bar, line, pie	Common types as well as tree maps, histogram, network, trellis, waterfall
Degree of interactivity for consumer	Initially and still often limited to refresh, but some vendors allow filter, sort, and drill on cached data set	Extensive and automatic filter, sort, lasso, drill, sliders, zoom

Table 3-2   Comparison of Business Query and Visual Data Discovery Tools

Popular tools in this category include Tableau and TIBCO Spotfire, as well as new solutions from BI platform vendors such as SAS Visual Analytics Explorer, MicroStrategy Visual Insight, and SAP Lumira. QlikTech QlikView is often positioned in this category because the applications built with QlikView facilitate explorations, but I think it is better viewed as a dashboard solution.

Figure 3-3 shows a visual data discovery created with Tableau Software and published on Tableau Public (a cloud-based solution where people can share data and visualizations) by Financial Genes. Financial Genes is a company that analyzes financial data from publicly held companies to explore which financial ratios best predict success. The Y axis shows net income, the X axis revenue, and the size of the bubble shows market capitalization. So, for example, Apple's revenues are much smaller than Exxon Mobile's, but the net income for both companies is just over $40 billion.

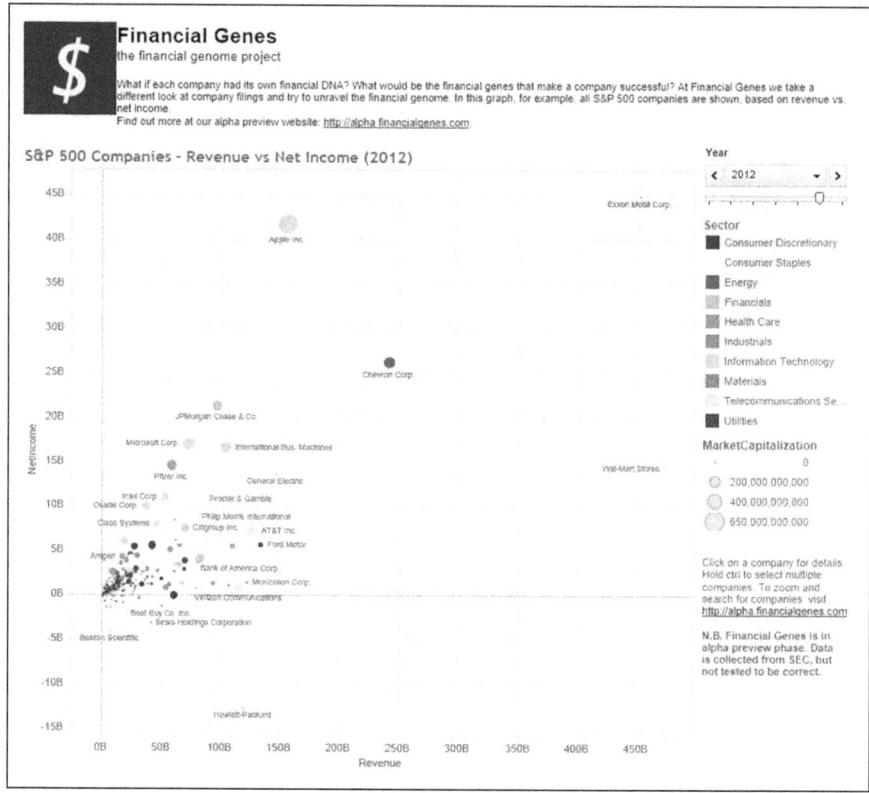

Figure 3-3   Tableau Software uses visualizations to reveal patterns in data. (Courtesy of Tableau Software)

Dashboards

Stephen Few, president of Perceptual Edge and author of a number of books on dashboard design, provides this definition of a dashboard:

> A dashboard is a visual display of the most important information needed to achieve one or more objectives, consolidated and arranged on a single screen so the information can be monitored at a glance.[1]

Wayne Eckerson, author of *Performance Dashboards*, expands on this definition to say, "A performance dashboard is a multilayered application built on a business intelligence and data integration infrastructure that enables organizations to measure, monitor, and manage business performance more effectively."[2]

BI dashboards are similar to car dashboards—they provide multiple indicators or reports in a highly visual way. A dashboard may be composed of

- A map that color-codes where sales are performing well or poorly
- A trend line that tracks stock outs
- A cross tab of top-selling products
- A key performance indicator with an arrow to show if sales are according to plan

Figure 3-4 shows an example of an executive dashboard created with QlikTech QlikView. This particular tab of the dashboard focuses on expenses and includes a column chart to compare actual expenses with budgets, a pie chart to show allocation of expenses, and a tabular display of year-over-year variances.

Ideally, users want to assemble their own dashboards with the information relevant to their job, and many visual data discovery tools allow for user-assembled dashboards. Other solutions are geared more for IT to design the dashboards. This is often preferred for operational dashboards that may access data in a source system (rather than a data

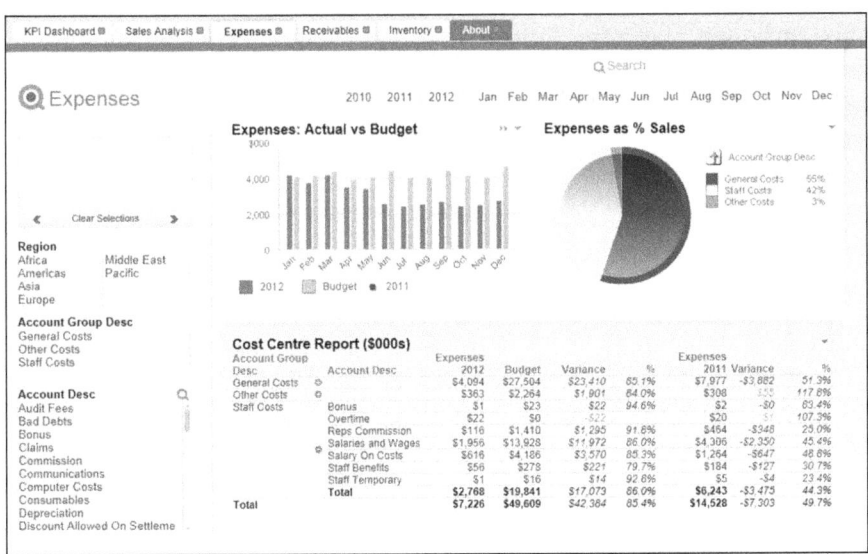

Figure 3-4   QlikTech QlikView dashboard allows users to view multiple indicators at a glance.

warehouse), are refreshed in real time, and support mission-critical operational tasks.

A key characteristic of dashboards is that they present information from multiple data sources. Exactly how they do this and what constraints there are in the accessibility and number of data sources vary widely from product to product.

The concept of dashboards is not new. Early Executive Information Systems (EIS) of the late 1980s tried to deliver similar capabilities. What has changed and continues to improve is the technology. EISs were often custom-coded, inflexible dashboards based on quarterly data. First-generation BI dashboards provided greater out-of-the box functionality. Next-generation dashboards provide greater interactivity and smarter visualizations, as well as linking insight to action. A few products will allow key performance indicators and strategy maps to be embedded within the dashboard.

All BI platform vendors support the creation of dashboards. QlikTech QlikView combines in-memory and visual discovery in their dashboard delivery.

Scorecards

The terms "dashboards" and "scorecards" are often used interchangeably, although they are indeed different things. A major difference between them is that a *scorecard* tracks a set of key performance indicators (KPIs) compared to a forecast or target, whereas a *dashboard* will present multiple numbers in different ways. Some dashboards may additionally display metrics and targets with visual traffic lighting to show the performance of that metric, but you should not assume that all dashboard tools support this capability.

Strategic scorecards contain metrics from the four key areas that drive the success of a business (people, customers, financial, operations) and will include strategy maps to show how the metrics relate to one another. Such scorecard products may be certified by Palladium Group, formerly the Balanced Scorecard Collaborative, an organization founded by management consultants Norton and Kaplan to further the education about and practical uses of strategic scorecards. Figure 3-5 shows an example of a strategy map created with Actuate BIRT 360.

Although there are a number of powerful scorecard products on the market, the biggest challenge in deploying scorecards is in getting the business to agree on common objectives, drivers, targets, and ownership for the KPIs.

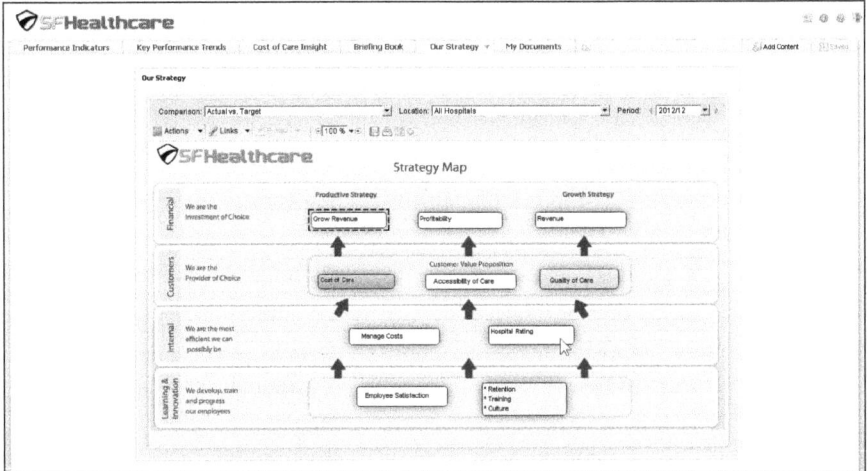

Figure 3-5   Actuate BIRT 360 allows executives to manage key performance indicators.

Production Reporting

Whereas business query and reporting tools allow for basic report formatting, production reporting tools have much more sophisticated formatting and design capabilities. Some people may refer to this category of tools as pixel perfect, operational, or enterprise reporting. Again, the terminology can be misleading, as some business query and reporting tools can create pixel-perfect reports, can be embedded in operational systems, and are used across an enterprise. For lack of a better term, I will refer to this module as "production" reporting. Examples of production reporting tools include SAP BusinessObjects Crystal Reports, Microsoft Reporting Services, Information Builders WebFocus, Jasper Reports, and Pentaho Report Designer.

A production reporting tool may access a transaction system directly to create a document such as an invoice, a bank statement, a check, or a list of open orders. When the reporting is not against a transaction system, it may be against an operational data store or detailed data within a data warehouse. IT usually develops these reports for the following reasons:

- The data source is an operational system in which you can't take the risk that "untrained" users may launch resource-intensive and runaway queries with a business query tool.
- Reports are often accessed through and embedded within the transaction system.

Characteristic	Production Reporting	Business Query and Reporting
Primary author	IT developer	Power user or business user
Primary purpose	Document preparation	Decision-making, management
Report delivery	Paper or e-bill, embedded in application	Portal, spreadsheet, e-mail
Print quality	Pixel perfect	Presentation quality
User base	Tens of thousands	Hundreds or thousands
Data source	Operational transaction system	Data warehouse or mart, occasionally transaction system
Level of data detail	Granular	Aggregated
Scope	Operational	Tactical, strategic
Usage	Often embedded within an application	Most often BI as separate application

Table 3-3   Differences Between Production Reporting Tools and Business Query Tools (Source: BIScorecard.com)

- The information requirements are common to all users and departments and often are static, such as for regulatory reports.

Because professional IT developers are often the users of production reporting tools, IT may also use these tools to develop management-style reports, particularly when a company does not have a business query tool.

Table 3-3 highlights some key differences between business query tools and production reporting tools. None of these differences is an absolute, except that they serve the needs of distinct user groups and, in many cases, distinct applications.

Mobile BI

I would rather not list mobile BI as a separate module here. In some respects, it would be like listing laptop or browser as separate BI modules! In theory, it shouldn't matter which device I use to access a report or dashboard, but with varying screen sizes and technologies in play, it does matter. For some BI products, you need a special application for tablet computers, such as the iPad or a smartphone, whether an Android-based device, an iPhone, or a BlackBerry.

There was a time in corporate life that IT could set standards on which devices they would support, and BlackBerry was considered the gold standard. Now, the predominant approach is one in which users bring their own devices (BYOD), iPads rule the tablet space, and Androids have taken over in the smartphone world. As market share in the smartphone and tablet space has been changing, so, too, has vendor support for particular devices and the approaches in which they deliver content. At a minimum, if you have a wireless signal, you can often use your browser to access BI content. This, however, does not typically provide the best user experience, so there are a number of native device-based apps for getting content. The degree that you can interact with, author new content, or access content offline in airplane mode varies significantly.

While the technology and requirements for mobile BI are changing, for sure the idea of accessing data "at the click of a mouse" has now been usurped with the notion of a "tap of fingertip."

Online Analytical Processing (OLAP)

Online Analytical Processing (OLAP) is a capability that focuses on *analyzing* and *exploring* data, whereas query and reporting tools put greater emphasis on accessing data for *monitoring* purposes. Wait! Doesn't that sound a lot like visual data discovery? It does. But the differences are in the underlying architecture and data models to support the exploration, with visual data discovery being more flexible and OLAP being more rigid.

OLAP provides interactive analysis by different dimensions (i.e., geography, product, time) and different levels of detail (year, quarter, month). For many users, OLAP has become synonymous with "drill-down" and "pivot" capabilities. Many BI products, though, will now provide drill-down and pivot capabilities without a full-blown OLAP engine or OLAP database on the back end. Instead of replicating and storing the data in an OLAP database, the BI vendor may use an in-memory engine or caching layer to ensure performance. If your data warehouse platform uses an analytic appliance, the query performance is also guaranteed, thus making OLAP less relevant.

As a technology, OLAP rose to prominence in the mid-1990s with solutions such as Essbase (now owned by Oracle), TM1 (now owned by IBM), and Microsoft Analysis Services. The following characteristics continue to distinguish OLAP tools from business query and reporting tools:

- **Multidimensional** Users analyze numerical values from different dimensions, such as product, time, and geography. A report, on the other hand, may be one-dimensional, such as a list of product prices at one point in time.

- **Consistently fast** As users navigate different dimensions and levels within a dimension, OLAP means fast—the speed of thought. If a user double-clicks to drill down from Year to Quarter, waiting 24 hours, 24 minutes, or even 24 seconds for an answer is not acceptable. Report users, of course, do not want slow reports either, but some reports take this long to run and must be scheduled.

- **Highly interactive** Drilling is one way users interact with OLAP data. *Pivoting* gives users the ability to view information from different perspectives, such as by geography or by product. *Slicing* allows users to filter the data within these dimensions, such as sales for New York only and then for New Jersey only, or crime statistics for Leeds only and then Manchester only. This kind of interactivity within a non-OLAP report ranges from nonexistent to only recently possible.

- **Varying levels of aggregation** To ensure predictable query times, OLAP products pre-aggregate data in different ways. Reporting, to the contrary, can be at the lowest level of detail: Rather than sales by product, you might have individual line items for a particular order number.

- **Cross-dimensional calculations** With multiple dimensions come more complex calculations. In OLAP, you might want to analyze percentage contribution or market share. These analyses require subtotaling sales for a particular state and then calculating percentage contribution for the total region, country, or world. Users may analyze this percentage market share by a number of other dimensions, such as actual versus budget, this year versus last year, or for a particular group of products. These calculations often must be performed in a particular order and involve input numbers that users might never see. Detailed reports, however, often rely on simple subtotals or calculations of values that are displayed on the report itself.

In understanding OLAP requirements, it's important to distinguish between OLAP platform issues and OLAP user interface issues.

OLAP Platforms

The OLAP platform is about how the data is stored to allow for multidimensional analysis. The cube shown in Figure 2-3 in Chapter 2 represents the OLAP database. On the one hand, business users should not have to care at all about how the data is stored, replicated, and cached, and yet the OLAP architecture greatly affects what you can analyze and how. The OLAP architecture also influences what OLAP front end you can use.

Architecture	Primary Difference	Vendor
ROLAP	Calculations done in a relational database, large data volumes, less predictable drill times.	Oracle BI EE, SAP BW, MicroStrategy
MOLAP	Calculations performed in a server-based multidimensional database. Cubes provide write access for inputting budget data or performing what-if analysis.	Oracle Essbase, Microsoft Analysis Services
DOLAP	Mini cache is built at query run time.	SAP BusinessObjects Web Intelligence
In-Memory	All data is loaded in-memory and does not need to be rigidly modeled as a cube.	QlikTech QlikView, SAP Hana, Oracle Exalytics, Microsoft PowerPivot and Analysis Services Tabular Data Models, IBM Cognos TM1, IBM Dynamic Cubes

Table 3-4   OLAP Architectures

There are four primary OLAP architectures, as described in Table 3-4. Relational OLAP (ROLAP) platforms store data in a relational database so data is not necessarily replicated into a separate storage for analysis. Multidimensional OLAP (MOLAP) platforms replicate data into a purpose-built storage that ensures fast analysis. Dynamic OLAP (DOLAP) will automatically generate a small multidimensional cache when users run a query. In-memory is a newer technology that may be used in conjunction with ROLAP and MOLAP or as an alternative.

With each OLAP architecture, there are trade-offs in performance, types of multidimensional calculations, amount of data that can be analyzed, timeliness of data updates, and interfaces through which the data can be accessed.

Historically, many OLAP products used MOLAP storage, which led to inflexible cube databases, management of more replicated data, and limitations on the data volumes and level of detail that can be analyzed. All of this has sometimes scared IT away from OLAP. Both the rise of in-memory BI tools as well as columnar databases and analytic appliances challenge the need for a MOLAP database.

What Are Multidimensional Expressions (MDX)?

MDX is a query language similar to SQL but used to manipulate data within an OLAP database. Microsoft created MDX as a language to work with its original OLAP server, now referred to as SQL Server Analysis Services. As MDX gained industry acceptance, a number of other OLAP databases added support for MDX such that today OLAP viewers will generate MDX to access and analyze data in a number of different OLAP databases.

OLAP Viewers

Microsoft Excel is one of the most popular interfaces to OLAP data. In fact, for three of the leading OLAP products (Oracle Essbase, Microsoft Analysis Services, SAP BW), the spreadsheet was initially the *only* interface. Users would open a spreadsheet and could immediately begin drilling within cells and Excel Pivot Tables to retrieve and explore their data.

Today, Excel continues to be an important OLAP interface, but in addition, users can explore data via OLAP viewers. These OLAP viewers may be web-based (whereas Excel is desktop-based) and will have advanced charting and navigation capabilities. In addition, business query tools and production reporting tools may also be able to access OLAP data sources and allow users to drill around with a report.

Just as business query and reporting tools allow users to retrieve data from relational databases without knowing SQL, OLAP viewers allow users to access data in an OLAP database without knowing MDX. Many of the leading BI platform vendors offer OLAP viewers to third-party OLAP data sources, sometimes via the business query and reporting tool, or via a production reporting tool, or via a special OLAP viewer. Examples of specialty OLAP viewers include arcplan, Strategy Companion, and Panorama.

Microsoft Office

It's often said that Microsoft Excel is unofficially the leading BI tool. Business intelligence teams have tried to ignore it and sometimes disable it, because it can wreak havoc on the one thing a data warehouse is supposed to provide: a single version of truth. Yet users are passionate about spreadsheet integration, and it may be the preferred interface for power users. The issue for BI teams and businesses, then, is how to facilitate the integration while managing its use. In the past, Excel "integration" was often limited to a one-time export of data from the BI tool to a disconnected spreadsheet. Most BI platform vendors support spreadsheet integration in ways that allow Excel and the BI environment to work better together, perhaps even extending BI's reach. SAS, for example offers an add-in that allows a user to refresh and interact with reports using Outlook, PowerPoint, or Excel. The theory is that anyone comfortable with e-mail can access and interact with a report.

Microsoft, as the maker of Office, clearly has a vested interest in surfacing data in Excel. To this end, Office 2013 now includes visualization capabilities for data exploration, and PowerPivot, an Excel add-in released in 2010, allows Excel users to mash together large data sources using in-memory technology. Static exports to Excel should not be considered business intelligence. It's not intelligence; it's chaos, and dangerous. Leveraging the power of a spreadsheet to access and explore data in a managed way, on the other hand, brings Excel into the spectrum of business intelligence.

Performance Management

Performance management and business intelligence are typically treated as separate applications, with the former being controlled primarily by finance and the latter by IT or individual business units. Some vendors will offer both BI and performance management tools because the information needs and purposes of both sets of tools are closely related. In rudimentary deployments, BI provides better access to data. In more focused initiatives, BI provides better access to data *so that an individual or an entire company can improve their performance.*

Performance management tools help optimize, manage, and measure that performance by providing the following key components: budgeting and planning capabilities, financial consolidation, and strategic or balanced scorecards. Business intelligence may provide the underpinnings for performance management in that (1) these applications need access to data for planning and measurement purposes and (2) what may start out as a simple BI initiative for "better data access" becomes more purpose driven when put in the context of optimizing performance according to the goals of the business.

Craig Schiff, a performance management expert and president of BPM Partners, describes the connection between performance management and BI as follows:

Business performance management is a set of integrated, closed-loop management and analytics processes that address financial as well as operational activities. Done properly, it enables business to define strategic goals and then measure and manage performance against those goals.[3]

Large BI platform vendors such as Oracle, IBM, and SAP all offer performance management solutions. However, other BI vendors such as MicroStrategy and Information Builders have elected not to pursue this related segment. Specialty vendors in this segment include Infor, Adaptive Planning, and Host Analytics.

NOTE While performance management may have its roots in finance, it is by no means limited to financial plans. Performance management may relate to workforce planning, supply chain optimization, capacity planning, and so on.

Planning

Many companies have manual planning processes compiled through thousands of disconnected spreadsheets. Planning tools help automate and control the process. Part of the planning process is reviewing historical actuals for a basis of comparison. These actuals most likely come from the data warehouse or a data mart (either OLAP or relational). An

---

Alphabet Soup: BPM, CPM, EPM, PM

Here come those acronyms again! Industry analysts, media, and vendors will refer to performance management with any number of acronyms: business performance management (BPM), corporate performance management (CPM), enterprise performance management (EPM), and performance management (PM). They all refer to the same things. The one major point of confusion is when "BPM" is used to refer to business *process* management, a completely different field. It is a shame that this acronym has become confusing because the BPM Standards Group, whose charter was to define standards and concepts pertaining to *performance* management, uses it as its name.

initial plan may be based on business rules such as percentage change from one year to another. Plans may be prepared either "bottom up," in which individual managers provide their plans to roll into a company-wide plan, or they may be "top down," in which plans are made at the highest level and individual units provide details on how that plan can be achieved. Here is where planning and BI show another point of integration: A number of planning tools use an OLAP database to capture plan data.

Once a plan has been finalized, managers want to monitor adherence to and progress toward the plan. Such monitoring can be part of a dashboard or a scorecard.

Financial Consolidation

As individual business units aggregate into a total company, financial consolidation tools help ensure things such as intercompany eliminations, currency conversion, and Sarbanes-Oxley compliance. A financial consolidation tool includes a chart of accounts (a specific dimension that defines, for example, how assets such as cash, inventory, and accounts receivable aggregate on a balance sheet). Financial consolidation may be provided by the enterprise resource planning (ERP) system or by a dedicated tool.

Financial consolidation tools differ from other aspects of a performance management or BI system in that their primary purpose is to produce the financial reports of a company, such as a balance sheet or income statement, whereas much of the other information is for management reporting and analysis.

Analytic Applications

Henry Morris of International Data Corporation (IDC) first coined the term *analytic application* in 1997.[4] According to IDC, for software to be considered an analytic application, it must have the following characteristics:

- Function independently of the transaction or source systems
- Extract, transform, and integrate data from multiple sources and allow for time-based analysis
- Automate a group of tasks related to optimizing particular business processes

Dashboards and reports may be components of an analytic application, but it is the optimization of a particular functional process or industry vertical that most sets an analytic application apart from other BI modules.

There are different types of analytic applications, including customer, financial, supply chain, production, and human resources applications. You can either buy or build an analytic application. When you "buy" an analytic application, you buy a range of prebuilt functionality such as the extract, transform, and load (ETL) routines; the physical data model; and prebuilt reports with functional metrics. When you "build" an analytic application, you determine how and whether to calculate "average sale per store visit" and in which reports you want this metric to appear. With a prebuilt analytic application, this and other metrics are provided for you. With "build" analytic applications, the development environment may provide templates and engines that allow you to assemble applications. A BI platform vendor may provide analytic applications, and numerous niche vendors also provide analytic applications for specific industries or functional areas. Oracle and SAP in particular have focused on delivering analytic applications for functional areas that align to their ERP modules.

Advanced and Predictive Analytics

Data mining and statistical analysis is a particular kind of analysis that describes patterns in data using various algorithms. Statisticians often work with granular data sets, whereas managers and decision-makers tend to work with aggregates to identify trends. A data scientist is a power user who may use statistical tools, custom SQL, programming languages, and BI tools to accomplish their analyses. Data scientists, dubbed the sexiest job of the 21st century by Tom Davenport in *Harvard Business Review*,[5] require a unique blend of math, computer, and business skills. A data scientist might be quite content, thrilled even, to have to install their own Hadoop cluster, write a MapReduce job, and then load the data into another tool to perform some analytics. A typical BI user would lament such a process, as the data is typically more prepared.

Predictive analytics allow users to create a model, test the model based on actual data, and then project future results. Data mining is used in predictive analysis, fraud detection, customer segmentation, and market basket analysis. Although predictive analytics is one segment of the BI market, it continues to be an application reserved for specialist users, with SAS, IBM SPSS, and open-source R leading the market.

Each vendor has a different approach in where the analytics should be done. In the past, statisticians have largely extracted data from source systems and data warehouses to perform analyses outside of the BI environment. Increasingly, the processing of the models is being pushed to the database, referred to as "in-database analytics."

In an effort to make BI more actionable, some BI vendors are incorporating data mining and predictive analytics into their BI platform. This does not mean that predictive analytics will become "mainstream," but rather, that the results of such analysis can be readily incorporated into everyday reports, dashboards, and decision-making.

Big Data Analytics

As discussed in the previous chapter, big data is not synonymous with Hadoop, but there is a new category of solutions that focus on exploring and analyzing data in Hadoop. Traditional BI vendors may provide connectivity to Hadoop, but their origins were in accessing and exploring data stored either in relational databases or OLAP databases using either SQL or MDX. Big data analytics, on the other end, may generate a MapReduce job to access the data. Such is the approach that DataMeer and Platfora take. Others, such as KarmaSphere, may use HiveQL to access the data. Because response time in a HDFS- or MapReduce-only world can be slow, these vendors also may load the data into their own in-memory solutions. In addition to differences in the technology, big data analytics may involve analyzing new types of data such as clicks from web site log files, positioning from radio frequency identification (RFID) devices, tweets, images, and so on.

Best Practices for Successful Business Intelligence

The BI front end consists of the tools and interfaces that business people use to access the data and monitor trends. These tools include business query and reporting, visual data discovery, dashboards and scorecards, mobile BI, production reporting, and Excel. Performance management tools are used in conjunction with BI tools and the BI architecture to improve planning, produce financial reports, and measure performance against the objectives and goals of the company. Because the BI tools provide the face for the business intelligence architecture and processes, it's easy for the tool to get an inordinate amount of attention. They are, however, only one aspect of a business intelligence solution, albeit an important one. As you work to exploit the full value of business intelligence

- Never underestimate the importance of these tools in engaging users to leverage data for competitive advantage. Ease of use and interface appeal matter!
- Understand that the business tools must work in conjunction with the underlying technical architecture; an intuitive tool is only as reliable and useful as the data that it accesses.
- Ensure the business and IT jointly develop a business-focused meta-data layer or business view upon which a number of the front-end tools rely.
- Consider the distinct capabilities of the different tool segments and offer the appropriate tool to the appropriate user group (discussed more in Chapter 12).
- Evolve your BI tool portfolio as technology and user requirements evolve.

Chapter 4

Measures of Success

There is no clear yardstick for *successful* business intelligence. While the industry would like to give a single, objective measure—such as return on investment (ROI)—the reality is that ROI is derived from imprecise inputs upon which few stakeholders agree. Interestingly, the most successful business intelligence deployments don't use ROI as a measure of success. Instead, there are multiple measures of success, with varying degrees of importance and accuracy.

> "We measure success by how fast we can get to a new insight. Speed to insight."
>
> —David Whiting, director of analytic technology solutions,
>
> Constant Contact

Success and Business Impact

In the Successful BI survey, I asked respondents to rate their BI deployment as very successful, moderately successful, slightly successful, or mostly a failure. As Figure 4-1 shows, the majority (51 percent) rated their deployments in the middle of the road as *moderately* successful. Only 24 percent considered their deployments as *very* successful. The good news is that only a very small percentage (3 percent) rated their deployment as mostly a failure. Some vendors (usually newer entrants), consultants, and media outlets claim the BI failure rate is significantly higher.[1] They have a built-in incentive to make you think that BI has been a disaster so that you will buy more tools and services to fix these failures. In truth, nowadays there are fewer spectacular failures than there were in the early days of BI and data warehousing. However, it remains true that most BI deployments have failed to reach their full

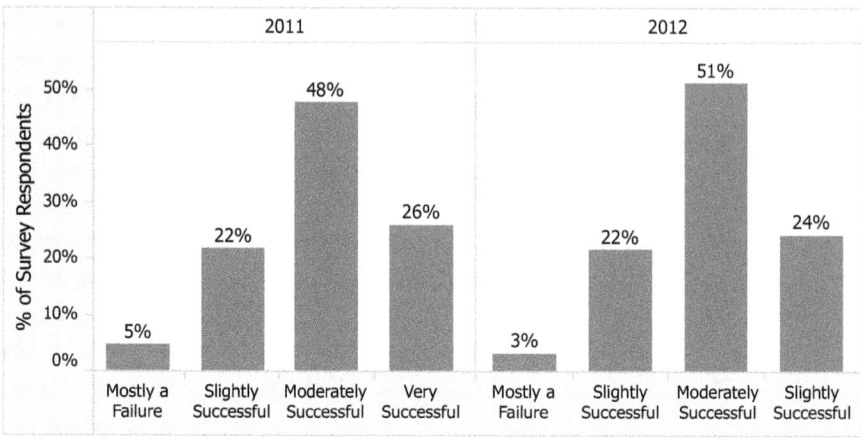

Figure 4-1   Assessment of BI success or failure

potential. This degree of very successful BI deployments has changed little since the original 2007 survey.

Some cynics would argue that only the people relatively happy with their BI deployment respond to these surveys, so failures might theoretically be underrepresented. Perhaps. However, some believe that dissatisfied people are more likely to complain than those who are satisfied. Regardless, mediocrity is not something to strive for, and while the failure rate is not catastrophic, the percentage of very successful deployments could and should be significantly higher.

One measure of BI success is how much business intelligence contributes to a company's performance, or business impact. Here, the results are slightly better, as shown in Figure 4-2. Thirty-four percent of respondents said their BI solution contributes *significantly* to company performance. That this is 10 percentage points higher than those who describe their solution as "very successful" shows an interesting dichotomy. A BI initiative may have a higher business impact than the degree that it is perceived as being successful.

Table 4-1 shows the correlations between how a respondent rates their BI deployment and the perceived business impact. (Note: Percentages are rounded to the nearest whole number.)

Business performance can be evaluated based on a number of different aspects. Which aspects are most important depends on the specific industry and whether you are a publicly held company, nonprofit, or government agency.

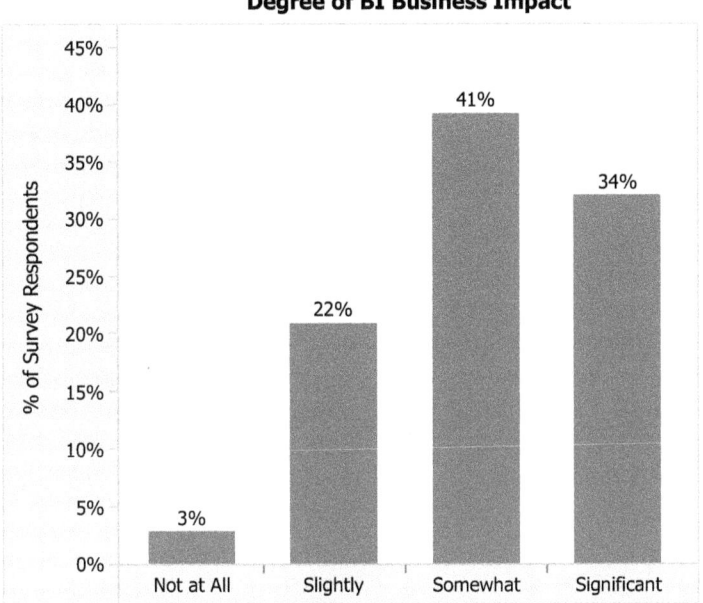

Figure 4-2   Degree to which BI contributes to company performance

	Significantly Contributes to Company Performance	Somewhat Contributes to Company Performance	Does Not Contribute at All	Contributes Slightly	Successful BI Deployment Totals
Very successful BI deployment	19%	5%	0%	0%	24%
Moderately successful	14%	31%	6%	0%	51%
Slightly successful	1%	6%	13%	2%	22%
Mostly a failure	0%	0%	2%	1%	3%
Contribution to company performance totals	34%	41%	22%	3%	100%

Table 4-1   Relationship Between Successful BI Deployment and Contribution to Company Performance

Why BI Success and Business Impact Are Not Synonymous

In crafting the survey and analyzing results, my initial expectation was that these two questions would be tightly correlated—that if your BI deployment were wildly successful, it would contribute significantly to business performance. Or conversely, if the BI solution is contributing significantly to the business, it would, of course, be viewed as very successful. However, these items are not synonymous. Often, survey respondents perceive BI success as relating to the correct technical implication, whereas business impact is reflective of how the data is used.

Further, there is sometimes a disappointment and gap between the vision of what's possible versus what has been achieved. For example, at The Learning Circle, there is clear evidence of three schools deriving measurable impact from the student dashboards, but as it's available to

---

About Learning Circle Education Services

Learning Circle began as a community outreach service within Nationwide Insurance in 2007.[3] The CEO at Nationwide had an interest in using data to improve educational outcomes—specifically, high school graduation rates in urban schools. In 2010, the group was spun off as a nonprofit organization serving three school districts, several communities, and 60,000 students.

About BI at Learning Circle

- **Start of BI efforts:** 2007
- **Executive-level sponsor:** CEO and superintendent of school district
- **Number of BI users:** 5,000
- **Number of source systems used for BI:** 30 data feeds from seven source systems
- **ETL/EIM tools:** Custom SQL and Information Builders MODIFY program
- **Data warehouse platform:** Microsoft SQL Server and Information Builders FOCUS
- **Frequency of updates:** Daily
- **BI tools:** Information Builders WebFOCUS
- **Big data:** Investigating, would like to bring in social data
- **Cloud:** Ohio Education Computer Network

117 schools, we should be able to cite all those schools as successes, says Barb Boyd, president of Learning Circle.[2] The other schools are using the dashboards, but it's not clear how much faculty are acting upon that information, with results bubbling up into improved grades, test scores, and graduation rates.

In the 2007 Successful BI survey, the percentage of business users seeing the business impact as significant was 15 percentage points higher than the percentage of IT professionals saying the impact on company performance was significant. In 2012, the view by different stakeholders reflected a greater consensus on impact; there was little difference of opinion by role, either business or IT. This seems to me to be a positive trend as IT shifts to a greater understanding of how BI is being used and where it is impactful, regardless of the myriad of technical and organizational challenges a BI team may face.

A small percentage of survey respondents (5 percent) consider the BI deployment as being very successful yet as having only moderate business impact. In this regard, it is possible to build a perfectly architected BI solution that has less impact on the business or on the way users leverage information.

How to Measure Success

There are a number of ways to measure the success of your BI deployment, some qualitative and some more quantitative and objective. Qualitative measures of success are used by more people than quantitative measures. For example, according to survey respondents (see Figure 4-3), better access to data was the number one measure of success (by 61 percent of respondents). The ability for BI to increase operating efficiencies (54 percent of respondents) and to manage the day-to-day business (51 percent) is an indicator of BI success. While BI is often used in marketing applications, marketing measures such as improvement in revenues and customer service were used in only a third of companies surveyed. In healthcare, measures such as improved patient outcomes and minimal emergency room wait times are objective measures of success. In education, many measures such as attendance rates, proficiency, and graduation rates can all ultimately be supported by data.

The challenge here is that qualitative benefits, such as "better access to data," are rarely a way of garnering executive-level support and funding for BI investments.

While measures such as ROI, cost savings, and number or percentage of active users are more objective measures, they appear to be used

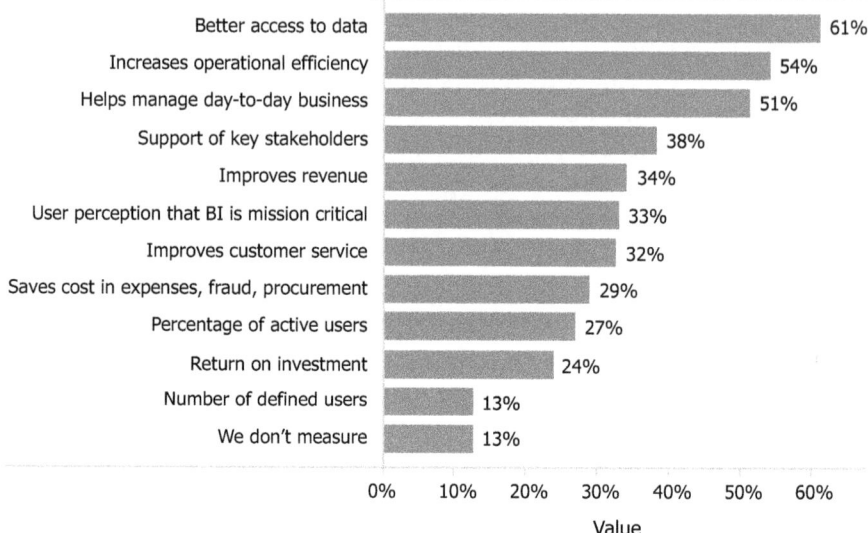

Figure 4-3   BI success is measured by both qualitative and quantitative measures.

less frequently as a measure of successful BI than qualitative measures such as better access to data and user perception.

Measures of Success at Netflix

Netflix has always been a data-centric company, and analytics is a part of its corporate DNA. "What's unique at Netflix is how integral data is with everything we do—the day-to-day business decisions," says Jonathan Liebtag, Senior Manager of DVD Financial Planning and Analysis at Netflix. Much of the success in the company's early years was about being able to buy and inventory movies cheaper than competitors, but more so, with a greater inventory, to get users' favorite movies in their hands faster. In my college years, I was a manager in a chain of video stores, and come Friday night, we could never keep enough copies of favorites like *Splash* or *Tootsie* in stock. We didn't have the technology to keep a wait list either. So indeed, while I mourn the demise of some local video stores, I admire Netflix's DVD rental optimization. For Netflix to succeed, both in DVD and streaming, they have to provide the best content, on the users' preferred device, at the lowest rate. One measure of success in DVD rentals, then, is how often a customer gets their first-choice DVD rental. On a daily basis, managers track across the 50 distribution centers the number of disks that were mailed and that were first in the customer's queue.[4]

Personalization is also key to keeping customers and enhancing customer loyalty when customers can so easily switch to competitors like Hulu and Amazon with a simple click or tap. In this regard, a

---

About Netflix

Netflix provides video and TV streaming and DVD rentals to 33 million members in 40 countries.[6] It became a public company in 2002, initially competing with mom-and-pop video stores and national chains such as Blockbuster. Instead of paying daily rental rates and high late fees, customers received DVDs via mail and could keep them as long as they wanted, for a low monthly subscription. With the rise of streaming video, Netflix separated its DVD and streaming subscriptions in late 2011.[7] After some initial customer backlash and loss of subscribers, Netflix has subsequently increased subscribers. As of June 2013, the streaming business unit accounted for 77% of the total revenues; however, the DVD business still accounted for 61% of the company's profitability.[8]

About BI at Netflix

- **Start of BI efforts:** When company was formed in 1997
- **Executive-level sponsor:** Multiple
- **BI center of excellence:** Per business unit, DVD, and global streaming
- **Adoption rate/number of BI users:** DVD: 60 percent of employees use BI directly; others may use secondarily via applications or in development; Streaming: 7,000+ clients.[9]
- **ETL/EIM tools:** Ab Initio
- **Data warehouse platform:** Teradata
- **Data warehouse size:** 40 TB in DVD
- **Frequency of update:** Near real-time
- **BI tools:** MicroStrategy
- **Predictive:** Open-source R
- **Big data:** Used in streaming business unit: Hadoop, Hive, Cassandra[10]
- **Cloud:** Used in streaming business unit: Amazon EC2

competitive edge is not only about having the best content, but also about the best use of the data to serve customers. Netflix is continually enhancing its recommendation and ranking algorithms. For several years, Netflix sponsored contests to engage the public in improving its movie rating engine. They are also a big proponent of A/B testing in which different sets of customers will receive a different sign-up page. Sign-up rates, viewing, and retention are all used in A/B metrics.[5] For example, Blu-ray customers seem to generate higher profit margins, but giving users too many options on viewing devices or disc types at sign-up can cause them to abandon a registration. Gut feel suggested the sign-up page should be simplified, so it was. When there was a drop in Blu-ray sign-ups, Netflix implemented an A/B test with a more detailed registration page and found that offering Blu-ray as a device choice at sign-ups resulted in an uptick in registrations.

Measures of Success at Learning Circle

At Learning Circle, the ultimate measure for success is whether the school, the teacher, or the community has enabled a child to be successful and move on to the next grade level. The state of Ohio uses the Education Value-Added Assessment System, a statistical model developed by SAS, to determine a school's effectiveness.[11] This measure is referred to as *value add*. If a school moves a child more than one year in the material for that grade, they get an "above" rating in the value-added assessment. Currently, the Learning Circle can cite three schools using the BI application that have rated "above."

There are multiple metrics that teachers can track in helping a child progress, including attendance rates, grades, and standardized tests. One of the benefits of the No Child Left Behind Act is that it forced educators to use data. (The No Child Left Behind Act was passed into law in the United States in 2002. It requires that states issue standardized tests to measure student progress and ensure that all students ultimately achieve proficiency at the respective grade level. If there is not a sufficient level of progress, then schools risk losing funding.) Many critics of the law, though, argue that it does not take into account factors that are beyond the teacher's control, such as discipline issues, chronic absenteeism, or lack of parental involvement. Test results alone don't show the full picture of a student.

As shown in Figure 4-4, the Individual Student Profile shows a teacher or administrator a full view of the student. Absenteeism is flagged as a caution, with eight unexcused absences. Discipline events

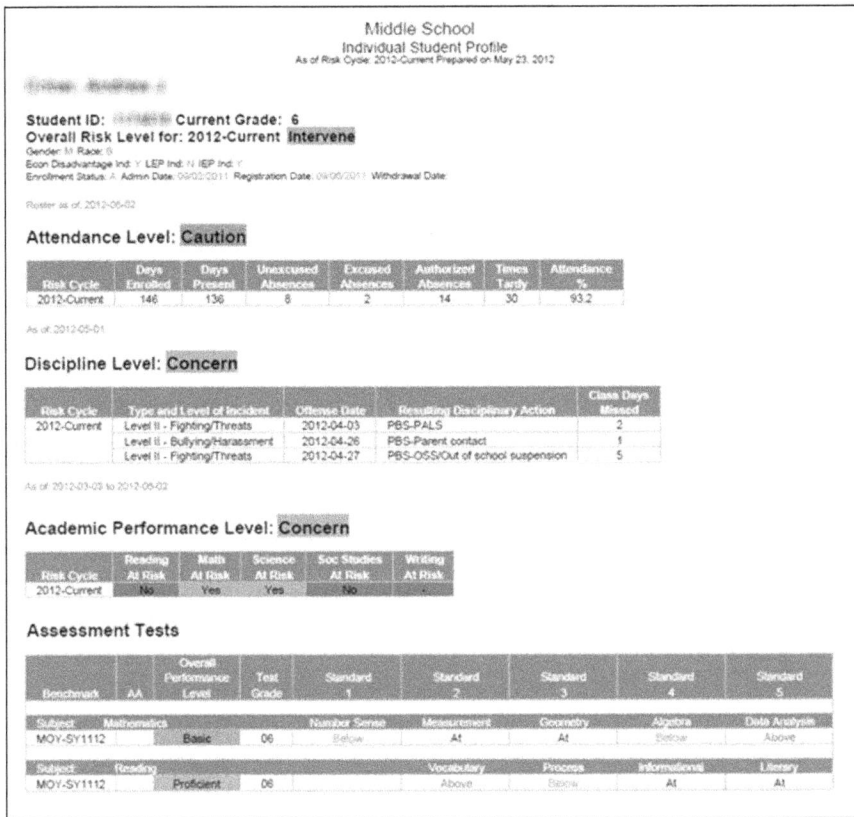

Figure 4-4 The Learning Circle's student profile report provides a full view of the student. *Note: Some information blurred to protect privacy.*

are reported and flagged as a concern. Math and science assessment tests are at risk of not being proficient for the grade level, so overall, the report suggests that the school should intervene.

Learning Circle President Barb Boyd explains that the data allows you to ask the next question and to have a conversation, not to place blame. Ed McLellan, Vice President of Product and Innovation, says, "It puts a lot of capability in the hands of the people who can make a difference on the success of those students."

Measures of Success at Constant Contact

David Whiting, director of analytic technology solutions at Constant Contact, echoes some of the same comments as other successful BI case studies when contemplating their degree of BI success. "We've accomplished a lot, but there is still so much more to do. We have an enormous appetite for information," explains Whiting. The company began investing more aggressively in BI in 2008.[12] Initially, they had a good data warehouse that was highly structured, but they didn't have the tools to be great at analytics. Since then, they implemented IBM Cognos and an analytic appliance, IBM Netezza. A big impetus for investing in BI was the ability to keep pace with the growth of the company. In 2008, Constant Contact had 200,000 customers; today it has over 500,000. In this regard, a key measure of BI success is how well the BI team is able to keep pace with the business requirements. Whiting says he doesn't have a formal KPI in mind, but focuses on the time to insight and the overall process to deliver that insight. There are some requests that used to take 15 hours—including analyst time to

About Constant Contact

Constant Contact was founded in 1998 and is a publicly traded company offering online marketing tools. As a cloud-based solution, its primary customer base is small to midsized companies and nonprofit organizations. The company's core product is email marketing but has recently expanded into online surveys, social media optimization, digital storefronts, and event management. They have over 500,000 customers.

About BI at Constant Contact

- **Start of BI efforts:** 2008
- **Executive-level sponsor:** CEO
- **Business Intelligence Competency Center:** Yes. Central BI team that is responsible for BI enablement reports to the CIO. There is also an analytics team that resides within finance.
- **Number of BI users:** 160
- **ETL/EIM tools:** IBM InfoSphere DataStage
- **Data warehouse platform:** IBM Netezza
- **Data warehouse size:** 45 TB
- **BI tools:** IBM Cognos
- **Big Data:** Hadoop
- **Mobile BI:** Not deployed
- **Advanced Analytics:** SAS and SPSS

understand and write a script, processing on the server, developing a report—that now only take 15 minutes. The faster time to insight can be attributed to a number of factors, including better self-service BI tools, the Netezza appliance, and expertise of BI team members. Whiting has been able to track quantitative measures from having implemented an analytic appliance such as[13]

- 60-fold improvement in partner reporting processes
- 44 times faster query performance for a product mix report
- 128 times faster performance to update an operational data store for rolling period reporting

Return on Investment

The projected ROI is often required to fund a BI project, but it is a measure that few companies calculate once BI capabilities have been provided or enhanced. One reason companies rarely calculate this is that while it is fairly easy to determine the cost or investment portion of a BI implementation, it is not easy to determine the return, a common challenge for many technology investments. There are some things that are simply part of the cost of doing business. Nowadays, no worker would be asked to justify the cost of having a phone, for example, and increasingly, BI falls into this category. And yet, ROI is a necessary requirement to get funding for projects and BI enhancements.

When assessing how much BI contributes to revenue improvement, it's debatable how much of a revenue increase or improvement can be attributed to BI versus other factors such as sales force training, merchandising, advertising, and so on. Identifying cost savings is easier when you eliminate specific reporting systems or reduce head count. However, even with cost savings, head count may not be reduced, but instead held constant while the business grows. In other words, there has been cost *avoidance* by providing a BI solution. How much cost has been avoided is yet another debatable number, ultimately making ROI a precise number derived from imprecise inputs.

There have been several industry studies to determine the average ROI for BI projects, typically in the 300 to 400 percent range, and some as high as 2,000 percent.[14] Of the more recent ROI analysis, in 2011, Nucleus Research reported that in its ROI case studies, for every $1 spent on analytics, organizations earned an average of $10.66. In 2012, Oracle commissioned Forrester Consulting to analyze the deployments of four customers who had purchased both the Oracle BI Foundation Suite and the prebuilt analytic applications. Based on those findings, Forrester developed a composite organization of 1,500 employees, $500 million in sales, and projected a 97 percent risk-adjusted ROI.[15] It's clear to me that while the use of ROI as a measure of success, or even a requirement for funding, has been declining, the returns for BI investments remain solid.

Calculating ROI

Despite the limitations of using ROI as a measure of success, it is a number that provides a basis for comparison to other BI implementations and IT initiatives. It also is a measure well understood by business sponsors who have to buy into the value of business intelligence. In this respect, even "guesstimating" your actual ROI can be helpful for internal promotion purposes. It's also interesting to note that while most survey respondents used multiple measures of success, a higher percentage of companies who said their BI had a significant impact on business performance also used ROI as a measure. This in no way suggests *cause,* but it might be an indication of the degree to which a company prioritizes technology investments and in which a measurable benefit must be demonstrated.

Use ROI as an objective measure of success, even if it's only a back-of-the-envelope calculation and not all stakeholders agree on the cost savings and revenue contribution from business intelligence.

The basic formula for calculating ROI over a three-year period is

$$ROI = [(NPV \text{ Cost Reduction} + \text{Revenue Contribution}) / \text{Initial Investment}] \times 100$$

Net present value (NPV) considers the time value of money. In simplistic terms, if you have $1 million to deposit in a bank today, next year, assuming 2 percent interest, it would be worth $1,020,000. The formula to calculate NPV of a three-year cost or revenue is

$$NPV = F / (1 + r) + F / (1 + r)^2 + F / (1 + r)^3$$

F is the future cash flow from the cost reductions and revenue contributions. R is the discount rate for your company. Five percent may be the interest a bank is willing to pay, but companies will have a different rate that takes into account the expected return for other investments and opportunity costs from investing in business intelligence versus other capital projects. In estimating the revenue improvement, take the amount revenue has actually increased and then assign a percentage of that for which BI has been a key enabler.

Anecdotes of Hard Business Benefits

If you are unable to calculate the ROI for a BI initiative, it is still important to cite any hard business benefits achieved from accessing and analyzing data. These anecdotes help motivate BI teams and foster ongoing executive support. Some additional examples of hard business benefits:

Novation is a healthcare supply chain and contracting company that serves hospitals such as Veterans Health Administration (VHA), University Healthsystem Consortium (UHC), and Provista. Novation's analytics capabilities identified approximately $850 million in supply chain cost reduction opportunities.[16]

The San Diego Unified School District in California gets funding according to the number of students attending school. It used Oracle BI to deliver reports and dashboards that allow administrators and guidance counselors to track daily attendance rates, contributing to a 1 percent improvement in attendance. Improved attendance generated $6 million in revenue for the district.[17]

The Austin, Texas, fire department implemented a data discovery tool, QlikView, and built dashboards to track and analyze head count, staffing, emergency calls, and education compliance. The previous approach to analyzing data was largely manual, but the QlikView solution allowed them to save 4,893 hours in data collection and formatting. Response time to 911 calls was reduced between 8 and 30 seconds.[18]

FleetRisk Advisors, a business unit of Omnitracs and a Qualcomm company, uses data to analyze and predict truck driver performance and safety. Their services have helped customers reduce the incidence of minor accidents by 20 percent and serious accidents by as much as 80 percent.[19]

Number of Users

While business impact may be in the eye of the beholder, you would think that the number of BI users is a much more objective measure of success. Yet here, too, there is room for debate and fudging of definitions. In discussing this statistic with experts, people have asked, "If a user receives a printout or static PDF (Portable Document Format) from a BI tool, should they be counted as a BI user?" This is a really tricky question. Some vendors would count this person as a user who would have to pay for a BI recipient license. If you use the concept I put forth in Chapter 1, that business intelligence is a set of technologies and processes that allow people of all levels of an organization to access, interact with, and analyze data . . . and that business intelligence is about creativity, culture, and whether people view information as a critical asset, then this person should be counted as a user if they can interact within the PDF or control how often they receive this information. So the operative words here are *static* and *interact*. Some BI tools do, in fact, allow users to sort and filter within a PDF, so I would consider a recipient of such a report a BI user. I would not consider a recipient of a static printout of a report a BI user.

BI Users as a Percentage of Employees

So let's assume there is direct access to the BI system or to the data warehouse. Here, too, companies may undercount users based on different definitions and ways in which BI is used and licensed.

Despite the discrepancies in what to count, there is a major difference between the case studies in this book and the industry as a whole, and that is in the degree of BI penetration. Historically, many in the BI industry still consider information workers as the only potential BI users, yet case after case in this book shows that information workers are only a portion of the total BI potential. With the rise of mobile devices, appealing dashboards, and easier BI tools, potential BI users may now include more diverse classes of users, such field salespeople, truck drivers, doctors, and teachers.

In the Successful BI survey, then, I specifically ask about the percentage of total *employees* (versus potential BI users) that have access to a BI tool; the average is 24 percent, only slightly higher than the initial 2007 survey and not statistically relevant. As Figure 4-5 illustrates, companies who describe their BI deployment as very successful have a 35 percent adoption rate, which is 9 percentage points higher of BI users than those of moderate success and 20 points higher than those who described their BI approach as slightly successful. In previous years, those companies rating their BI deployment as a failure also showed a significantly lower adoption rate. In 2012, responses from two companies with pervasive deployments described as failures skewed results

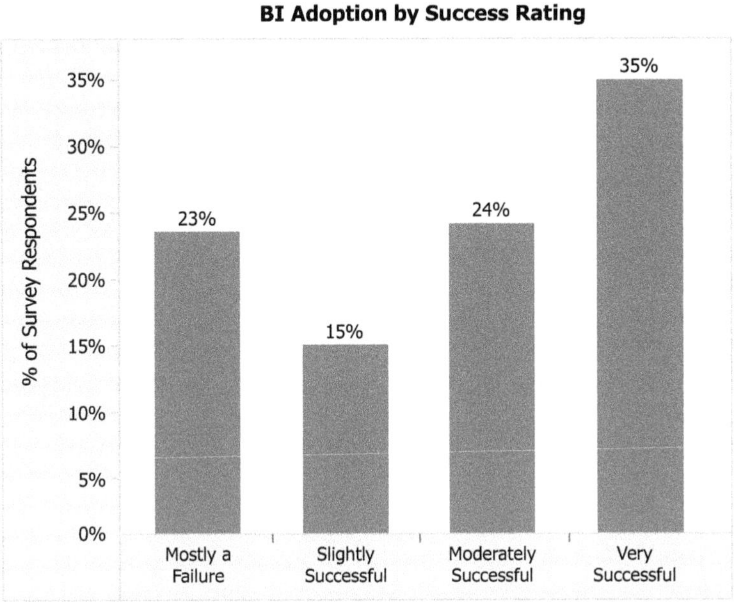

BI Adoption by Success Rating

Figure 4-5   BI success and adoption are related.

for that category; when omitting those records, the adoption rate for companies described as BI failures is 13 percent, well below the overall average of 24 percent.

Indicating that the industry has not yet fully realized how wide a net BI can cast, when asked if the BI deployment were wildly successful and budget were not an issue, what percentage of employees *should* have access to a BI tool, respondents said they thought only 54 percent of employees *should* have access to a BI tool (versus 24 percent currently using). The large gap between currently using and perceived potential shows that BI is not reaching everyone it should and not providing BI's full value. Further, that the perceived potential according to survey respondents is not closer to 100 percent and has not changed in five years, shows the industry still has a long journey to make data relevant to everyone.

To be successful with business intelligence, you need to be thinking about deploying BI to 100 percent of your employees as well as beyond organizational boundaries to customers and suppliers.

Business intelligence as a set of technologies and processes is still relatively young, at less than 20 years old. A number of technical innovations, as well as improving data literacy and technical proficiencies in the workforce, will allow BI penetration to be 100 percent of employees. Think about it: Does everyone in your company have a cell phone? Did they 20 years ago? Yet portable phones (more the size of briefcases) existed in the late 1980s. Such "portable" phones had little adoption due to usability and cost reasons. BI eventually will be viewed in the same way. If you think this sounds too technocratic or too futuristic, consider how absurd these quotes appear with the clarity of hindsight:

> "There's no reason anyone would want a computer in their home."
> —Ken Olson, founder of Digital Equipment Corporation (DEC), 1977

> "I think there is a world market for maybe five computers."
> —Thomas Watson, chairman of IBM, 1943[20]

Some argue that certain users will never need BI. Indeed, this may be partly true, but currently we just haven't made BI relevant enough for all users, particularly beyond information workers. Don't imagine 100 percent of employees using traditional business query and reporting tools, designed for power users. Instead, picture all employees having access to information to support their daily decisions and actions, with tools that work in ways they need them to. For some users, that's a business query tool; for others, it's a dashboard; and for still others, it's a widget of information. When BI is made relevant and accessible to front-line and field workers as well as externally to customers and suppliers, then BI usage will be closer to 100 percent of employees. The concept and importance of relevance are discussed further in Chapter 9.

No matter what you think the total BI potential is—100 percent of employees or only 54 percent of employees as shown in the earlier chart—the survey results clearly show that there is huge untapped potential.

BI for Everyone or for Only Certain User Segments?

When analyzing the percentage of BI users according to different user segments, the information workers or business and financial analysts have the highest penetration at 67 percent of the total, as shown in

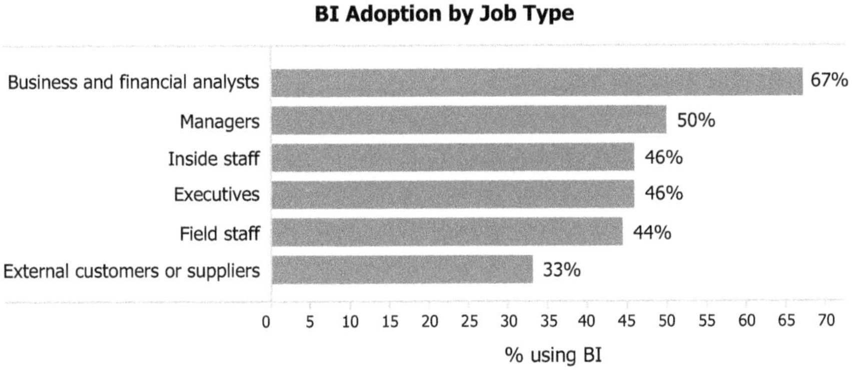

BI Adoption by Job Type

Figure 4-6   Of the percentage of total employees by user segment, information workers show the highest BI penetration.

Figure 4-6. Executives and managers are the next highest segments, followed by inside staff such as customer service representatives, accountants, and administrative assistants.

External users such as customers and suppliers show the lowest deployment rates at 33 percent, but a marked increase from the 10 percent adoption rate in 2007. There are some technical issues when BI reaches beyond company boundaries, and cloud-based BI is an enabler to extranet deployments. However, some of the larger barriers are organizational and a matter of being aware of the benefits of sharing data with external stakeholders.

Percentage of Active Users

I was pleasantly surprised by the survey results that the percentage of *active* users is a more often cited measure of success than the number of *defined* users (27 percent track active users versus 13 percent defined users). The reason for my surprise has little to do with this measure's importance, but rather, how difficult it is to determine. Then again, less than a third of companies do measure this!

Historically, business intelligence tools were implemented primarily on a departmental basis, where there is little attention paid to monitoring the system. As deployments scale to the enterprise and become more mission critical, monitoring system performance and usage is key to scaling to increased analytic requirements and numbers of users. The ability to monitor activity for the entire BI platform (from data warehouse to BI front-end tools—see Figure 2-3 in Chapter 2) has been somewhat lacking in the industry, either for historical usage reporting or for real-time monitoring.

Other Measures of Success

Other ways to measure the success of your BI initiative include the following:

- **Number of business intelligence applications**   This includes dashboards, business views, and custom applications, such as BI content embedded in an operational system.
- **Number of new requests**   A challenge to successful companies is that the demand for new applications, data sources, enhancements, and so on, significantly outpaces the BI team's ability to deliver enhancements. Business users want more, faster, as they are constantly coming up with new ways to exploit their BI capabilities. This is not the same measure as a "report backlog." Instead, it is a measure of requests that the BI team should fulfill rather than requests for capabilities business users should be able to do themselves.
- **Number of standard and ad hoc reports**   While this is an interesting number, be careful, as more is not always better. If one standard report with greater interactivity and better prompting can serve the needs of hundreds of users (versus having 100 different reports for 100 users), then a single report is better. It is extremely difficult, if not impossible, to assess the number of truly useful versus redundant reports. Having a lower number of reports that are more useful provides a lower cost of ownership and an easier ability for information consumers to know where to find relevant information. Usage monitoring capabilities within a BI solution allow system administrators to track how often particular reports are accessed.
- **Elimination of *independent* spreadsheets**   "Independent" is a key word here, as delivering BI via spreadsheets may be an enabler to user adoption, as long as a live link is maintained back to the BI platform. Even though I don't survey people on this aspect as a measure of success, a number of respondents wrote this factor in free-form comments. At the same time, Microsoft is increasingly pushing spreadsheets as the preferred BI interface but managed via its SharePoint portal.

- **Increased employee satisfaction**   This is achieved by empowering employees to get the information they need to do their jobs well.
- **Increased customer service**   This has an impact on revenues, so here, too, assign a percentage for how much BI contributed to improved customer service.
- **Time reduced in any process**   BI can help reduce the time to complete a number of processes, whether product time to market, order fulfillment, application approval, and so on.

Best Practices for Successful Business Intelligence

The success of a BI deployment can be measured by both intangible criteria, such as better access to data, and user and stakeholder perception. Of greater import are objective business measures, such as revenue improvement, costs saved, better patient outcomes, improved test scores and graduation rates, and return on investment. Other objective measures include number of active users and BI applications. The impact on the organizational performance and support of business goals should be the ultimate criteria of BI success, keeping in mind that how that performance is measured depends on the specific industry and whether you are a publicly held company, nonprofit, or government agency. In evaluating the success of your business intelligence deployment,

- Be able to cite measurable benefits as anecdotes in conversations with stakeholders and new BI users. Anecdotes can go a long way in engaging BI skeptics.
- Use ROI as an objective measure of success, even if this is only calculated on the back of an envelope.
- Don't underestimate the value of intangible, nonquantifiable benefits, such as better access to data and positive user perception. Do try to assign a dollar value to these softer benefits, and state the value in terms of how they align with the strategic goals of the business.
- Use multiple measures of success.
- When initially embarking on your project, agree to and build into the program or project plan the measures of success and progress. Ensure that the sponsors, stakeholders, and project team all agree to the measures.
- Always keep in mind the ultimate goals of BI—insight and action.

Chapter 5

Catalysts for Success: The LOFT Effect

As I analyzed trends from the successful BI companies, a consistent theme emerged. Many had been plugging along at business intelligence to varying degrees for years, and there were a variety of factors that catapulted them from BI mediocrity to success. A few people described the change as "an aligning of the stars" or "a perfect storm." When I look closely at the factors that led to the change from mediocre business intelligence to greater success, there were varying degrees of Luck, Opportunity, Frustration, and Threat: LOFT.

The Role of Luck

The funny thing about luck is that you never really know if a positive outcome truly arises from luck or if it is from fortuitous timing and exceptional insight. While working at Dow Chemical, there were times I felt luck played a big role in our BI efforts, but in hindsight, perhaps it wasn't luck at all. Perhaps it was the effect of some very smart people working toward a common goal.

> "Luck is what happens when preparation meets opportunity."
>
> —Elmer G. Letterman[1]

When Dow first began its BI initiative in 1993, it was an IT-driven project designed to reduce the costs associated with multiple custom reporting systems. There were three aspects to Dow's information management strategy then, all of which played major roles in business intelligence:

- Dow Diamond Systems, which involved implementing SAP globally as its primary enterprise resource planning (ERP) system, replacing numerous custom applications. The breadth of the implementation was enormous, and it encompassed all of Dow's major work processes, including supply chain logistics, customer service, manufacturing, inventory management, accounting, and finance.[2] Not only was this a systems implementation, but it also was a work process redesign and optimization effort. Diamond Systems allowed Dow to reduce its systems by 80 percent and cut its sales and general administration costs by 50 percent.[3]

- Dow Workstation, which involved standardizing all desktop computers and operating systems globally. Up until this point, if a business unit or functional department felt like buying from IBM, HP, Gateway, Dell, or any mom-and-pop build-it-yourself computer outlet, they could. Without a standard workstation, implementing a global client/server BI solution would have had even more technical barriers to overcome than those brought by the newness of data warehousing and business intelligence. With most BI tools now web-enabled, a standard workstation might not have a big influence on a new BI implementation. However, in the mid-1990s, client/server computing was the norm for BI tools, making Dow Workstation a critical enabler to wide-scale deployment.

- The Global Reporting Project, whose charter was to build a global data warehouse with standard access tools to replace multiple regional custom reporting and decision support systems. Initially, Dow thought reporting and analysis would come directly from SAP. However, as sites came online, the regional decision support systems that had previously served the businesses so well began to degrade, and IT could not keep pace with the demand for custom-built reports within SAP.

When I first began working on the Global Reporting Project in 1993, I had never even heard the term "data warehouse." My indoctrination into the project was a gift from my boss: a just-published book by Bill Inmon, *Building the Data Warehouse*. Management reporting was not new to me, but up until this point, my work—and most everyone else's in information systems—was regionally focused. Located in Horgen, Switzerland, I did what my individual business unit (hydrocarbons) in Europe wanted to do. I was unaware of and pretty much ignored what my counterparts in the same business unit in Texas were doing.

Meanwhile, the Global Reporting Project was not in the least bit regionalized. It was our business to know what all the regions and

About the Dow Chemical Company

Dow Chemical is one of the world's largest chemical companies, with $56 billion in annual sales in 2012 and operations in 160 countries around the world. Its products are used in a wide range of goods, including toys, tools, textiles, pharmaceuticals, personal care items, and water purification technologies. In 2001, Dow merged with Union Carbide, consolidating its position in the chemical industry. In 2009, Dow acquired a privately held company, Rohm and Haas. With the rise in petrochemical feedstock costs and increasing world demand for chemicals and plastics, the company must continually look for more efficient ways to operate to ensure profitability and preserve availability of natural resources. All shared services (finance, supply chain, customer services, purchasing) and the commercial divisions rely on business intelligence for strategic, tactical, and operational decisions.

About BI at Dow

- **Start of BI efforts:** 1993
- **Executive-level sponsor:** CIO
- **Business intelligence competency center:** Yes
- **Number of BI users:** ~3,000 concurrent users (more than 10,000 named users), plus an additional 10,000 customers
- **Number of source systems used for BI:** 5
- **ETL/EIM tools:** Currently custom, beginning to use IBM DataStage
- **Data warehouse platform:** Oracle, SAP BW, SAP BW Accelerator
- **Data warehouse size:** 13 TB, with 70 percent updated daily
- **BI tools:** SAP BEx, Web Application Designer, and BusinessObjects
- **Advanced Analytic Tools:** IBM SPSS, SAS JMP

business units were doing in terms of reporting and analysis. Team leaders came from the United States, locations throughout Europe, and later Hong Kong. This global focus was a major organizational and cultural shift from a work perspective. Indeed, we also had cultural "national" barriers to overcome—the Europeans laughed at some of the U.S. counterparts who canceled meetings abroad at the last minute for lack of having a passport. Despite these profound changes and logistical hiccups, we quickly adapted and took advantage of an almost 24-hour work window. Whatever work I started in the morning, a counterpart in the United States added to in his time zone, and yet another continued in Hong Kong. The Dow Workstation and global area network allowed us to share files easily and seamlessly.

While the Global Reporting Project seemed like a good idea at the time, what none of us fully realized was that the regional businesses didn't want what we were building.

SUCCESS: An Idea from Frankfurt, Germany

Prior to the SAP implementation, Dow Europe had an easy-to-use reporting system it called simply decision support system (DSS). It was mainframe-based and might be deemed archaic with today's rich web, Windows, and iOS interfaces, but at the time, it had all the key elements sales and marketing wanted: good data with easy drill-down. As the contrast to newer tools such as Microsoft Excel revealed the limitations of DSS, the Frankfurt, Germany, sales office came up with its own reporting solution. It was a custom-built client/server application, optimized for field sellers, with personalized data and an intuitive, graphical interface. Jens Garby, global director of commercial IT and e-business, then the sales director for Germany, showed it to the European polyethylene director. The executives saw the potential of information technology. They had power and influence, where the information systems department had none. So they decided to make the Frankfurt initiative bigger, better, and broader, with the new reporting application boldly named SUCCESS.

While the SUCCESS team rapidly delivered a slick interface, with flashy charts and fast drill-down times, the Global Reporting Project floundered amid data quality issues and queries that ran for hours. "Global" was not all it was cracked up to be. We held a meeting with European executives and their business analysts to give a status update. For lunch, we served spaghetti to convey the theme of how messy it was to merge information globally.

Dow Globalizes

About 18 months into the project, we got lucky. Very lucky! Under the leadership of a newly appointed CEO, Dow globalized its 15 business units. As the global reporting team learned the news in the cafeteria, many echoed a similar thought, "Wow, did we get lucky!" No longer would businesses be run on a regional basis, but rather, on a truly global basis. Overnight, the global data warehouse became the *only* source of information for managers to run their businesses. Regional DSSs became useless overnight. The original SUCCESS project? It served the needs of field sellers for a while, but data quality declined as regional transaction systems were phased out, and maintenance for the application was problematic when the original programmer left the company. The experience with the SUCCESS initiative, however, provided critical lessons to everyone on the Global Reporting Project that continue to hold true today for anyone in the BI industry:

> (1) Business intelligence has to be fast, easy, and tailored. (2) Great ideas often come from prototypes built within individual business units, which can be more agile and focused on the needs of a smaller constituency.

Rather than viewing departmental initiatives as a threat to enterprise efforts or dismissing them as only point solutions, they should be considered for inspiration and a way to understand the business requirements.

The truly global aspect of the Global Reporting Project was one step ahead of Dow's regional businesses that subsequently globalized 18 months into the BI project. With the clarity of hindsight, perhaps this globalization had little to do with luck. Perhaps it had everything to do with the forward thinking of the IT leaders and having a visionary project manager—Dave Kepler, the original Global Reporting Project manager, went on to become CIO just a few years after he started the Global Reporting Project. At the time, it certainly felt like luck!

In 2009, Dow embarked on its second-biggest acquisition in the history of the company: Rohm and Haas. There were many in the industry who did not think that the acquisition should go through, that it would overstretch the liquidity and debt ratio of the firm. Acquisitions are driven by the business value and product synergies a combined company can deliver, and often the fit from a culture and technology perspective is secondary. However, perhaps luck again played a role in Dow's BI evolution, as Rohm and Haas had both a mature and complementary BI platform and a culture similar to that of Dow's. Rohm and Haas used SAP ERP as its source systems and the packaged data warehouse SAP Business Warehouse (BW). Rohm and Haas' BI leader, Mike Masciandaro, held a similar view to Dow's Dave Kepler—that while technology plays a role in analytics, it's secondary to the business value.

If I think about the technical and cultural clashes of other mergers—United Airlines and Continental, for example—I would say that the Dow and Rohm and Haas teams were lucky that the BI technology, vision, and culture were so compatible.

Opportunity

FlightStats' foray into business intelligence has been evolutionary. Starting originally as an interactive multimedia company, it designed a dial-up travel booking system for American Airlines rewards members in the mid-1990s and later developed the booking engine that powered American's web site for over four years.[4] As that business was acquired by a competitor and spun off, the company changed focus from booking engines to air freight forwarding. In its effort to determine which were the best flights to put freight on, the company began acquiring statistical information on flight performance, weather, and airport delays. Much of the publicly available data is too old and limited to be useful for booking purposes. For example, the Department of Transportation (DOT) provides information for a limited number of airlines, but only two months after the flight.[5] In 2004, as it was improving its database for its freight customers, the company realized that nobody was collecting and mining real-time flight data for external use.[6]

CEO Jeff Kennedy saw an opportunity to exploit this data. What started as a database to optimize air freight logistics morphed into FlightStats, a platform and set of services to "transform information into travel intelligence."[7] FlightStats collects worldwide data from multiple data sources, including airlines, the U.S. Federal Aviation Administration (FAA), global distribution systems (such as Sabre, Amadeus, and Galileo), weather providers, airports, and other third-party data providers. Data is updated in near real time, and a historical reporting and analysis data mart is updated daily.

With planes operating at higher capacities, routes overscheduled with little margin for error, and an antiquated air traffic control system in the U.S., FlightStats has a unique opportunity to help solve passenger woes by providing travel agents and consumers access to near real-time flight performance information. It also publishes airport and airline score cards to help travelers determine the best route, carrier, and time of day to travel.

As an example, Figure 5-1 shows flight performance for the Newark, New Jersey, to Orlando, Florida, route during the two-month period of March 1 to April 30, 2013, during many schools' spring breaks and the

About FlightStats

FlightStats is a privately held company and the leading provider of worldwide flight performance information to the global travel and transportation industries. The FlightStats platform delivers real-time and historical flight information that lowers travel-related costs and improves the travel experience. The company's roots go back to the early 1990s, when they developed a dial-up booking system for American Airlines and the booking engine for several other airlines. The company later moved into providing air freight forwarding decision support tools and applications. In its effort to determine which were the best flights for freight, the company began acquiring statistical information on flight performance. FlightStats has provided this information to airlines, airports, travel agents, search engines, mobile application developers, and media companies since 2005. The consumer-facing solution was launched in May 2006. FlightStats has the most extensive and timely information on U.S.-based flights and 80 percent of international flights. Airlines, consumers, and third parties such as travel agents use the data from FlightStats to monitor and predict flight delays and to send alerts to travelers and travel agents.

About BI at FlightStats

- **Start of BI efforts:** 2001
- **Executive-level sponsor:** CEO
- **Number of BI users:** 57 internal users, with more than 100 million application programming interface (API) requests a month, 5 million external users per month
- **Number of source systems used for BI:** Dozens of real-time flight sources external to FlightStats. These include flight schedules, runway and positional data, gate status, gate assignment, weather, and airport delay information.
- **ETL/EIM tools:** Pentaho Kettle
- **Data warehouse platform:** PostgreSQL
- **Data warehouse size:** mult-TB, with 150,000 flight records and more than 10 million flight events daily
- **Number of subject areas:** Two: historical and real-time
- **BI tools:** JasperReports with OpenReports
- **Big Data:** MongoDB, Hadoop
- **Advance Analytics:** Open-source R and Weka, Python, Numpy, and Scipy for statistical and algorithmic work, Celery for distributed task management, NetworkX for graph processing, MATLAB for statistics and plotting, Gephi for graph processing and visualization
- **Cloud:** Amazon EC2

EWR to MCO Historical On-time Performance Ratings

Route: Date Range: Airline(s):	Newark to Orlando March 1, 2013 to April 30, 2013 All Airlines	This Route Time of Day Flight Status
Departure Airport: Departure City	(EWR) Newark Liberty International Airport Newark, NJ, US	Departures On-time Performance Scorecard
Arrival Airport: Arrival City:	(MCO) Orlando International Airport Orlando, FL, US	Arrivals On-time Performance Scorecard

EWR to MCO On-time Performance

Click flight number for details about the rating   Canceled / Diverted > 4%

On-time Performance	Rating On-time Performance	Carrier	# Flights		On-time %	Delay		Canceled		Diverted	
			Operated	Codeshare	%	Avg	Max	Flights		Flights	
Average	(3.4)	(CM) Copa Airlines	0	576	84%	24	199	0	0%	0	0%
	(3.2)	(UA) United Airlines	604	0	85%	24	199	0	0%	0	0%
	(3.0)	(LO) LOT - Polish Airlines	0	16	81%	25	36	0	0%	0	0%
	(2.9)	(TP) TAP-Portugal	0	108	77%	24	127	0	0%	0	0%
	(2.6)	(SK) SAS - Scandinavian Airlines	0	165	77%	25	148	0	0%	0	0%
	(2.5)	(SN) Brussels Airlines	0	60	80%	31	199	0	0%	0	0%
Poor	(1.3)	(B6) JetBlue Airways	311	0	67%	43	328	4	1%	0	0%

Figure 5-1   FlightStats performance ratings show airline performance out of Newark during FAA furloughs in April 2013.

FAA furloughs, where air traffic controllers were forced to take time off due to mandatory budget cuts. Notice along the left side of the figure a five-point scoring system. The scores consider not only how many flights were late, but also the magnitude of the lateness.

The level of detail that FlightStats provides makes the information actionable. JetBlue has better on-time performance, for example, out of John F. Kennedy Airport than Newark Airport. The time of day and day of week also affect on-time performance. If you are a frequent business traveler, you assume—by experience or gut feel—that the first few flights out are more often on time and less impacted by bump-on delays. It turns out, though, that this is only true on certain days. As Figure 5-2 shows, 73 percent of flights from 6 A.M. to 9 A.M. on Saturdays were significantly delayed.

For FlightStats, successful business intelligence comes with recognizing a unique opportunity in the data they've amassed and enhanced. Initially, such data was only available to freight customers, but availability was expanded, first to travel agencies and airlines, and then,

EWR to MCO Historical On-time Performance Ratings

Route:	Newark to Orlando	This Route Time of Day	
Date Range:	March 1, 2013 to April 30, 2013	Flight Status	
Airline(s):	All Airlines		
Departure Airport:	(EWR) Newark Liberty International Airport	Departures	
Departure City	Newark, NJ, US	On-time Performance Scorecard	
Arrival Airport:	(MCO) Orlando International Airport	Arrivals	
Arrival City:	Orlando, FL, US	On-time Performance Scorecard	

EWR to MCO On-time Performance

The following section is broken down by flights departing Newark in the various time periods. The on-time information is based on whether the flights arrived at Orlando on-time or if they were late.

Time		Mon	Tues	Wed	Thurs	Fri	Sat	Sun	Total
12 AM - 3 AM	Observations								
	On-time %								
	Avg Delay								
	Rating								
3 AM - 6 AM	Observations								
	On-time %								
	Avg Delay								
	Rating								
6 AM - 9 AM	Observations	61	56	52	53	62	55	57	396
	On-time %	93%	100%	90%	100%	85%	73%	95%	91%
	Avg Delay	36.4	4.92	14.09	5.33	14.6	47.74	34	24.38
	Rating	3.11	4.56	4	4.38	4.13	1.16	3.34	3.52
9 AM - 12 PM	Observations	39	34	34	34	38	24	39	242
	On-time %	100%	94%	88%	100%	74%	100%	90%	92%
	Avg Delay	7	12.38	31	5.22	21.58	6.67	20	15.77
	Rating	4.32	4.26	3.15	4.5	2.83	4.43	3.48	3.82

Figure 5-2   FlightStats performance ratings show historical performance by day of week and time of day.

as of late 2006, to consumers. Since first launching the application to customers, FlightStats now uniquely has flight performance on code share partners, something the airlines often cannot provide to its passengers. So if you have a connecting flight with a code share, FlightStats can provide such an alert to the traveler or the agent.

The number of third-party firms using FlightStats data has also expanded. FlightCaster is a third-party application that uses the FlightStats data to predict delays long before an airline will inform its passengers. In addition, multiple mobile application developers, travel agencies, airlines, airports, and search engines rely on FlightStats data to inform their customers.

With advances in mobile technology, FlightStats is furthering its capabilities in providing travelers with tailored, actionable information via the FlightStats mobile web site and mobile apps.[8] In addition to providing travel delay alerts on the smartphone, it will display which baggage carousel luggage is arriving on. Interestingly, on a recent trip to Las Vegas, the FlightStats app gave me this information before it appeared on the airport monitors. For many consumers, pop-up advertisements can be annoying, so leveraging content with personalization and targeted advertisements has to be useful. To this end, FlightStats has added targeted ads to their app, providing things such as a discount coupon for local airport parking or car hire. Mobile technologies, then, are allowing FlightStats to further extend opportunities to leverage the data.

Opportunity at Emergency Medical Associates

Emergency Medical Associates (EMA), which operates emergency rooms in the New York metro area and New Jersey, echoed a similar theme of opportunity as FlightStats. The healthcare industry is not known for being leaders in business intelligence or information technology, yet Emergency Medical Associates is. EMA differentiated itself based on a unique electronic patient management system that few emergency rooms had.[9] Through this system, EMA amassed data related to emergency room diagnosis and operations well before electronic medical records were prevalent. One of EMA's senior physicians had a vision of using this data for the patients' good. He saw an opportunity to leverage the unique data EMA had amassed. Jonathan Rothman, then director of data management, explains, "EMA is fortunate in its ability to take data and turn it into actionable information. By improving emergency room operations, our patients benefit, the physicians benefit, and our whole organization benefits."[10]

In a life-threatening emergency, a patient will be rushed to the nearest hospital. However, many emergency room (ER) visits are non-life-threatening. As wait times in emergency rooms increase, patient health may decline or the patient may leave and risk a health complication. Wait times during flu outbreaks reflect this difficult problem. The opportunity to reduce wait times allows the hospital to improve patient care. While nationally, wait times in hospitals may average three hours, in EMA-operated hospitals, the wait times average 30 minutes. To be honest, I didn't fully believe these patterns or these metrics, until I experienced them first hand with my two children: one non-life-threatening incident with my daughter who was triaged and seen by a doctor in less than 30 minutes in an EMA-operated hospital, compared to hours in a closer, but non-EMA-operated hospital. For my son, it didn't seem to matter that it was his appendix the one time or a sports injury on

About Emergency Medical Associates and Emergency Medicine BI

Emergency Medical Associates (EMA) is a group of emergency physicians who are contracted to manage and staff emergency departments at 30 hospitals throughout New Jersey and New York, recently expanding to Rhode Island and North Carolina. They treat more than 1 million patients per year. The data warehouse contains information on over 14 million ER visits, making it one of the largest sources of ER data in the world. Based on the BI success at EMA, the BI leaders formed a new company in 2010, Emergency Medicine BI (EMBI), to build and introduce a performance dashboard and key metric solution for the broader market. In less than three years, EMBI has installed 21 performance dashboards at 18 hospitals throughout the United States.[11] EMA and EMBI use business intelligence to provide emergency departments (EDs) the information they need to enhance the quality of patient care, improve productivity, and better manage their EDs.

About BI at EMA[12]

- **Start of BI efforts:** 1999
- **Executive-level sponsor:** Chief technology officer
- **Number of BI users:** 250 users, which include the company's employees as well as external hospital staff
- **Number of source systems used for BI:** 25
- **ETL/EIM tools:** Custom and SAP BusinessObjects Data Integrator
- **Data warehouse platform:** Oracle
- **Data warehouse size:** 550 GB, updated daily
- **Number of subject areas:** Three
- **BI tools:** SAP BusinessObjects

About EMBI

- **Start of BI efforts:** 2010 formed new company
- **Executive-level sponsor:** President
- **Number of BI users:** 80 users across 18 hospitals
- **ETL/EIM tools:** SQL Server Integration Services
- **Data warehouse platform:** Microsoft SQL Server
- **Data warehouse size:** 20 GB, updated monthly
- **BI tools:** SAP BusinessObjects and Information Builders WebFOCUS
- **Cloud EMBI:** Amazon Web Services

another occasion. With his appendix, of course, I wasn't about to leave, but with the sports injury, after three hours of boredom on a sunny Saturday afternoon, indeed, I was ready to walk out and diagnose the injury myself as a sprain. Our closest hospital is less efficient than the farther away but more efficient EMA-operated hospital.

Just as digital medical records allowed EMA to exploit the data for patient benefit, the emergence of cloud BI has allowed the BI capabilities to expand. In 2010, the architects of the internal EMA solution formed a separate company, Emergency Medicine BI, to bring a similar vision, value, and BI capabilities to other hospitals. The BI solution runs in the cloud, providing a flexibility and scalability that would be more challenging if the solution were only on premise.

Opportunity at Dow

Whether it was luck or foresight that gave Dow's global data warehouse more acceptance is debatable. However, the degree to which Dow exploited this asset and realized its importance only came with the merger of Union Carbide in 2001, which made the Dow Chemical Company the largest chemical company in the world. The merger promised a number of synergies, and when the deal finally closed, the expected synergies were even greater than originally anticipated. Dow employees who had taken their information systems somewhat for granted up until this point now realized just how good they had had it compared with Union Carbide's antiquated systems. Dow quickly updated its estimated merger savings to double that of the original estimates.[13] The opportunities for synergy were there; could Dow exploit them?

Dow's CIO Dave Kepler explains that the operational systems and global data warehouse were key requirements to drive the synergies from the merger with Union Carbide. "We had to improve the way people worked, made decisions, and interacted with customers."[14]

However, in 2007, with the original Dow data warehouse and BI platform more than a decade old, the enterprise architecture needed an update. Dow was also running on an unsupported version of SAP (R/2), but identifying the hard business benefits of such a major upgrade to the latest release (ECC) was difficult. Rohm and Haas, meanwhile, was on the latest release and leveraging SAP's packaged data warehouse, BW. At the vendor's annual industry conference, Rohm and Haas was often showcased as a model deployment. When Dow acquired Rohm and Haas in 2009, it gained expertise in ECC and BW. Dow had already begun its next enterprise architecture (NEA) and initially thought BW would not be part of that architecture. It had planned to upgrade its custom data warehouse. "BW is not easy," explains Masciandaro, "and it's difficult outside of an SAP ERP. There was a lot of internal debate."[15] However, the Rohm and Haas acquisition gave Dow the opportunity to revisit the initial BW decision and to learn from an early adopter. BW is now a core part of the next-generation architecture.

Opportunity at Macy's

In recent years, retail sales at brick-and-mortar stores have been limping along at single-digit growth rates, while e-commerce has been growing at double digits. In the early days of e-commerce, some predicted the demise of brick-and-mortar stores. Retailers now recognize that online and in-store presences strongly complement each other, bringing the best of both shopping venues to offer both convenience and choice. The ability to buy something online and then be able to return or exchange it at a nearby store can provide an edge in loyalty over an online-only store. Executives at retailer Macy's suspected there were some synergies, but as data for online and in-store sales were largely separate, the correlation remained only a hunch.

In May 2010, Kerem Tomak was recruited by Macy's to build a world-class analytics organization that could provide visibility into consumer buying patterns, marketing effectiveness, and merchandizing. Tomak had previously built out the analytics program at Yahoo!, a pioneer in large-scale data analytics and e-commerce. Tomak explains, "Macy's already had a data-driven culture, and the president of Macy's set down a mandate to improve analytics. I was basically given a blank check to make it happen. We went from three people in marketing analytics to a group of 21 experts."[16]

Macy's reflects an interesting trend related to big data: Much of the value in mining big data still is an unknown. It's often new data that has never been tapped before. There are opportunities to exploit the value of this new data, but in discovering those opportunities, you have to expect some failures and misses.

Tomak had to be pragmatic about which opportunities he pursued, choosing those that would be most impactful, and he had to move fast—at the pace of business. By combining store sales with .com sales, they can now identify which online marketing tactic (such as an e-mail or web site coupon or display) had a related impact in the store and how online browsing and in-store sales may relate. The analytics have proved their value many times over, although he can't publicly share the hard numbers. In comparing Macy's financial data with the retail industry, the retail industry had an average annual growth of 4.1 percent since 2010.[17] Macy's outperformed the industry with an average annual growth of 5.6 percent,[18] and has certainly outperformed its department store peers, some of whom are struggling to achieve a profit.

In addition to mining its own web site and sales data, Macy's is mining social data to better predict customer behavior, preferences, and trends. Retailers operate on razor-thin margins, so having the right product on hand can be the difference between customer loyalty and profitability, on the one hand, and excessive inventory and losses on the other. As shoppers discuss their favorite jeans or colors on Twitter and Facebook, recognizing these patterns allows Macy's to better optimize its merchandizing.

About Macy's

Macy's is one of the oldest department stores in the United States and opened its first store in New York in 1858.[19] It is iconic for its Thanksgiving Day parade and Fourth of July fireworks show. Macy's Corporation also owns the Bloomingdale's department stores. Once branded Federated Department Stores, the company filed for bankruptcy in 1990. Following the bankruptcy, Federated acquired Macy's in 1994 and adopted the Macy's name in 2007.[20] The company now operates 850 stores with annual revenues in 2012 of $27.7 billion.

About BI at Macy's

- **Start of BI efforts:** 1998
- **Executive-level sponsor:** CEO
- **Business intelligence competency center:** BI center of excellence reports to IT; marketing analytics reports to CEO
- **Data warehouse platform:** Oracle, Teradata, DB2
- **Data warehouse size:** 100 TB
- **BI tools:** MicroStrategy, SAP BusinessObjects, and Tableau
- **Big data:** Hadoop and Hive
- **Cloud:** PivotLink
- **Mobile:** Yes
- **Advanced analytics:** SAS Enterprise Miner and open-source R

Do Business Requirements Always Map to Opportunities?

Often with business intelligence projects, business users first must define their requirements and IT then builds a solution. FlightStats, EMA and EMBI, Dow Chemical, and Macy's all illustrate a different paradigm, though.

Whenever a new opportunity presents itself, the requirements may not be well known. The business users may first have to test new processes and business models as part of pursuing the opportunity. IT must learn to expect that precise requirements will change on a daily basis, but always within the framework of the broader vision. This can be a frustrating process for IT staff, who need to know exactly which fields to extract from a source system and how to transform them onto a dashboard or a report. The reality is that the business users may only know detailed requirements once they've been able to experiment with different tools and explore information to determine what most supports their vision. For example, EMA knew their patient data presented a unique business opportunity to improve care and emergency room operations. However, it was only after exploring the data and prototyping different reports and dashboards that the team arrived at the final metrics that provided the best insights and benefits.

> Successful BI companies start with a vision—whether it's to improve air travel, improve patient care, or drive synergies. The business sees an opportunity to exploit the data to fulfill a broader vision. The detail requirements are not precisely known. Creativity and exploration are necessary ingredients to unlock these business opportunities and fulfill those visions.

Frustration

When companies first embark on business intelligence, a frequent starting point is to address the biggest pains. Sometimes the degree of frustration has to reach a boiling point before business intelligence becomes a priority. Frustration can come in many forms, whether it's the inability to answer simple questions, being held accountable for things without the right tools to do a job well, or, as many managers describe, the frustration at managing blindly without facts to support their decisions.

Frustration was a driver for BI at 1-800 CONTACTS. 1-800 CONTACTS has been selling contact lenses via mail order, phone, and the Internet since 1995.[21] It has a unique challenge, though, in that its customers must go to a competitor—eye doctors—to receive a prescription.[22] A key differentiator for 1-800 CONTACTS is customer service. The company first released its data warehouse in early 2005 as a way of addressing growing frustration among its customer service representatives. "All the agents were clamoring for information. We hire competitive people. The biggest dissatisfaction in their job was to have to wait until the next morning to look at a piece of paper taped to the wall to see how they were performing," recalls Dave Walker, vice president of operations. Employee turnover was high, and on exit interviews, agents

About 1-800 CONTACTS

1-800 CONTACTS is the world's largest supplier of contact lenses, with inventories over 15 million. Orders are placed by phone or via the Web (www.1800contacts.com). On any given day, the company delivers over 250,000 lenses to customers. 1-800 CONTACTS was founded in 1995 by two entrepreneurs. Insurance provider WellPoint acquired 1-800 CONTACTS in 2012 for an estimated $900 million.[23]

About BI at 1-800 CONTACTS

- **Start of BI efforts:** 2004
- **Executive-level sponsor:** CFO
- **Business intelligence competency center:** Yes
- **Number of BI users:** 700 users, or 75 percent of division employees
- **Number of source systems used for BI:** Nine
- **ETL/EIM tools:** Microsoft Integration Services and Informatica
- **Data warehouse platform:** Microsoft SQL Server
- **Data warehouse size:** 1.3 TB, with 80 percent updated every 15 minutes
- **Number of subject areas:** Seven
- **BI tools:** Microsoft BI
- **Mobile BI:** Custom HTML5 and JavaScript
- **Big data:** Splunk for web server analytics

complained most about being held accountable for things they couldn't control without access to information to improve their performance.

In many companies, a common complaint is having multiple versions of the truth. Executive meetings start with a debate about how numbers are compiled and whose are correct rather than with a discussion of the insights such numbers provide. Frustration at the amount of time reconciling differences in numbers can be a catalyst to improve BI capabilities. Frustration may also intensify from the degree of manual effort to analyze data. In many companies, the precursor to a formal BI initiative may be manual and spreadsheet-based analyses. Macy's estimates it is saving $500,000 annually in full-time equivalents (FTEs) by eliminating manual processes to create reports that were spreadsheet based.[24]

Opportunity and Frustration in Public Education

The quality of public school education has been a sore point across the country. America is now ranked 17th overall in reading, math, and sciences scores of industrialized nations.[25] Declining test scores and tightening budgets led to a showdown between government, citizens, and teachers' unions in Wisconsin in 2011, ultimately leading to a recall election of Governor Scott Walker (Walker won).

While emotions run high, how best to solve our educational woes is unclear. In 2006, high school graduation rates within some inner-city schools in Columbus, Ohio, were less than 50 percent.[26] Then CEO of Nationwide Jerry Jurgensen understood both the value of data and the importance of education. Jurgensen and Nationwide as a company are very active in the local community. Frustrated by poor school performance, then Columbus City Schools Superintendent Dr. Gene Harris was open to the idea of using data to identify patterns, root causes, and opportunities for improvement. "The initiative started as our CEO's curiosity," recalls Learning Circle President Barbara Boyd.[27] "Could data help improve the district? In education, there is a lot of data, but not a lot of information." Figure 5-3 shows reading rates for one elementary school the Learning Circle has worked with. In the 2005–2006 school year, reading rates for third through fifth graders were below 30 percent proficient, and in fifth grade, only 19 percent were proficient (the name of the elementary school is omitted for privacy reasons). In the 2010–2011 school year, the elementary school used Learning Circle's formative assessment process and leveraged data to drive instruction. "Data coupled with great teaching enabled them to make a dramatic improvement," says Boyd. Similar trends are reflected in math scores and in the

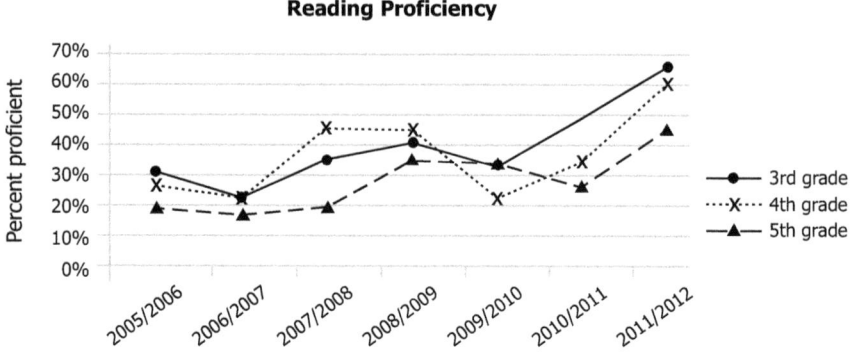

Figure 5-3 Reading proficiency has improved dramatically in select elementary schools in Columbus, Ohio.

other schools using the data. As with any BI initiative, data alone cannot be credited with improving performance, but it's an important enabler to identifying attendance issues, intervening early when grades and test scores are declining, and tracking progress toward a common goal.

One of the things that most caught my attention in the use of data in Columbus, Ohio, was a dramatic improvement in high school graduation rates. It is a publicly reported figure I have tracked for several years since I first learned about the Nationwide partnership with Columbus city schools. The results appeared dramatic, with graduation rates in 2010–2011 over 80 percent and above the national average of 78 percent. Unfortunately, a state investigation and now an FBI investigation have revealed the data cannot be trusted.[28] Certain schools within the district have been involved in "data scrubbing" in which data for chronically absent students was systematically deleted. Whether or not the data should have been deleted is debatable: Did the student drop out or move out of the school system? There is a lot at stake with school performance, with everything ranging from federal and state funding to whether or not a parent is allowed to use school vouchers to fund education at a private school. The developing story in Columbus and in other districts within the United States provides a cautionary tale about the role of data, how it can be manipulated, and how incentives influence behavior. If the data reveals problems that are beyond an individual's control and those people are either punished for negative results or falsely rewarded for positive ones, there will be a host of negative behaviors. The schools and data that Learning Circle has shared as models of success are outside the scope of the investigation.

Threat

Threats that propel a company to more successfully leverage business intelligence can come in the form of reduced margins, regulatory compliance, increased competition, reduced public funding, or even bankruptcy.

Rising healthcare costs have reached crisis levels in the United States. Healthcare costs are increasing, while people are living longer and unemployment rates are at record highs, leaving many people uninsured. The state of New Jersey, where EMA operates a number of emergency rooms, has a Charity Care Law that requires hospitals to treat patients, regardless of their ability to pay.[29] Under this law, the state will reimburse these hospitals, but the formula for reimbursement has changed significantly in the past several years such that hospitals, on average, are reimbursed only a third of the $1.6 billion spent annually.[30] Reimbursements under Medicare (U.S. government program to provide healthcare for seniors) and Medicaid (U.S. government program for health insurance for low-income families and individuals) have also not kept pace with hospital costs or inflation, paying only 89 cents and 73 cents, respectively, for every dollar spent. The Affordable Care Act (passed in 2010 and sometimes referred to as ObamaCare) is expected to increase the number of people using Medicaid. There is no effort to reduce the gap between actual cost and what the government reimburses healthcare providers. The rise of managed care has further challenged hospitals. Under all these threats, patient care is threatened as hospital income declines and some are forced to close.

In addition to financial threats, the healthcare industry faces regulatory pressures. The Joint Commission is a national organization that provides hospitals and healthcare providers with measurements for accreditation, accountability, and public reporting.[31] Now patients can see which hospitals are performing above, equal to, or below other accredited hospitals. EMA responded to these multiple threats by providing doctors and hospital administrators access to information to manage emergency rooms more efficiently.

Denise Shepherd, vice president for patient care services at Saint Barnabas Health Care System (a nonprofit hospital in New Jersey), describes how EMA's business intelligence solution called WEBeMARS has helped their emergency room.

> WEBeMARS has and continues to provide invaluable data management services to the Saint Barnabas Health Care System and our Emergency Departments. Information provided by WEBeMARS is used at each Saint Barnabas Health

Care System hospital and across the system to drive performance improvement and ensure the highest quality of care for our Emergency Department patients.[32]

At Netflix, meanwhile, changes in technology and new forms of competition provide a constant threat. When Netflix first started, their main competition was local mom-and-pop video stores and big physical chains such as Blockbuster and WalMart. As online streaming has grown in popularity, the threats have shifted from physical DVD competitors to start-ups such as Hulu and Amazon, as well as TV networks and movie studios that also provide content to Netflix. This threat from competitors has forced Netflix to change its business model as well as its BI architecture. It's no longer enough to monitor if customers are getting their first-choice movie via a DVD; it's now also about ensuring they have the best content and reliable streaming on what may be a range of devices, including smart TVs, computers, iPads, and smartphones, in a single household. In assessing the constant but changing threats, CEO Reed Hastings says,

> The most difficult thing is anticipating the threats ahead of time. We've got a great head of steam, fast growth, big earnings, customer growth, all kinds of good things, but we've watched a lot of companies rise and then fall, especially in Silicon Valley. So we work very hard to kind of game-theory it out: what could happen if all of these things happened, how we'd react in that scenario, strategic planning, anticipating what will come up.[33]

In the retail industry, threats from competitors, fickle shoppers, and higher costs pose the ultimate threat: bankruptcy. The retail industry saw bankruptcies and the loss of a number of long-time chains during the Great Recession from the likes of Circuit City, Borders, and Linens N Things (now an online-only store). In 2008, as Macy's posted losses for the first time in decades (see Figure 5-4), rumors swirled that it would be the death of the chain department store as we know it.

While retail organizations may face competitive and financial threats, in the medical device industry regulatory compliance is another type of threat that can increase the need for better BI. The medical device industry is regulated by the Food and Drug Administration (FDA). Medtronic's global complaint handling (GCH) project was initiated in 2007 by corporate quality to develop and deploy a global system to improve product complaint processing and associated international regulatory reporting activities. This system established Medtronic's first

About Medtronic

Medtronic is a medical device manufacturer, founded in 1949, and headquartered in Minneapolis, Minnesota. Its devices are used by 7 million people, ranging from those needing cardiac pacemakers, spinal discs, and insulin pumps to manage diabetes to neurostimulators for brain stimulation.[34] Medtronic devices serve a patient every three seconds. In 2012, it had $16 billion in revenues and operated in 120 countries worldwide. A city-wide power outage in 1957 provided the creative spark for the first battery-operated pacemaker.[35] Previously, the pacemakers had to be plugged into an electrical outlet.

About BI at Medtronic

- **Start of BI efforts:** Mid-1990s
- **Executive-level sponsor:** CIO
- **Business intelligence competency center:** Central team of BI experts staff projects, implementing a BI council for ongoing support and vision beyond projects.
- **Number of BI users:** 15,000, or one-third of employees
- **Number of source systems used for BI:** 160, including legacy; 50 active
- **ETL/EIM tools:** Informatica, SAP Data Services, SAP SLT, IBM IRS, Oracle Stored Procs
- **Data warehouse platform:** Custom Oracle, SAP BW, and SAP Hana
- **Data warehouse size:** 46TB
- **Frequency of updates:** Ranges from near real-time at three seconds to monthly, depending on business needs
- **BI tools:** SAP BusinessObjects, TIBCO Spotfire
- **Big data:** SAP Hana
- **Mobile BI:** Yes
- **Advanced analytics and predictive tools:** SPSS and SAS

global, enterprise-wide repository for complaints and medical device reports (MDRs). GCH enables consistent, timely, and effective handling of complaints, as well as submission of international regulatory reporting. With the new system, users have much greater data mining and analytics capabilities, allowing for rapid identification of product performance trends and ensuring greater regulatory compliance.

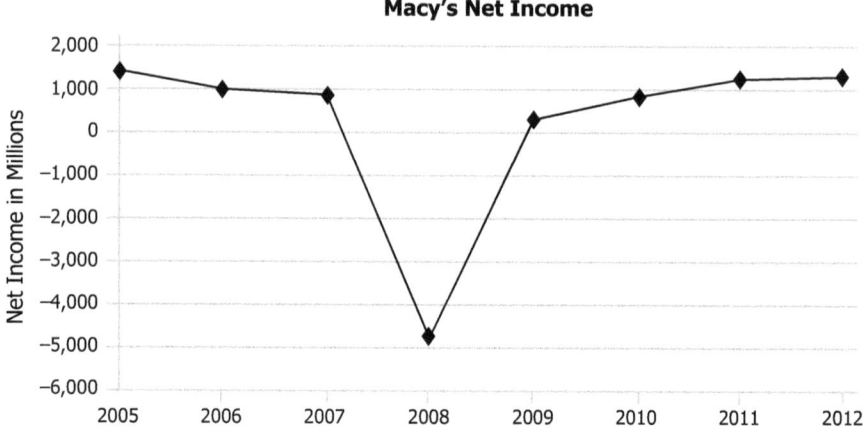

Figure 5-4   Macy's has steadily improved profitability despite a global recession.

"Complaints are often the first area for an FDA auditor to pull on a thread and see where it leads," explains Sarah Nieters, IT Director at Medtronic.[36] A delay in responding to an auditor question can raise a red flag. So at Medtronic, regulatory compliance needs put pressure on the BI capabilities. Opportunity also played a role in Medtronic's BI upgrade in that they were able to leverage a new in-memory technology, SAP Hana. This technology has allowed ad hoc queries to be fast and for the company to access and analyze textual data that was not previously readily accessible.

The Role of Time

With some of the successful BI companies, it seems that time has played a role in their success, that BI had to be failing or mediocre for a period before these companies learned how to use business intelligence more effectively. There does seem to be a maturity evolution in transitioning from straightforward reporting to advanced analytics. However, time is not a prerequisite for significant impact. 1-800 CONTACTS, for example, saw success and impact from the call center application immediately, less than a year into the deployment.

Figure 5-5 shows the relationship between the length of a BI deployment and the degree of impact. The survey responses show that having a significant impact is indeed possible within the first year of deployment. Twenty percent of first-year BI deployments rate their projects as being

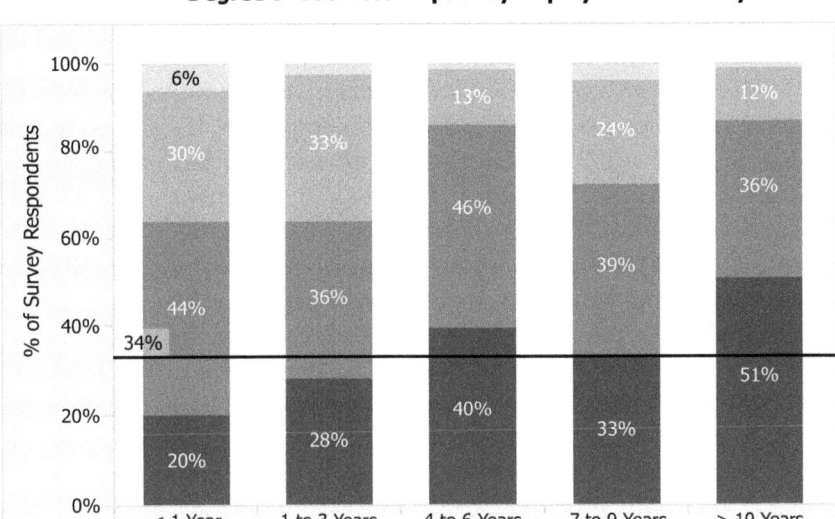

Degree of Business Impact by Deployment Maturity

Business impact
- Not at all
- Slightly
- Somewhat
- Signficant

Figure 5-5   Business impact increases with time.

very impactful. However, this is the largest proportion of failures, at 6 percent of first-year projects having no impact and 30 percent only a slight impact. The rate of impact is highest (51 percent of companies have significant impact) for deployments ten years or older.

Figure 5-5 also shows a reduced impact in the five-to-seven year range. We can't attribute a particular cause to this pattern. However, as many BI programs go through a second-generation architecture, there is sometimes a disruption as efforts shift to updating technology and processes as opposed to providing business value. This dip in impact, however, did not appear in the initial 2007 survey or subsequent 2011 survey.

If There Is No LOFT Effect, Is Successful BI Still Possible?

As a business intelligence consultant, I was bothered by the concept of the LOFT effect: I didn't like the idea that a BI team could do everything else right—executive sponsorship, alignment with the business, solid data architecture—and the BI initiative might only be moderately successful. At this point, there is not enough data to say that the LOFT effect is a *prerequisite* for wild success. It is, however, a common characteristic among the more successful companies. It's also clear that the degree to which BI best practices are followed has an impact on the degree of success, so even if there is a LOFT effect present, don't expect success unless you are applying other best practices. As shown in Figure 5-6, the LOFT effect amplifies the benefits of following BI best practices, allowing for greater success and business value.

Discussing the role of "threats" on BI success, one BI manager said, "Well, when people are fat and happy, you don't have to be as smart." Supporting this point, when survey respondents described their company as lean and operating efficiently, they also had a higher impact and success rate. There is not enough data to determine if business intelligence *enabled* this efficiency or if efficiency happened first, and thus better BI use *followed*.

Also, it's important to note that not all the successful BI case studies showed *all* aspects of the LOFT effect, but they did show more than one element. BI teams can use the LOFT effect as a way of

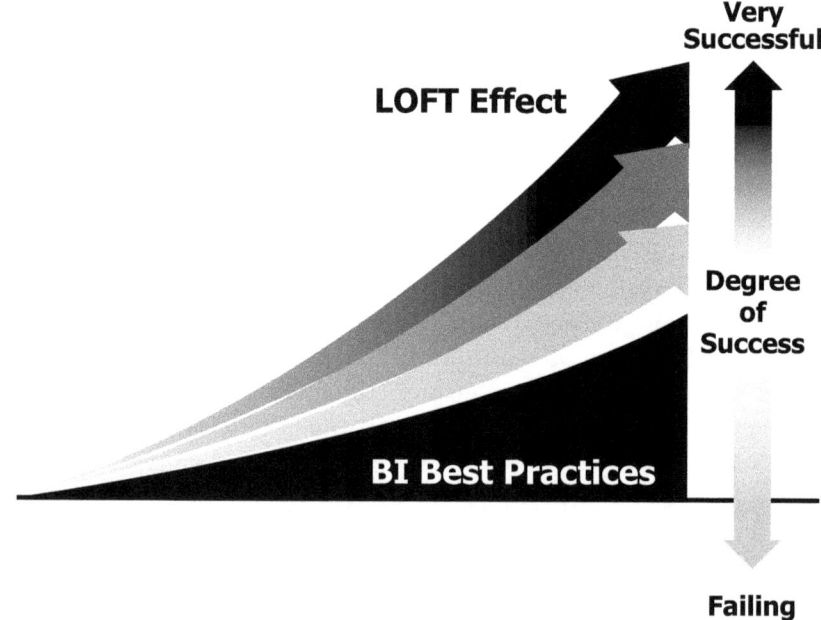

Figure 5-6   The LOFT effect (Luck, Opportunity, Frustration, Threat)

communicating with the business to see how business intelligence can be used more effectively. Most business units and companies routinely perform a SWOT analysis—strengths, weaknesses, opportunities, and threats. BI teams can study the opportunities and threats portions to understand where BI can help the business pursue opportunities and address threats.

Best Practices for Successful Business Intelligence

The degree to which a company is successful with business intelligence is influenced by forces beyond the direct control of the BI team, whether luck, opportunity, frustration, or threat (LOFT). In the most successful BI companies, a LOFT effect has moved them from being moderately successful with business intelligence to extremely successful and having a profound impact on the business.

To move your BI efforts from one of moderate success to wild success

- Understand the LOFT effect and proactively look for these elements that affect your company or business unit. The business and BI teams should explore the role that business intelligence can play in exploiting business opportunities, addressing frustration or pain, and squashing the threats.
- Don't use the longevity of your BI program as an excuse for lack of success and impact. Successful BI is possible within a short time frame. Focus on anecdotal, measurable quick wins.
- Do continue to follow all the other BI best practices described in this book, recognizing that the LOFT effect is only an *intensifying* effect.

Chapter 6

Executive Support
and Culture

If you ask people what the number one enabler for a successful BI deployment is, most will respond "executive support." It's an easy answer, as executive support is key to the success for almost any company-wide initiative—change in business strategy, new product launch, or reorganization. Executives can clear the path for many political, organizational, and technical obstacles. They also are the key people who influence that subtle but essential analytical enabler: culture. However, getting and maintaining that executive support may not be easy, particularly if senior executives don't believe in or understand the value of business intelligence.

> "Our BI initiative is not successful or fully utilized because of the lack of vision, sponsorship, and leadership from the executive level."
> —Hybrid business/IT professional, transportation industry

Executive Support and Success

BI success and impact hinge on both technical issues and organizational issues, but an overwhelming majority of survey respondents (86 percent) attribute greater impact (and failure) to organizational factors.

When survey respondents were asked to rate the importance of various cultural and organizational aspects that affect the success of a BI project, executive support consistently ranked at the top of the list, followed closely by alignment to business goals (see Figure 6-1). A large portion of survey respondents (45 percent) rated executive-level support as essential. There was little difference in this ranking regardless of the

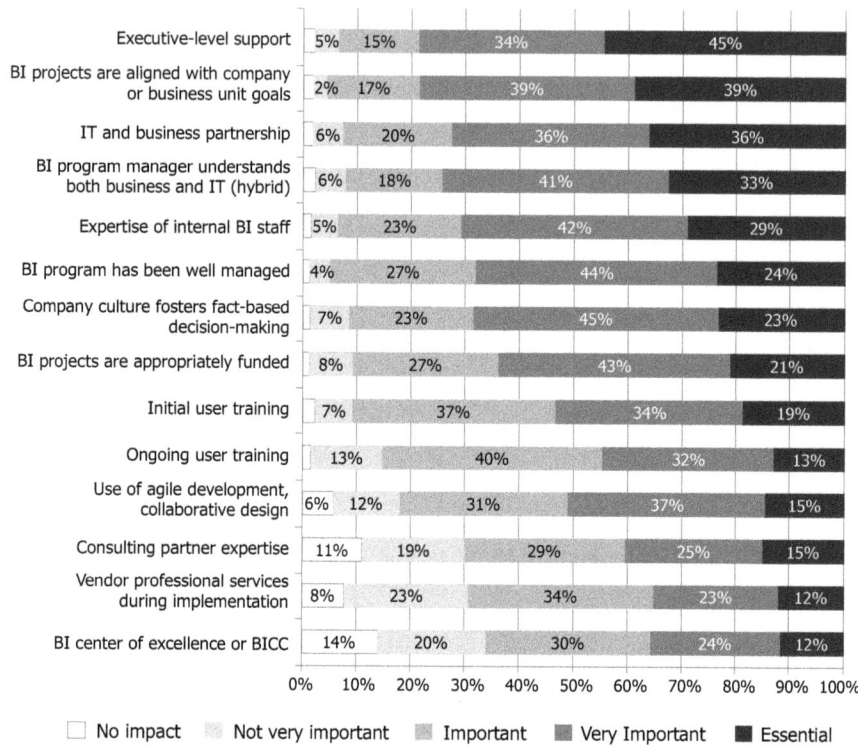

Figure 6-1   Executive support is one of the most important aspects to successful BI.

company size or duration of the BI program. If a project was deemed a failure, a respondent was more likely to rate the importance and role of executive sponsorship even higher.

Consistent with the survey results, the successful BI case studies often cited—unprompted—executive support as one of the reasons they have been so successful and a reason for evolving from simple reporting to sophisticated analytics.

Despite the relative importance of this, not all BI initiatives have executive-level sponsorship. The majority of BI deployments (85 percent) now have executive sponsorship, an increase from 74 percent in 2007. As shown in Figure 6-2, the influence on a project's business impact is noticeable: Of the companies who describe their BI projects as having significant impact, 92 percent have executive sponsorship, whereas in the projects described as having no impact, only 75 percent had executive sponsorship.

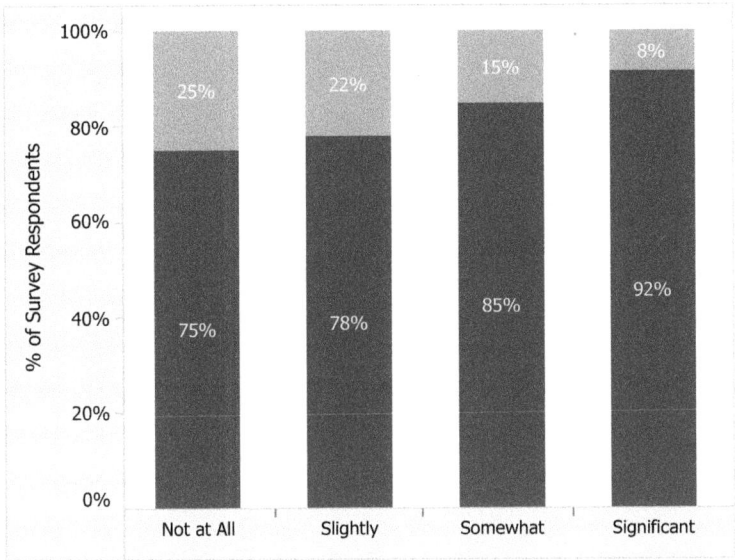

Figure 6-2   Companies with greater business impact have a higher rate of executive sponsorship.

Which Executive Is the Best Sponsor?

Business intelligence projects can be sponsored by any executive: the chief executive officer (CEO), the chief operating officer (COO), the chief financial officer (CFO), the chief information officer (CIO) or IT manager, the VP of marketing, or another line-of-business leader. As Figure 6-3 shows, the CIO is most often (in 30 percent of projects) the sponsor of a BI initiative, followed by a line-of-business leader (18 percent).

While the CIO may often be the sponsor for business intelligence, this executive does not appear to be the most effective sponsor on average. Figure 6-4 shows the relationship between the sponsoring executive and the business impact of the BI initiative. The portion of companies who have the CEO or COO as their sponsor and classify their project as having significant business impact is 40 percent. This is higher than

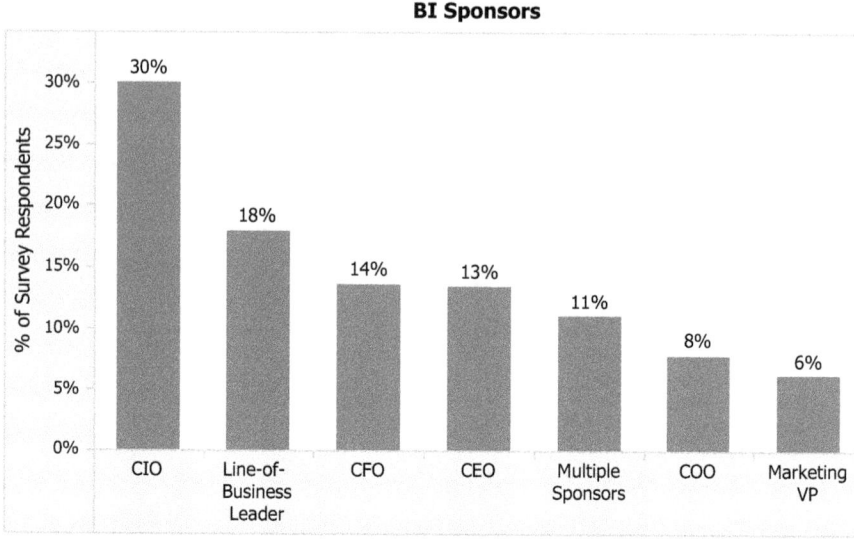

Figure 6-3   The CIO most often sponsors a BI initiative.

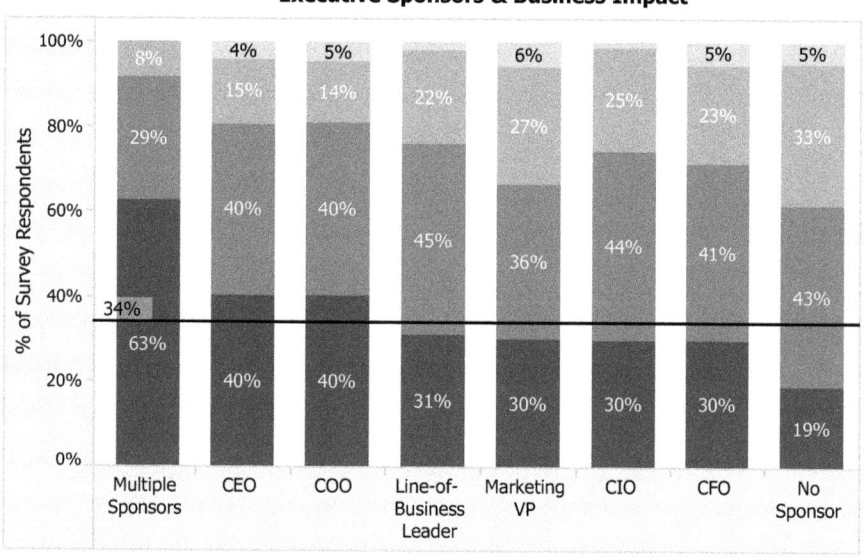

Business impact

- Not at all
- Slightly
- Somewhat
- Signficantly

Figure 6-4   The CEO as the BI sponsor has the highest rate of BI success.

the average rate of significant business impact (34 percent of survey respondents). Contrast this with the portion of companies who have the CIO as the sponsor and describe the project as having significant impact (only 30 percent, slightly lower than the average). The greatest degree of impact comes when multiple executives sponsor the BI initiative (63 percent).

If you are a CIO reading this book, don't panic (yet). While it's not good news that the CIO is not necessarily an ideal sponsor, the problem is not with the individual executive per se but rather with the degree of influence the CIO wields with the business. If the CIO is viewed as a technocrat rather than a core member of the business team, then this lack of business alignment will get reflected in lower BI success rates and lower overall effective use of technology.

The role of the CIO has been transitioning to the point that *Information Week* described the next era of the CIO as a four-headed monster: Chief innovation officer. Chief infrastructure officer. Chief integration officer. Chief intelligence officer.[1] It's difficult to lead and align with the business when what you are most measured on is the least cost to compute. In this way, the degree that the CIO is a business-savvy executive with the trust of the CEO is strongly correlated with the degree of impact from BI. There is, however, a difference between membership on a board of directors and being an *influential* member of the company's executive or operating committee. In 2003, less than 10 percent of CIOs were members of the board. However, in the 2012 Successful BI survey, 63 percent of respondents said their CIOs are active members of the business team or operating committee. Despite a growing number of CIOs in executive board rooms, a majority of CEOs consider their CIOs too technical and unable to align IT with the business, according to a Gartner survey of 220 CEOs.[2]

These survey findings reveal an important point: If the CIO is not involved in the strategy of the business and is also the executive sponsor for a business intelligence initiative, the initiative will be met with less success; the company also may have lower financial performance overall.

Ultimately, the most effective sponsors for a business intelligence initiative are the leaders who understand the full value of data and who wield influence, instill credibility, and foster trust with all of the business and functional executives.

The Role of an Executive Sponsor

Executive sponsors support the BI effort in the following ways:

- Articulate commitment to the initiative and to the impact it will have on the organization.
- State the business intelligence vision in the context of the company's strategy. They may help craft this vision.
- Approve the budget.
- Clear political barriers.
- Act as the go-to person for ultimate resolution of issues that cannot be resolved by the BI team or the BI steering committee (see Chapter 11). Such issues are rarely technical in nature and more often involve prioritization, organizational issues, and project scope.
- Set an example by using the BI tools, asking analytical questions, supporting those who challenge the status quo, and encouraging different perspectives.

Executive sponsors are seldom involved in the day-to-day tasks and issues of the BI team.

Kay Van De Vanter, BICC Director at Boeing, says, "You need to make sure the key stakeholders understand and invest in the BI strategy. Otherwise, you are constantly pushing against the mountain."[3]

At Constant Contact, the CEO has been pivotal in bringing the full potential of BI to bear on the organization. One of the influences on the CEO's view of data, and on many analytic leaders, has been the work of Tom Davenport, a speaker, author, and professor, whose *Harvard Business Review* article on analytics eventually led to the book *Competing on Analytics*. David Whiting, director of analytic technology solutions, explains: "Our CEO Neal Goodman is very data focused. He read Davenport's book, was inspired, and took it to heart. So he had a lot of influence, but the conversation around data started with marketing."[4] It seems to me that in the information and technology era, CEOs at so many technology startups are data centric. Perhaps in the industrial age, CEOs who saw opportunities to automate things were the visionaries. In the information age, the visionary CEOs are exploiting the value of data for optimized insights.

The Changing Role of the CIO

The role of the CIO is undergoing a transformation in many companies. This change can be attributed to the greater role technology plays in business. In the past, CIOs may have been viewed only as the technology keepers and data center managers. This may still be the case in companies and industries in which technology is viewed as an operational necessity but not necessarily an enabler or as a provider of competitive advantage. If the CIO's role is largely left to overseeing maintenance of systems, this type of CIO is not an ideal sponsor for a business intelligence initiative, as BI is less about technology and more about business. In *Managing IT as a Business* (Wiley, 2003), author Mark Lutchen explains that some CIOs may stay in the predominantly technology role for personality reasons on the part of both the CIO and the CEO: If the CIO lacks interpersonal skills or an understanding of the business, that CIO will not become an integral part of the business committee. Conversely, if the CEO does not value or understand information technology, the CEO may not want someone on the business team who can make him or her feel stupid. Lutchen explains, "Most CIOs have not done a very good job of communication in ways that make CEOs comfortable. Thus, a CEO who is already less than conversant in technology does not want to demonstrate further public weakness (or possibly be humiliated) concerning IT should he or she fail to understand what the CIO is talking about (even though that may be entirely the CIO's fault)."[5]

With technology touching all facets of our lives from home to consumer to business, I sometimes struggle to believe that there are still executive leaders who don't embrace technology and BI. Haven't their companies gone bankrupt or haven't they retired by now? But then I encounter a client or course attendee who is grappling with this issue, and they muddle along, frustrated and discouraged, in the hopes that their bosses will one day get it . . . or move on. So while executive skepticism may be less of a challenge today than ten years ago, it seems some organizations still lag.

The executive sponsor for a BI initiative may change throughout the BI life cycle, whether due to a change in personnel or a change in business emphasis. As with any change, it may be necessary to re-engage with the new sponsor, re-educate, and re-prove the value of the BI efforts.

The Chief Analytics Officer

With the changing role of the CIO, some industry experts and thought leaders have advocated for a new C-level executive: the chief analytics officer (CAO). Whereas the CIO may be most concerned with how data is captured and stored, as well as system uptime, the CAO is most concerned with exploiting the value of data and analytics. Like the CIO, the CAO has authority and influence across departments and individual lines of business.

As part of Constant Contact's vision to improve its use of data, in 2012, the CEO hired a CAO, Jesse Harriott, who had built an analytics division at Monster Worldwide, the job and resume posting site. At Constant Contact, Harriott is building out the analytics culture and roles across the business, moving from what was primarily a centralized team to a more federated approach.[6] The BI team, meanwhile, focuses on the technology, data, and tools that support the analytic requirements. Organizationally, the analytics function resides within finance, not within IT, although at other firms, such as Macy's, the analytics function may reside within marketing.

Getting and Keeping Executive Buy-In

While most recognize the importance of executive-level support for BI, getting that support can be difficult. In some companies, "data warehouse" is a dirty word, and business intelligence is synonymous with expensive, never-ending projects. Business intelligence *is* a never-ending initiative, but that doesn't mean working endlessly without delivering business value.

A BI analyst at a telecommunications firm expressed his frustration: "The political issues are show stoppers without CXO edicts. Another issue is getting all levels of management to 'get it' as they tend to lack the big picture. It seems that they do not lead but instead are reacting to their environment." At this company, the BI team tried the "guerilla marketing as long as we could, but without executive-level support, we got nowhere." Like most good people who get frustrated at lack of progress and vision, this particular analyst eventually moved to a company who saw the value of BI.

Some have it easier than others. The arrival of a technically savvy executive who has encountered BI success elsewhere may make life easier for the BI team. In many cases, however, executive support has to be earned, even re-earned. Some specific things the BI team can do to earn executive-level support:

- Demonstrate small successes and communicate the business benefits.
- Manage expectations.
- Exploit frustration (the LOFT effect) in which BI can address the pain.
- Evolve the capabilities and organization, and continuously engage executive stakeholders.

Demonstrate Small Successes

When you have completed a successful project—however small you must start—you will earn the trust and support of whichever executive or business unit derives the benefits from that first project. This executive will quickly become your BI champion and advocate for promoting BI to other departments, functions, and business units (absent political power struggles and assuming they are strategically aligned).

As an example, ENECO Energie is one of the top gas and electricity suppliers in the Netherlands. ENECO executives initially frowned upon BI. According to Ton van den Dungen, former manager, Business Intelligence Center of Excellence, the attitude was "There is not one successful BI project. It's too expensive." So with an entrepreneurial approach, ENECO's initial BI project consisted of manual extracts from source systems and Microsoft Excel PivotTables. Accounts receivable was the only subject area with the goals of better understanding why receivables were high and identifying opportunities to reduce them. The pilot cost only 350,000 euros (EUR) and helped ENECO save 4 million EUR ($5 million). Following the pilot's success, the BI team could get support and funding for a full BI architecture that included a data warehouse and suite of BI tools.

ENECO's initiative demonstrates a key secret to success: Successful BI companies start their BI initiative with or without executive sponsorship. They demonstrate success early and ramp up only once they've garnered that executive buy-in. Success at this early stage has to be measured in hard business benefits. ENECO could cite a specific value saved in millions of euros.

Small successes are important to engage executive support for an overarching BI initiative, but also for any change in strategy or new initiative. For example, if your BI program plans to adopt support for mobile BI, cloud, or big data sources, then you will want to demonstrate small, measurable successes before embarking on wider deployments. These small successes are important for learning, managing risk, and proving to those who fund your initiatives that there is clear business value.

Use the measurable business benefits that leading companies describe throughout this book—improved patient care, faster synergies following a merger, increased customer satisfaction, immediate sales lift, cost reductions in advertising campaigns—to inspire conversations with your executives on how your company can exploit business intelligence.

Manage Expectations

Managing expectations is paramount in earning and retaining executive support. Never overpromise and underdeliver. Particularly if you are starting out without executive support, position your efforts as only a prototype or point solution. Communicate clearly that the BI deployment will not be scaled up or out without an executive champion. This can be a difficult balancing act, particularly when vendors undermine your efforts. A BI project manager for a medical center expressed frustration:

> All the BI vendors come in and show these executives a bunch of eye-candy and make it sound easy when it's not. So we had no funding, no resources for our project. The BI vendors set us up for failure. An executive will have a team of ten analysts that he can ask a question of. The executive has no idea how their staff gets the numbers, the manual processes, the data manipulation. So the comparison is that it takes their staff an hour to give an answer versus a BI project that takes six months. Nobody has a handle on what it costs to do manually and how vulnerable they are.

Exploit Frustration

Recall the discussion of the LOFT effect in Chapter 5. If you currently lack executive-level sponsorship, ask the sought-for sponsor this: "How much time do you spend in meetings arguing about the numbers?" Find out the degree of pain and frustration.

How you frame the frustration is important. Executives don't want to hear about what a mess the data is or how tightly locked it is in the operational system. The focus has to be on the degree of frustration and that business intelligence—done well—can relieve that frustration and provide measurable business value. You have to be able to fill in the blank:

The *frustration* is killing us, and business intelligence can provide *benefit*.

For example: "The *time we spend debating numbers* (frustration) is a problem, and business intelligence can provide a *single set of numbers and allow us to focus more on innovation* (benefits)." Or "We are *losing market share*, and business intelligence can help us *increase sales by 5 percent*."

Evolve and Engage

As with any project, there is often initial excitement and dedicated efforts to get executive support at the onset. However, as business intelligence is a continuous process, that executive support needs to be nurtured on an ongoing basis. To ensure ongoing support, the BI team has to show ongoing benefits. Oftentimes, those benefits are achieved but may not be well communicated (see Chapter 13 for a discussion on marketing your BI efforts). In addition, the organization will change over time as you experience successes, setbacks, and technical changes. All these factors mean your BI team cannot stand still. At the beginning, you may have a dedicated organization for BI that resides within the technology group. To take BI impact to the next level, over time, you may decide that certain BI people need to reside within the lines of business. As the focus moves from reporting to self-service to sophisticated analytics, the company may decide that it needs a chief analytics officer in the board room, not just a CIO. With this evolution, the more you can provide executives tools that help them execute, the greater the chances they will stay engaged in the BI efforts. A tangible way to do this is by delivering a dashboard of key performance indicators on a tablet such as the iPad. Perhaps mobile is not the highest priority for your overall deliverables, but it should be viewed as a way of fostering ongoing executive engagement.

Brian Green, BI director at Blue Cross Blue Shield of Tennessee, states, "Gaining buy-in is ongoing, It's definitely not something you achieve and then put on the back burner. You have to constantly keep the value-add focused on your key business objectives if you're going to keep their buy-in."[7]

Culture

Culture is one of those hard-to-define yet critical aspects to powerful business intelligence. The attitudes and interactions of employees reflect a company's culture, but it is usually the executive leaders who establish and enable a company's analytic culture. Conversely, it can also be the executive who is skeptical of data, or who fears the impact of sharing data with rank and file, that can sabotage a company's BI initiative.

Picture the founder of Facebook, Mark Zuckerberg, in his hallmark hoodie in a room full of Wall Street executives, dressed in conservative navy blue suits. Zuckerberg's dress style reflects Facebook's culture. His readiness to challenge traditional ways of doing business and to take risks is part of Facebook's culture. It is in part that culture that explains why Facebook's initial analytic architecture was new and unconventional: open-source Hadoop. The current data volume would also justify the use of Hadoop, but even when Facebook was just a small company with a few members, it did not initially embrace a traditional relational data warehouse. This was a technical component that Facebook only added later.

At consumer goods manufacturer Procter & Gamble, the CEO describes a cultural revolution to shift the company from reacting to historical results to using more real-time and predictive analytics.[8] "We have to move business intelligence from the periphery of operations to the center of how business gets done," says CEO Bob McDonald. Part of that cultural shift includes tools and technologies that allow decision-makers to visualize and analyze data interactively during meetings, a degree of openness that fosters an analytic culture and that would be discouraged if anyone was afraid of exposing negative results. The role of social media is also driving the demand for more real-time data so that P&G can see how customers are commenting on Twitter and Facebook to new ads. For example, during the 2012 summer Olympics, P&G ran a new "Thank you, Mom" campaign that showed athletes thanking their mothers for years of nurturing their talent.

An analytic culture seems to be the biggest catalyst for big impact and is at the heart of many other best practices of BI success, including executive sponsorship, business–IT partnership, and agile development. The survey results reflect this impact. An analytic culture requires that executives be willing to share data, that fact-based decision-making is valued over gut feel, and a belief that data and technology can provide a competitive advantage. Figure 6-5 shows the degree that companies have this kind of culture. The good news is that approximately half of the companies surveyed agree or strongly agree their companies have these cultural factors. Fact-based decision-making had the lowest adoption, with only 42 percent saying their company had this kind of culture, compared to 29 percent of companies who say they operate mainly on gut-feel decision-making.

When a company has an analytic culture, there is a greater degree of impact. Not surprisingly, if a company believed that data and technology

Analytic Culture

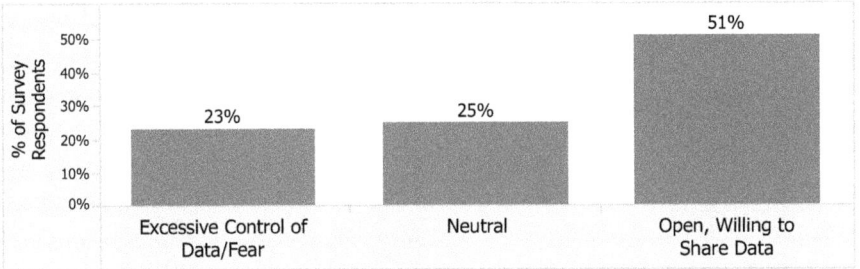

Degree Executives Control Access to Data, Fear Sharing

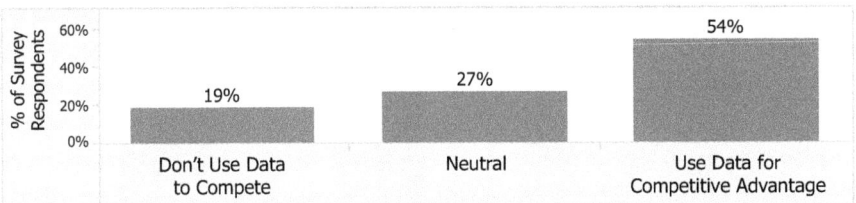

Use of Data and Technology for Competitive Advantage

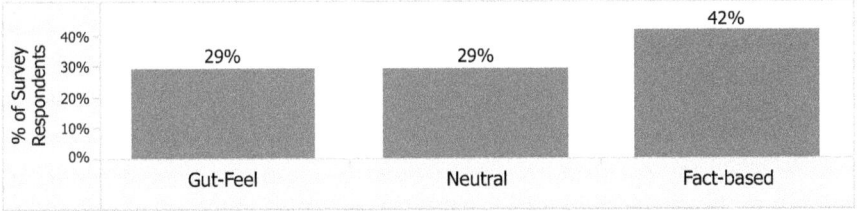

Fact-based Decisions

Figure 6-5   Degree that companies have an analytic culture

provided a competitive advantage, there was a significantly higher business impact from BI, at 49 percent, versus the industry average of 34
percent. (See Figure 6-6.)

And yet, there is no clear recipe for how to create such a culture.
Is it like the chicken and the egg, that you first need access to data to
be able to exploit data for competitive advantage? Or do you need first
to *value* fact-based decisions before leaders are willing to invest in the
BI technologies?

Contrasts are sometimes enlightening in how or whether an analytic
culture exists and how it can evolve. Jonathan Liebtag is the manager
of financial planning and analysis at Netflix, a company that has an

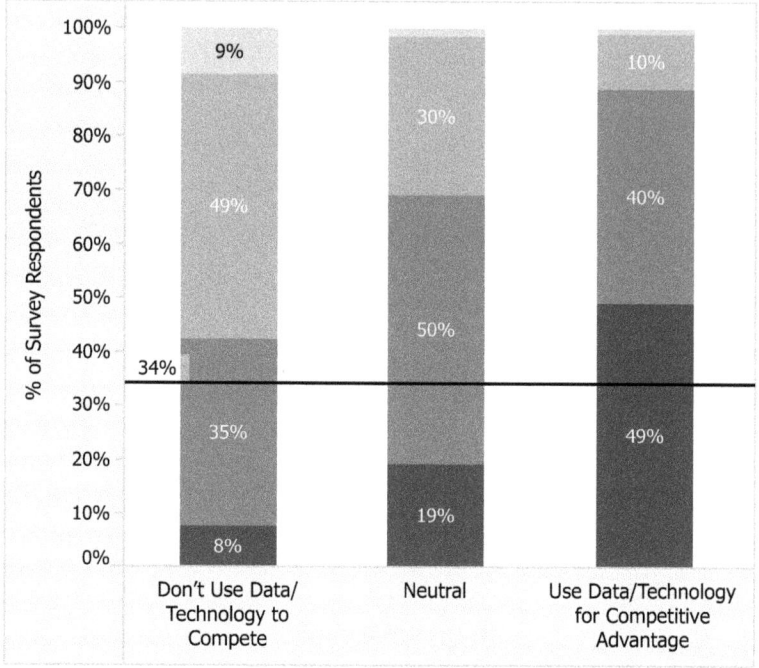

Figure 6-6 Companies who see a competitive advantage in the use of data and technology report the highest business impact from BI.

analytic culture. Liebtag spent most of his career in the banking industry. With so much data available and a clear focus on financial results, I would have thought banking might inherently have an analytic culture. Liebtag says that in his banking days, IT often simply passed the data off, whereas at Netflix, there is more of a conversation. "The people in the BI team are thoughtful and insightful. They really think about what the *question* is, rather than what the *request* is."[9]

So having that data first is not what makes an analytic culture. And if I think about it, banking is one of the oldest industries, having started with pen, paper, and manual ledgers. Decades of a culture that started with oak-paneled offices, strict hierarchies in decision-making, and repetitive processes cannot be transformed at the same pace as a start-up company.

"Culture, more than rule books, determines how an organization behaves."

—Warren Buffet

The Right People

Recruiting and retaining the right people can help foster an analytic culture. In *Analytics at Work* (Harvard Business Review Press, 2010), the authors Tom Davenport and Jeanne Harris describe the following behaviors and traits of analytical people:

- Search for truth and tenacious in that search
- Find patterns and root causes
- Granular in their analysis
- Seek data to analyze a question or issue
- Value negative results as well as positive
- Use results to make decisions and take action
- Pragmatic about trade-offs in decision-making

Management expert Jim Collins in his book *Good to Great* identifies one of the key characteristics of companies with sustained competitive advantage as the ability to "confront the brutal facts . . . You absolutely cannot make a series of good decisions without first confronting the brutal facts. The good-to-great companies operated in accordance with this principle, and the comparison companies generally did not."[10]

The CIO of Dow Chemical, Dave Kepler, explains how creating a culture where people can confront the "brutal facts" can take time:

> Information is still power, so you need a culture where people can be open. Analytics started out with a technical guy giving data to the boss, but that's not analytics anymore. That's history. We need to bring information much more into the executive suite and make it available to everyone. There's good news and bad news with reporting information. The executives have to be comfortable. How you respond to that information is pretty important and a big part of enabling an analytic culture. Everyone should be immersed in it so it's real time. You don't want any hoarders, or that only the boss should see the information first. It's become too dynamic a world not to be transparent.[11]

"It's become too dynamic a world not to be transparent."

—Dave Kepler, Dow Chemical CIO

However, the benefits of gut-feel decision-making should not be dismissed entirely. Sometimes experience and numerous facts may get synthesized into what is our "gut" feel. For doctors in emergency rooms, gut-feel decision-making may be all that time allows for. As Jonathan Rothman, a principal at EMBI, says, "Doctors often have to rely more on experience than fact-based decision-making. They get so used to making big decisions based on so little information. In the emergency room, you may not have time to run a lot of tests, and you have to make fast decisions. So for other things like the efficiency of the emergency room, we have to teach them the importance of getting the complete picture."[12]

The problem is when biases and inaccurate data also get filtered into the gut. In this case, the gut-feel decision-making should be supported with objective data, or errors in decision-making may occur.

Take the case of a small plastics packaging business. One of their most important national customers was consolidating suppliers, and the plastics packaging company was about to lose one of their best long-time customers. Or so they thought. At the threat of losing this customer, the company began looking for ways to retain the customer. With a new purchasing manager in place at the customer, it seemed a long-standing relationship was not an influencing factor in the decision to change suppliers. It was price and price alone. While this customer accounted for a significant portion of the supplier's revenue, when the supplier analyzed the profit margin for this customer, they found little to none. This customer was certainly keeping the supplier busy, but they were not helping them improve profitability. The supplier only realized this when they began studying the data to understand the impact of this customer loss. Based on the facts, the plastics company decided to let this customer go without a battle and without further cutting their prices.

Even when company culture encourages fact-based decision-making, recognize that facts can still be misinterpreted, misrepresented, or buried. Experts in decision-making describe one of the common errors in decision-making as the "confirming evidence trap."[13] The confirming evidence trap causes decision-makers to seek information that supports a decision they have already made (by gut or intuition or personal agenda) and to ignore facts that may contradict that decision. In the case of the plastics packaging company, the analysis of the customer profitability was specifically performed by someone who did not have a personal or long-term relationship with the customer. During the analysis, there were lively debates about how much fixed and overhead cost should really be allocated to the customer; any underallocation would make retaining the customer seemingly more attractive.

> Business intelligence tools can only present the facts. Removing biases and other errors in decision-making are dynamics of company culture that affect how well business intelligence is used.

Sometimes the facts are available but they are so buried that information is not actionable. In his article "The Formula," Malcolm Gladwell recounts all the warning signs of a pending catastrophic failure at Enron.[14] Some may argue that the "confirming evidence trap" was somewhat in play at Enron. Banks with sizable investments in the company would not want to see their money so at risk. Employees with sizable pensions and stock investments would also not want to contemplate the extent of the risk. A bigger problem, though, is that the facts were so convoluted and ineffectively presented that the poor financial health of the company was not readily discernible. Frankly, with more and more data being collected in the age of big data, I am concerned that the noise can often drown out the important facts.

In another example of how culture led to important facts being ignored, consider the BP oil spill disaster. The root cause of the oil spill was attributed to a failure in cement at the well's base. A subcontractor had data from a pressure gauge that warned of a problem, but management chose to ignore the warnings in an effort to speed drilling and cut costs. Industry experts say there was a culture of greed that led to the disaster. But imagine instead an executive willing to face the "brutal facts" that there was a major problem. Imagine, too, if the work environment was one in which the low-level worker who identified the problem could safely share this data more widely. Had this information been clearly communicated, the drilling might have been temporarily halted, the problem fixed, and the whole disaster averted.

> Knowledge workers and BI experts must continually evaluate the reports, dashboards, alerts, and other mechanisms for disseminating factual information to ensure the presentation facilitates insight.

Fostering Fact-Based Decision-Making

Decision-making experts say that being aware of decision-making traps is the most important first step to improving decision-making. "At every stage of the decision-making process, misperceptions, biases, and other tricks of the mind can influence the choices we make . . . the best protection against all psychological traps . . . is awareness."[15] Beyond that, encouraging fact-based decision-making is taking root in management literature and in business schools around the world. The number of MBA programs that offer business intelligence and statistical analysis courses increases each year.

Best Practices for Successful Business Intelligence

Executive support is one of the most important secrets to successful BI and the degree to which BI contributes to business performance. Fail to garner executive-level support, and your project will be met with only moderate success, perhaps in isolated deployments. Executive support is not guaranteed and is something that must be earned and continually ensured.

- Recognize that the best executive sponsor is one who has credibility and influence with all the business units and functions, not just with IT or just with finance.
- The sponsoring executive may change throughout the BI life cycle.
- Until you can prove the value of BI, some executives will skeptically think that BI is just another IT drain on investment dollars.
- Encourage your executives to read stories on how data and culture contribute to value as in Chapters 5 and 6 of this book, or in books and movies such as *Analytics at Work*, *Moneyball*, or *Zero Dark Thirty*.

If you have been diligently following all the other best practices in this book and still don't have executive-level support, face the harsh reality that your company may never fully appreciate the value of business intelligence without exogenous change.

Chapter 7

The Business–IT Partnership

Business and information technology (IT) professionals can become equally exasperated with one another, as they are often such opposites. However, the degree to which business and IT can partner together is a critical organizational aspect to successful business intelligence (see Chapter 6, Figure 6-1). According to the Successful BI survey, 36 percent identified the business–IT partnership as essential for success, and 36 percent say it is very important. For the sake of impactful business intelligence, then, opposites better attract!

Voices of Frustration . . . and Hope

In the Successful BI survey, respondents from both the business side and the IT side expressed frustration with one another, regardless whether their BI deployment was a failure or a success, but there are signs that partnership is improving as both sides recognize the importance of partnership in achieving BI success.

Frustration

"Business and IT have a great deal of difficulty communicating, clearly because of different language and different mind-sets."
—*A hybrid business–IT person from a major insurance company*

"IT is the main reason why our BI effort failed."
—*A business user from a utility company*

"IT and business are marching to different drums. Business moves with a sense of urgency, and IT moves with a sense of perfection."
—*Hybrid/business solutions architect in manufacturing*

"BI is failing. Time and resources are not allocated fully. IT and business don't see eye to eye on issues."
—*Manager, commercial analytics in energy industry*

"Our BI is failing due to years of neglect and underspending, coupled with the fact that IT will not release tools to allow business users access to data unless it has been developed through IT."
                                                        —*IT person in energy industry*

Hope

"The partnership and trust between the information systems BI team and the business is essential. Information systems must understand the business and be involved in what they are trying to achieve."
            —*Margie Lekien, a BI leader with Landstar System, Inc.,
                who describes their BI project as very successful*

"You don't build BI solutions without engaging the business/end user. In other words, if you build without user input, they will *not* come."
    —*Jagannathan Santhanam, solutions architect, Columbian Chemicals
        Company, who describes BI as having a significant impact*

"We are successful because of our self-service model, enforced with excellent training and IT/departmental partnerships."
            —*Charles Boicey, informatics solutions architect, University of
            California-Irvine, who describes BI as having a significant impact*

"BI has finally hit mainstream, and the business is finally driving this versus IT. The success of a BI project is much greater when the business is driving."
                —*BI architect in manufacturing who describes
                        BI as having a significant impact*

The frustration and divide between the business and IT has ramifications far beyond business intelligence. Yet given the distinct aspects of BI technology, lack of partnership has a more profound effect on BI's success than other organizational and technical factors. As both sides blame one another, a key secret to reducing blame and increasing understanding is to recognize how these two sides are different.

The Business–IT Yin-Yang

The concept of yin and yang originated in ancient Chinese philosophy.[1] The yin—the black portion of the symbol—represents passiveness, cold, and water. The yang—the white portion of the symbol—represents movement, initiative, heat, and fire. The yin-yang is a good symbol for the business–IT relationship because while it does reflect opposites, it is said the yin-yang also conveys "balance" and "a duality that cannot exist without both parts."[2] Within the white yang portion of the symbol, there is also a small black circle (and the black yin portion has a small white circle) to show that each side has elements of the other and is stronger when they interact. The differences are not absolute.

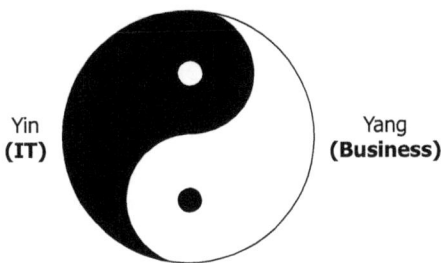

Table 7-1 compares characteristics of businesspeople and IT people. They are archetypes, and as with any archetype, there are exceptions, but I would suspect that if each group of professionals were given a personality test, consistent traits would emerge. As an example, when an archetypal businessperson wants to address a problem, he or she will schedule a face-to-face meeting so differences, opinions, and ideas can be shared. An IT person, on the other hand, might prefer to fire off an e-mail, avoiding direct interaction (and providing documentation on the disagreement). A businessperson would comfortably skip documenting and testing a system and happily just install the latest version of software. The prospect of doing this might cause heart palpitations for an IT professional—the risks and lack of a systematic approach are overwhelming. Okay, perhaps both archetypes would like to skip documenting the system, but it illustrates the extreme differences in work styles.

In reviewing drafts of this chapter, I and my editors were concerned that my proposed archetypes would offend some readers. While they agreed with my observations, we wanted to support these archetypes with hard data. So I turned to one of the most widely used personality tests: the Myers-Briggs Type Indicator (MBTI). MBTI breaks personalities into four aspects:[3]

Businessperson Archetype	IT Professional Archetype
Extrovert	Introvert
Sociable	Solitary
Freewheeling	Methodical, systematic, disciplined
Risk taking	Risk averse
Prefers face-to-face meetings	Minimal face-to-face communication; e-mail and instant messaging are fine

Table 5-1   Archetype characteristics of businesspeople and IT professionals

- **Energy**   Introverts (I) draw their energy from themselves and solitary activities, whereas extroverts (E) draw their energy from being with other people.
- **Perception**   Sensing types (S) prefer to deal with reality, whereas intuitive (N) types are more imaginative and future focused.
- **Judgment**   Thinkers (T) are more objective and logical in assessing a situation, whereas feelers (F) are people who will judge a situation more by how people are affected.
- **World orientation**   Judging (J) personality types like structure in their world, whereas perceiving (P) types are more spontaneous, flexible, and thrive on change.

In considering the business archetypes described in the earlier table, the businessperson shows a personality type that is extroverted, feeling, and perceiving, or EFP. The IT archetype is more introverted, thinking, and judging, or an ITJ personality type. Now, don't let some of the Myers-Brigg terminology lose you here—everyone is a "thinker," but from a personality point of view, a T-type suggests an approach to decisions from a more logical, almost clinical, point of view, whereas F-types consider more the impact their decisions have on people. I don't think the personality extremes for perception (sensing or S and intuitive or N) are distinguishing characteristics in the business and IT archetypes.

The Center for Applications of Psychological Type (CAPT) analyzed more than 60,000 MBTI test results that determine a person's personality type with the selected careers of those individuals. Sure enough, ITJ types (which correspond to my IT archetype) more often choose technical careers, and a career in computer science, data analysis, or mathematics appears at the top of the list for this personality type.[4] Specifically, ISTJs and INTJs are most likely to find interesting and satisfying careers that make use of their depth of concentration, reliance on facts, use of logic and analysis, and ability to organize.[5]

Meanwhile, EFP types most often choose careers that have more people interaction and breadth of skills; careers like marketing and management professionals moved to the top of the list for this type.[6] Specifically, ESFP and ENFP are most likely to pursue careers that use their breadth of interests, grasp of possibilities, reliance on facts, warmth and sympathy (emphasis on interpersonal skills), and adaptability.[7] These personality types may hate jobs that require technical analysis and significant attention to detail, so it's not a far leap to say that these personality types may find it difficult to work with people who do like analysis and details.

This is not to say that you won't find an EFP type in IT or an ITJ type as a business user; it simply means that the distinct personality types are indeed more prevalent in each role (think the larger black area of the yin-yang versus the small black circle). It's not a baseless stereotype.

Facebook Director of Analytics Ken Rudin has also noted this yin-yang and describes the different personalities as the hippo and the groundhog. The hippo is the "highest-paid person's opinion." They may have too much art and not enough science in their decision-making. The hippos can be bullies. The groundhogs, in the meantime, prefer the science that goes into a decision. Rudin recalls the themes from the movie *Groundhog Day*, in which the main character is caught in a time loop, and each day, he gets another chance to win over the girl, guessing at what she likes and wants in a date. Their dates are like a series of A/B tests, a type of controlled experiment used in marketing and advertising to see which approach yields the best outcome. Explains Rudin, "Science has its limits. A/B testing has its limits and helps you get to a local maximum, but it won't get you to the creative breakthrough . . . You want the yin- yang tension."[8]

Despite the MBTI research, some may still dismiss these differences in work styles and personalities as stereotypes. However, one difference that cannot be so easily dismissed is that of incentives. In many companies, the business is motivated and rewarded for behavior that increases revenue. Increasing revenue may involve designing new products and testing new market segments, all with a lot of risk. IT, meanwhile, is often rewarded for cutting costs and providing a stable IT environment, where risk is discouraged. To a degree, this dichotomy is necessary. You can't swap out systems on a regular basis and expect the company to continue to operate. As with most things, the solution to closing this incentive gap lies in the middle.

IT people should be rewarded for being responsive to business requests that improve business performance. Providing a stable, low-cost
computing environment should be only a *portion* of their total variable
compensation and performance evaluation.

Meet the Hybrid Business–IT Person

One way in which business and IT people are bridging the gap is by
cultivating hybrid business–IT people. These hybrids are typically businesspeople by training or career who gain technology skills. They may
not be programmers or systems engineers, but they speak enough of
the IT language to translate business needs, opportunities, and requirements in ways that IT traditionalists understand. They also look for ways
in which information technology is a business enabler. As shown in the
Appendix, 24 percent of the survey respondents describe themselves as
hybrid business–IT persons.

A hybrid business–IT person can act as a powerful bridge between
the different business intelligence stakeholders: The business derives
the value and IT enables the systems. Hybrid business–IT persons understand the business and how to leverage technology to improve it.
Conversely, they also understand enough of the technology to identify
opportunities to apply new technology to solve business problems.

I would also describe myself as one of these hybrids. I stumbled into
the field of IT in the 1980s. While I excelled at math, computer science
at the time was not the place for women, so I pursued my other passion:
writing. Being a lousy typist (then and now), I developed a knack for this
new thing: word processing. When the university network kept crashing,
I had to find innovative ways to recover corrupted files (what—retype an
entire paper?!?!?) and discovered the world of personal computers and
local area networks. Fortunately for me, training in those days meant
vendor-specific certifications in tools like Lotus 123 and dBASE rather
than in hard-core programming. Given how newfangled some of this
technology was, nobody laughed at my bachelor's degree in English, but
I entered the workforce already in the middle of two disciplines.

Dow Chemical was my second job out of college, and in an unusual twist, I was hired directly by a business unit (not the information systems department) to fill a newly created role as a business systems specialist. So here is an easy way to ensure business–IT partnership: Make sure IT personnel are directly on your payroll and not a chargeback or overhead cost. (I only later learned all the political consequences of this unusual reporting line.) The business unit I worked for, hydrocarbons, gave me only broad guidelines to work within, and I answered only to this business unit. When we wanted a local area network, I defined the requirements, bought the system, and installed it. I *might* compare requirements with the central information systems group (out of diplomacy or curiosity), but I didn't have to follow any of their standards back then. The hydrocarbons business even went so far as to buy our own meeting scheduler (pre–Microsoft Outlook) and to build an integrated transaction system (pre-SAP). As much of what the hydrocarbons business did was ahead of what the European information systems department was offering other business units at the time, there was an enormous amount of friction between the two. Describing the dynamics as an "us versus them" mentality was an understatement.

My business users were happy, and the hydrocarbons unit was using information technology in ways that provided real business value. It was rewarding, exciting, and challenging, but offered absolutely no career progression. So when the Global Reporting Project came along in 1993, it seemed like a smart career move. It was my first glimpse into the "other side," though, of being a cost center and of having to satisfy the greatest common denominator of not 1, but 15 different business units and multiple functions. If the yang is like the fire of the business, my move into IT certainly was like walking into the yin of winter. Overnight, I had become a "them."

I went from the hydrocarbons way of minimal requirements analysis for fast delivery of capabilities to an excruciating level of project planning down to the hour. In hydrocarbons, the technology investments were approved by a business team when something sounded reasonable enough. Within information systems, I had to do a full economic analysis before buying a packaged business intelligence solution, calculated by return on investment (ROI) and payback period, when I was frankly guessing at benefits. I was out of my league.

Eventually, I got past my panic attacks. Through the Global Reporting Project, I learned the discipline within information systems that is necessary when building solutions for thousands of users; in hydrocarbons, the users were fewer than 200. I also learned that while

I had gained an understanding of the hydrocarbons business unit, my knowledge of business in general was lacking. For the Global Reporting Project, two of the initial subject areas included a product income statement and a business balance sheet. I had no idea what these terms meant, let alone why they were important. So I did what any stubborn person determined to understand the purpose in all this would do: I quit my career of eight years, left the company that I referred to as my "extended family," and pursued my MBA, albeit with a focus on management information systems.

As my own experience illustrates, the career path for a hybrid business–IT person is often unclear. Do you align more with the business or with IT? What is clear is that such hybrid people benefit from indoctrination and training in both disciplines.

Over the years, since the first edition of this book was released, people have asked me what is better and easier: to hire an IT person and cross-train them in business, or to hire a businessperson and cross-train them in technology? I have not found an overarching trend. But hybrids are motivated to understand "the other side." So a businessperson, frustrated by lack of responsiveness in IT, will go out and learn the technology. Hybrids that come from the business often benefit from already having the respect of the business community. The converse may not be true of a technology person; that respect by business leaders will have to be earned as they develop a deeper understanding of the business.

The need for hybrid business–IT people is something that business schools throughout the United States increasingly recognize. The importance of this dual skill set is most apparent at the CIO level (see Chapter 6). However, it is also important at lower levels and, I would advocate, at any intersecting points in which businesspeople and IT people must communicate directly with one another.

How to Be a Better Partner

An effective partnership is a relationship in which both are jointly committed to the success of a particular process or goal.

This doesn't mean the business can define their requirements, throw them over the fence, and hope to get a usable business intelligence solution in return. Nor does it mean that the IT personnel can approach the business with a degree of wariness, the "them" in the "us versus them" relationship of people who don't know what they want and are never satisfied. Partnership starts with a positive attitude. Describing 1-800

CONTACTS' business–IT partnership, Jim Hill, the data warehouse manager, says, "We are equal partners with the call center. The business comes here and says, 'Here's what we are trying to accomplish. What do you think?' ... If the business feels they are a partner in solution, you get the desired results." Confirming that this idea of partnership must come from both sides, and also that it exists with the business users at 1-800 CONTACTS, Dave Walker, vice president of operations, attributes their BI success to this partnership: "The IT people in the data warehouse team understand the call center so well, they could probably take some calls. They are a life-saver for so many things. I've never felt an 'us' versus 'them' mentality. The issue is always 'we' not 'they.'"

The first step to building such a partnership is to recognize its importance in successful business intelligence. Business intelligence is a technology that lies at the heart of the intersection between business and technology; without the partnership, your efforts will be met with moderate success at best.

Some specific things that both the business and IT can do to develop a stronger partnership:

- **Develop an understanding of each other** Recognize the different personalities, work approaches, and constraints under which each works. For the business, this may mean recognizing that IT must deliver common solutions and not business-specific solutions. For IT, this may mean greater recognition of why a timely delivery is so critical to the livelihood of the business (see the section on enterprise versus departmental BI in Chapter 11).
- **Recruit hybrid business–IT people** Whether you identify and develop these people internally or hire from the outside, ensuring some hybrid business–IT people are involved in your business intelligence initiative will help foster a greater partnership.
- **Ban the technobabble!** IT people tend to overuse acronyms. As a courtesy to businesspeople, all acronyms should be banned. You wouldn't speak a foreign language in a room otherwise filled with only English-speaking colleagues, so don't revert to technobabble. Chapter 13 contains techniques on how to better frame business intelligence in terms of the business benefits rather than the technical terms. Practice an elevator pitch that describes briefly what business intelligence is all about in business terms.
- **Team building** Work with your human resources department to bring both IT and businesspeople together for team-building

exercises, particularly if you use agile development techniques (see Chapter 10). This might include a personality assessment such as the Myers-Briggs Type Indicator so that team members recognize and understand people's unique motivators and styles of working.

- **Change incentive compensation** Most people have a portion of their salary also tied to performance and accomplishment of certain goals. For IT people, it's important that the goals are not only related to cost containment, but also to business enablement.

- **Consider organizational structures** As my own experience demonstrates, reporting lines do affect the business–IT partnership. Consider alternative organizational structures that provide the appropriate partnership and balance for fulfilling career paths, shared resources, knowledge sharing, and expertise as they relate to business intelligence. For example, a strong steering committee and business users that reside within the central BI team help foster partnership. In other organizational models, the BI experts reside within the individual business units for maximum alignment and collaboration. These organizational aspects are discussed further in Chapter 11.

- **Involve one another** Business units will periodically have staff meetings, an ideal forum for an IT person to gain a greater understanding of the business, and conversely, for a BI representative to provide an update on the business intelligence initiative. IT personnel should study the company's mission statement as well as individual business unit plans.

- **Have lunch together** Study the corporate cafeteria, and you will find the cliques of high school echoed. The IT department sits with themselves, and businesspeople sit with each other—that is, when people even eat lunch together! It is an unfortunate situation that lunchtime, particularly in the United States, is often relegated to a quick sandwich eaten in isolation at one's desk or in a cubicle. Lunchtime is an ideal time to build a partnership more casually.

- **Hire a woman** I recognize that this recommendation may be perceived as sexist and self-serving. But consider this: Women in IT make up less than 25 percent of the workforce, and that percentage has been declining. Building bridges and gathering requirements demand strong listening skills, empathy, and intuition—traits more often associated with females. If you don't have a diverse BI team in terms of gender, skills, and work styles, creativity may suffer. In terms of the business–IT partnership, be sure that you have a team member who is a good listener.

Partnership and BI Success

So we know that partnership is important and difficult to achieve, but how bad is the disconnect? At first blush, the survey results revealed some positives. As shown in Figure 7-1, overall, the majority of companies surveyed say there is a partnership between business and IT, with 25 percent citing a strong partnership. It is the minority, or 23 percent, who say there is no partnership. Given how much people seem to complain about this issue, I thought perhaps it was just the disgruntled who were being louder than the satisfied.

Figure 7-2 shows the assessment of partnership according to a person's role in the company. For the most part, IT perceives there is a partnership. But it is the hybrid business/IT person and business user who have a higher rate of saying there is an "us versus them" mentality (36 percent and 30 percent, respectively). I suspect the businesspeople perceive a greater disconnect because they feel the brunt of the pain when IT is either not responsive or simply doesn't understand the business requirements. IT is more often forced into the position of saying "no" to the business rather than the business saying "no" to IT.

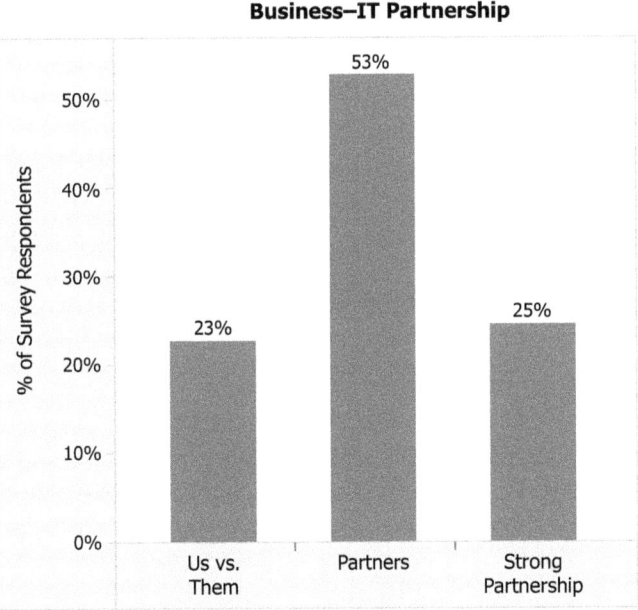

Figure 7-1 The majority of companies say there is a partnership between business and IT.

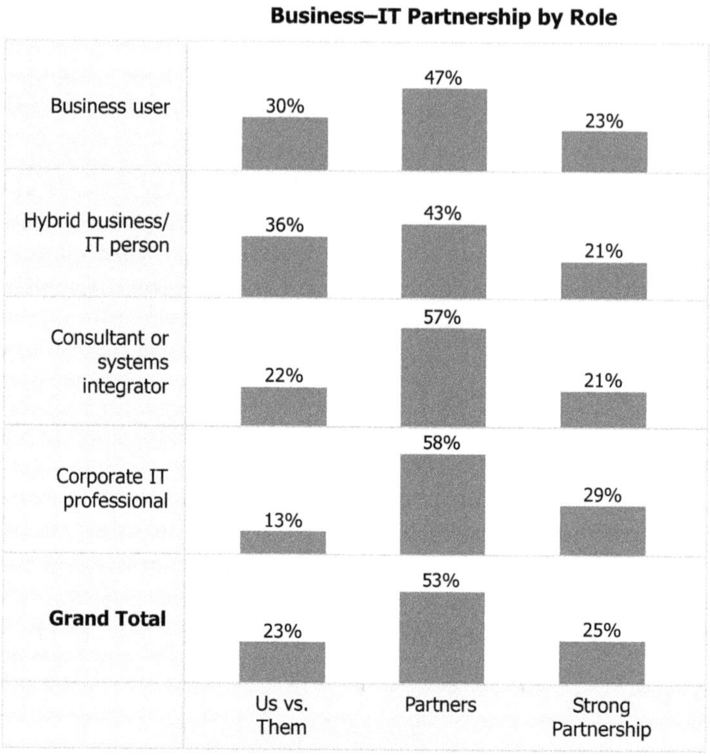

Business–IT Partnership by Role

	Us vs. Them	Partners	Strong Partnership
Business user	30%	47%	23%
Hybrid business/ IT person	36%	43%	21%
Consultant or systems integrator	22%	57%	21%
Corporate IT professional	13%	58%	29%
Grand Total	23%	53%	25%

Figure 7-2   IT perceives a better partnership than business users.

The impact a lack of partnership has on BI's contribution to the business is noteworthy. As shown in Figure 7-3, when there is a strong business–IT partnership, the percentage of companies achieving significant business impact from BI is 54 percent. This is a substantially higher impact than the survey average of 34 percent.

Partnership at Netflix

The concept of partnership at Netflix extends beyond the internal business–IT relationship and even beyond corporate boundaries to other service providers on which Netflix's business model depends: the U.S. Postal Service (USPS) for delivering DVDs, Amazon for streaming content, and content producers. Danny Jackson is the director of postal and security operations at Netflix on the business side. He is also a retired postal executive, having worked in the Postal Service for 37 years. He credits the BI success at Netflix to the partnership with IT and the type

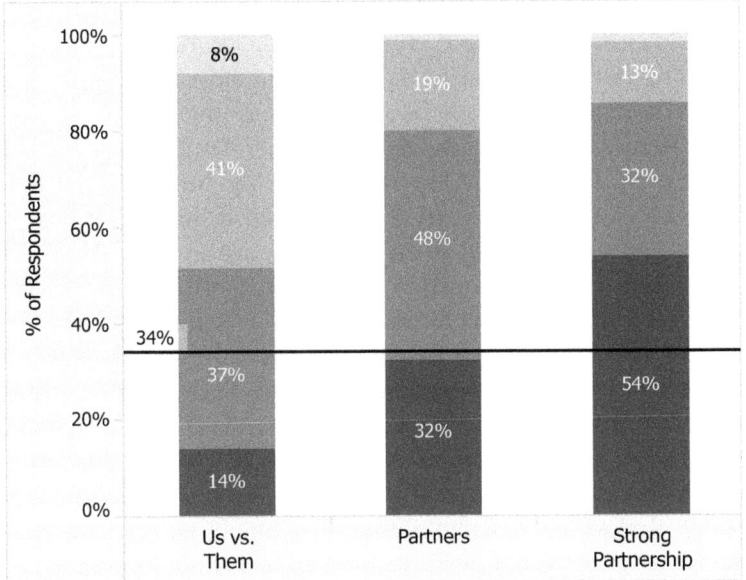

Figure 7-3   BI has a more significant business impact at companies with a strong business–IT partnership.

of people on the BI team. "I have to give kudos to the hiring folks who select people in the BI world. I am overwhelmed by how bright they are. They are hungry to look at data, how best to provide it, and when. They are very focused on me as a user and that I have a good experience with it."[9] Jackson adds that he is not a very technical person and in dealing with IT people in the postal world, "they spoke another language. At Netflix, the IT people are gifted with numbers, data, systems, but they have very good people skills as well. They are articulate and listen well."

As I listed earlier and as Jackson's thoughts reinforce, IT needs to ban the technobabble and ensure members of the BI team are good listeners.

In fostering a partnership with the U.S. Postal Service, it helps that Jackson had a career in the Postal Service, allowing for a greater understanding of the constraints and capabilities of the USPS. Likewise, a number of the operations managers are former postal employees. Two factors that can impact Netflix costs and customer service are when DVDs go missing or break. Blaming it on the Postal Service can be a delicate accusation. Blaming it on the customer can be even more delicate. Avoiding loss altogether is, of course, the best alternative, but not realistic. So when more people began watching Blu-ray DVDs, the data revealed a higher breakage rate than for other DVD types. Each DVD envelope has its own unique bar code, allowing Netflix to get detailed information about where the DVD was mailed from, which post office handled it, and even which postal machine scanned it. After further analysis, Jackson's team identified certain post offices, and eventually certain postal processing machines, that had a higher breakage rate.

Because the relationship between Netflix and the Postal Service is a positive one, Netflix shares data with the Postal Service. Explains Jackson, "They have welcomed that feedback, and we have coached them on how to build service into their own systems. It's been a good relationship." With this data, Netflix and the Postal Service worked together to identify the design issue in the automation machine, and the breakage rate on DVDs went from 4 percent down to less than 1 percent.

This whole dynamic also reflects how culture, discussed in Chapter 6, has a significant impact on the use of data and the degree that different stakeholders can partner together. Imagine if either side of this relationship, either Netflix operations or the U.S. Postal Service, had a culture of fear and territorial wars. Exposing the data of breakage rates could have been a blame game, but this example had a positive outcome because of the culture and alignment toward achieving a common goal: reducing the breakage.

Alignment

While business alignment and business partnership are closely related, they are not the same thing. *Alignment* involves IT and the business working toward a common goal; *partnership* has more to do with commitment and recognition that both stakeholders have an interest in each other's success. The business intelligence initiative must support the company's or business unit's objectives, whether to be a low-cost provider, best in class service, and so on. Ideally, even when BI is delivered for a new subject area for a particular business unit, those capabilities are aligned with the goals of the company overall. In some cases, they aren't. Individual business units may be at odds with another, putting IT resources in the difficult middle position. In this case, IT and that particular business unit may be working as partners, but they are not aligned. Balanced scorecard experts Robert Kaplan and David Norton describe this alignment "much like the synchronization achieved by a high-performance rowing crew."[10] Partnership is a commitment to achieving this synergy.

When the business and IT are aligned, both add value to each other, consistent with the concept of the yin-yang. In this way, the business sees IT as a trusted partner to ensure that technology is considered in developing a business's strategic direction and that IT delivers an architecture and set of services consistent with this direction (see Figure 7-4). Alignment should not be construed as an excuse for IT to *react* to all business requests. The former CIO of Westchester County, New York, Dr. Norman Janis, says, "Too often, the phrase 'aligning IT with the business' implies that IT must breathlessly run to catch up with the business as it goes in whatever direction someone else has determined. True alignment means IT and the business units together define the best direction for the organization to go—and IT shouldn't be afraid to take the lead."[11]

The dynamic of defining the best direction together, as opposed to reacting to business demands, is a subtle but important dynamic of a partnership. A partnership suggests that IT can in fact say "no" to something. One of my clients suggested that it is because people in IT have

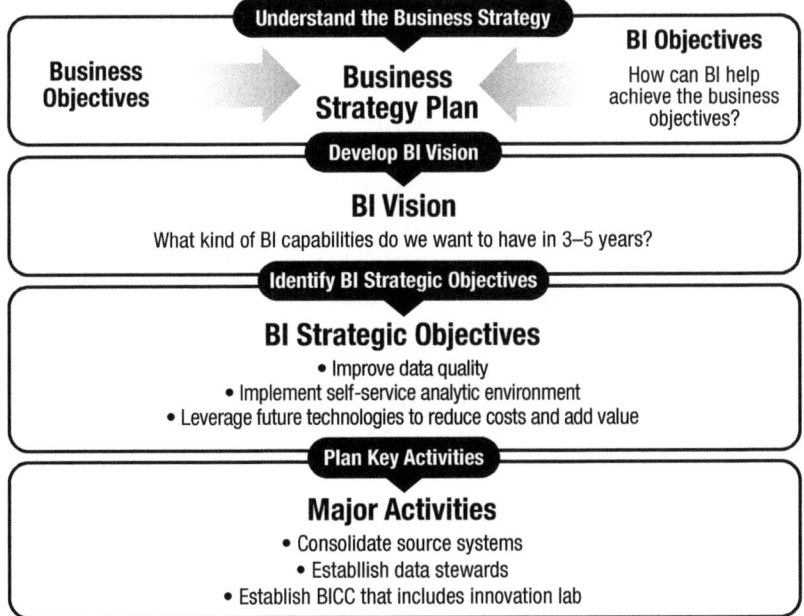

Figure 7-4 Aligning business intelligence with the business

been taught to think of their internal users as "customers," leading to a mentality of "the customer is always right." However, in business and in BI, the "customer," or user, is not always right. For example, business users may start their BI journey in spreadsheets, but downloading massive amounts of data to spreadsheets that grow into inconsistent data marts is not always the best practice.

It can be difficult for a low-level BI developer to say "no" to a user, and this is why it's important to have the right people and organizational structures in place so that stakeholders at all levels can trust that they are working toward the same goals.

While alignment is an important ingredient for successful business intelligence, the business intelligence architecture and solution need to be flexible enough to change when the business strategy changes. In this way, Mike Costa, former corporate director of quality process and architecture at Dow Chemical, cautions, "The strategy of the company can change overnight. Business intelligence should be able to react quickly."[12] While the initial technology and architecture Dow established in 1994, when it first began the Global Reporting Project, continues to be used today, Dow is implementing a second-generation analytic environment that allows greater agility. The aspects that have changed the most are the data warehouse platform to include SAP BW and BW Accelerator, the applications (reports, cubes, business views), and the organization to bring traditional BI analysts and statisticians together.[13] When Dow started on its BI efforts in the early 1990s, the concept of a packaged data warehouse did not exist, so all of the data extraction from SAP was custom-written. The use of BW as a prebuilt data warehouse and the BW Accelerator have brought greater agility into the BI environment, says Mark Carter, a systems architect at Dow. "In 2009, we set a goal to reduce our turn-around time to 30 days, and to put more analytics in the hands of the users." With the initial custom-developed data warehouse, changes often took months to implement.

Alignment of the BI program to business goals can be easier when the CEO is driving the initiative and when data is your product. This is the case with FlightStats. While the airlines may have started as the primary customer base to FlightStats, the ultimate business objective is to help the traveler.[14] One of their taglines is "When the travel gets tough, the tough fly smarter." This can be in the form of direct communication, such as letting them know a flight will be late or which route is best, or indirectly, by helping airlines better manage on-time performance. A third customer segment comprises those firms that consume the data,

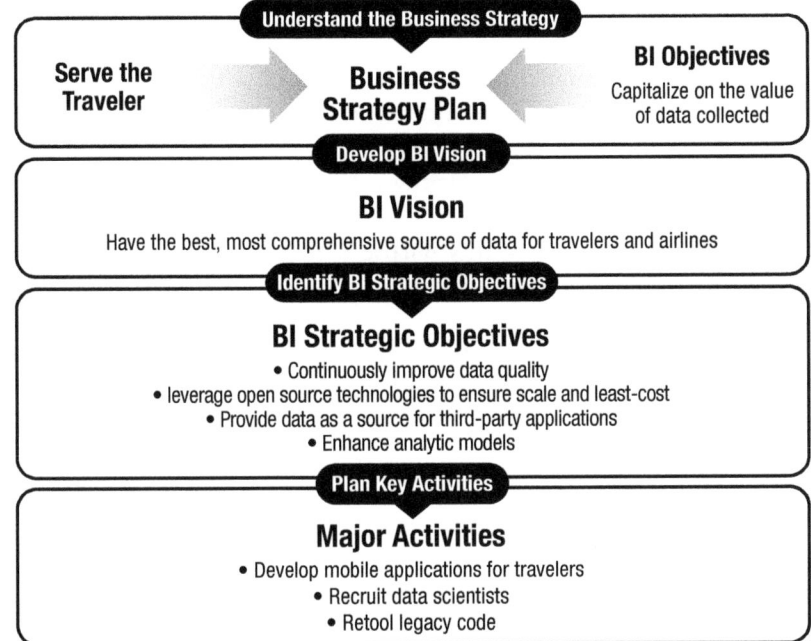

Figure 7-5 FlightStats BI efforts align to the company's goal to help air travelers

also to help airlines. For example, Flightcaster uses the FlightStats' data to build predictive models of potential delays, whereas masFlight, a cloud-based flight analytics platform, uses the data for flight operations. Figure 7-5 shows how the BI vision, objectives, and activities are aligned to the overall business strategy of focusing on the traveler. Jeff Kennedy, CEO of FlightStats, explains, "On-time performance is a single number of so many people doing their jobs correctly, so it's something everyone can rally around."

Best Practices for Successful Business Intelligence

The business–IT partnership is one of the most important aspects in succeeding with business intelligence. To foster this partnership and to ensure greater alignment

- Recognize the importance of the business–IT partnership in successful business intelligence.
- If you feel like the other side seldom understands you, has a radically different way of working, and is motivated by different forces, then

congratulate yourself for recognizing some significant differences. They are real!

- Evaluate variable compensation such that the BI team is rewarded not only for cost containment and reduction, but also for the business value added.
- Recruit and develop hybrid business–IT personnel to play a pivotal role in your BI effort.
- Be proactive in developing this partnership by communicating regularly, banning technobabble, studying the business goals, and occasionally having lunch together.
- Align the vision and deliverables for business intelligence with the goals of the company and individual business units that BI serves.

Chapter 8

D Is for Data

Data is the fundamental building block for a business intelligence application. Successful business intelligence is influenced by both technical aspects and organizational aspects. In general, companies rate organizational aspects, such as executive-level sponsorship, culture, and the business–IT partnership, as having a higher impact on success than technical aspects. And yet, even if you do everything right from an organizational perspective, if you don't have data, you can't do business intelligence. If you don't have high-quality, relevant data, with the breadth of data sources needed to support a decision, your BI initiative will have minimal success.

Figure 8-1 shows how the data architecture provides the pillars for BI front-end tools and applications. Each pillar within the data architecture

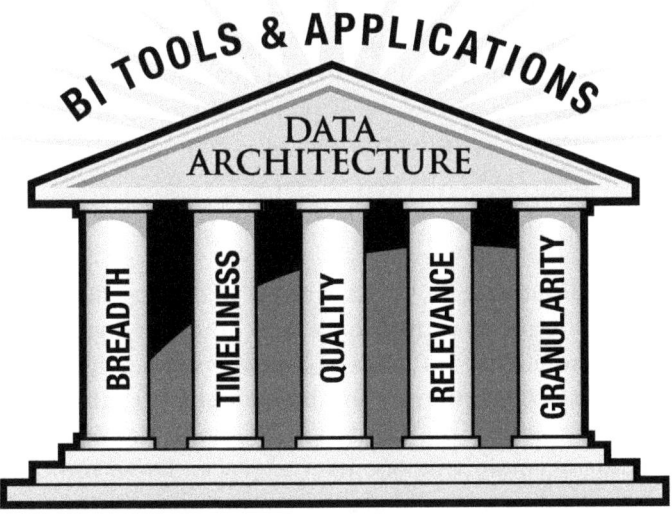

Figure 8-1 The data architecture is the foundation for successful business intelligence.

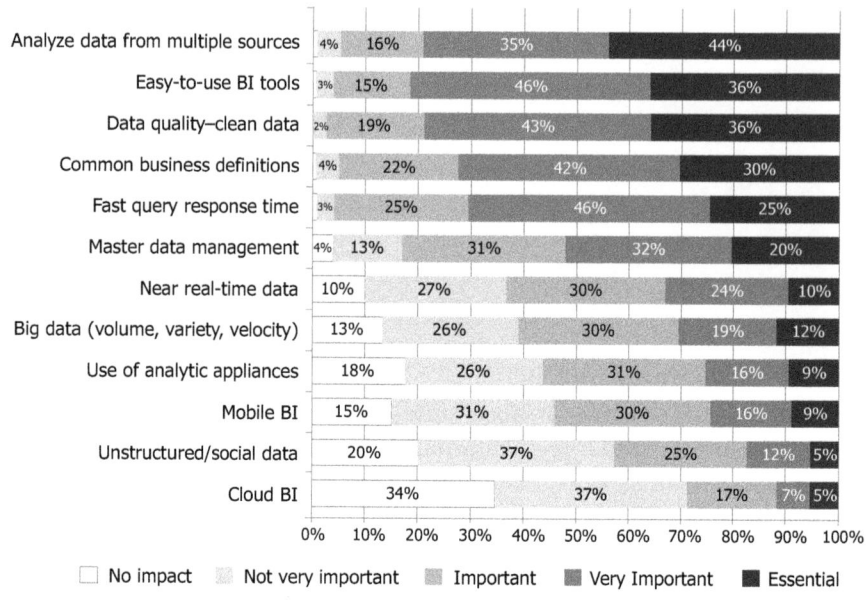

Figure 8-2 The ability to analyze data from multiple data sources is the most important technical criterion for BI success.

is important. Data quality is the center pillar. So much effort goes into ensuring and improving data quality, long before that data reaches a decision-maker in a report or dashboard. However, for the first time since I began surveying companies on the importance of these technical factors, data quality has declined from the top ranking to now third in priorities (see Figure 8-2). The ability to get to multiple data sources, or breadth, was ranked number one in terms of technical factors for success, with 44 percent of survey respondents saying it is essential.

Data Breadth

With early BI initiatives, the focus was on unlocking data captured in transactional systems. A central data warehouse or independent data mart provides a safe place for users to query, report, analyze, and explore the data without impacting the transaction system. With a central data warehouse, information has been extracted from multiple source systems and made accessible in one central place. These multiple source systems may include a general ledger, payroll, orders, customer relationship management, and so on.

In the era of big data, the source of data is no longer just an internal transaction system. New data sources such as web click-stream, smart meters, cloud-based systems, and social data are data repositories that users want to combine with transactional data. The breadth of data has increased at a faster pace than many BI teams have been able to adapt to bring them into the existing, centralized information architectures.

Data Quality

Data is considered to have a high level of quality when it is consistent, complete, and accurate. Thirty-six percent of survey respondents rated data quality as essential to a successful BI deployment. This is a lower portion than in the original 2007 book, and I suspect the reasons for the decline in importance relative to other factors is multifaceted:

- First, 68 percent of companies said they now have a high degree of data quality. As data quality has improved over time, the degree of pain inflicted by poor data quality has subsided. (See Figure 8-3.)
- Second, many new data sources do not have the same levels and measures of quality that can be expected from a transactional system. Textual data entered in a comment field that wasn't accessible before does not have a clear "good data" or "bad data" qualifier. Similarly,

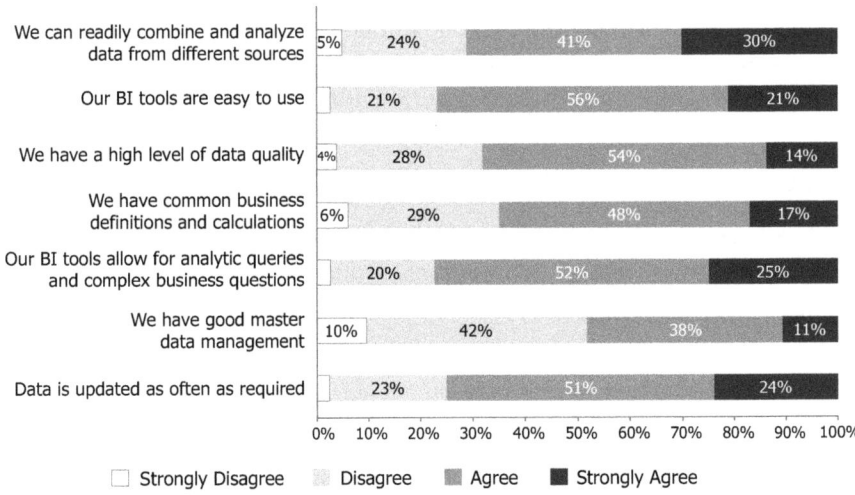

Figure 8-3 Status of technical factors affecting BI success

the quality of customer-created social data is highly variable. Teens sometimes enter information in a loose context, naming siblings and spouses that are not truly siblings and spouses. Others have said they enter minimal information and will intentionally provide false demographics out of privacy concerns when they suspect data is being used by marketers.

- Last, as BI deployments have matured, they have moved beyond only transactional data that has often initially been centered around financial systems. In accounting, raw data is transformed and aggregated with the intent of creating and reporting financial results. This data has to be right, or there may be legal consequences. However, for decision-making, users may want the more granular data that is not necessarily as cleansed or transformed to an accounting view. There is a greater acceptance that granular data may be dirtier, but also may reveal an important insight. Similarly, in healthcare, certain data elements such as patient blood type have to be accurate, but the quality of data pertaining to time to wait to see a doctor does not require the same accuracy.

Data quality, then, is an important issue, but the degree of quality necessary will depend on the type of data source and application. Achieving a high degree of data quality is a challenge that is not well understood or exciting to business users. It's often perceived as being a problem for IT to handle. But it's not: Data quality is something only the business can truly own and correct. IT can only bandage data quality problems, usually during the extract, transform, and load (ETL) process (see Figure 2-3, Chapter 2). Addressing the root cause of data quality issues, at the source, is a business responsibility.

Achieving a high level of data quality is hard and is affected significantly by organizational and ownership issues. In the short term, bandaging problems rather than addressing the root causes is often the path of least resistance.

Bad data can be a big business problem. Larry English is one of the leading experts on information quality and once ranked information quality as the second biggest threat to humankind, second only to global warming.[1] Initially, I thought his comments were hyperbole, framed to garner readership interest. Yet he cites compelling statistics to support his dire claim. As an example, he notes that 96,000 hospital patients die each year from errors arising out of poor data quality. In 2007, he estimated that the cost of process failure and rework from poor data quality in the United States alone was $1.5 trillion or more.[2] In 2011, a data quality software vendor pegged that loss at $3.1 trillion a year.[3] In a 2012 survey, analyst firm Gartner reported that 38 percent of companies don't know what bad data costs them, but more than 33 percent say bad data costs more than $1 million annually.[4]

Getting to the heart of data quality problems is complex, spanning business and technology, work processes and systems, and inevitably, politics. Data governance recognizes that data is as an asset to be managed. Jill Dyche, author of *Customer Data Integration* (Wiley, 2006) and a fellow The Data Warehousing Institute (TDWI) instructor, defines data governance as follows:

> Data governance is the organizing framework for establishing strategy, objectives, and policies for corporate data. It pervades the enterprise, crossing lines of business, data subject areas, and individual skill sets.[5]

Rarely does a company start out with data governance. Instead, as data is collected and analyzed, companies will evolve to recognize the importance of data governance to ensure data quality and reusability. As business user Eric Bachenheimer, director of client account management at Emergency Medical Associates (EMA), describes, "If you don't have trust or faith in your data, you're dead in the water. It will take you a long time to get that faith back." Early in EMA's business intelligence deployment, there was little data governance. The BI application manager got dragged into data validation in the source systems simply because the data appeared to be incorrect in the business intelligence reports. Ultimately, the cause of the data quality problems was not because of the ETL process, or the way data was modeled in the data warehouse or represented in the reports: It was because two hospitals submitted data in the source systems differently. However, because it was the reports that displayed the bad data, the BI administrator was forced to develop a stopgap solution. Getting businesspeople to understand the issues that affect data integrity can be a slow process. There sometimes has to be a degree of pain or a major business impact before it becomes a priority.

Establishing a data governance program will also be a low priority if the BI team is stretched for resources, a common problem for a fast-growing company. 1-800 CONTACTS started its BI program when it was a small, privately held company. When it was acquired by WellPoint, its customer base grew rapidly. Later, it formed an alliance with Wal-Mart, doubling its order volume. In 2011, it expanded beyond contact lenses into eyeglasses. Ideally, the company would like to be able to offer customers a consistent experience when ordering glasses and contact lenses at the same time. And yet, the back-end applications were developed by different teams, at different points of time. The customer ID may not be the same in each system. While it would have been ideal to start with consistent master data and a formal data governance process, there just wasn't time to do so. Jim Hill, director of data management, explains, "We would get bogged down with forcing that onto the organization. I tried to convince them to tackle master data immediately when we launched glasses.com. There almost has to be a degree of pain before it becomes a priority."[6]

Data Problems Start at the Source

Data quality problems frequently start in the source systems. A client in the oil and gas industry had significant data quality problems following the merger of multiple companies. While all the companies used SAP as the enterprise resource planning (ERP) system, they had deployed SAP in slightly different ways with company-specific data-capture rules. When business users wanted to report information by bill of lading—a fairly important and routine way of tracking materials—they couldn't. Bill of lading was not mandatory in the source systems! If it were captured, it could appear in any one of a number of fields: bill of lading (an obvious choice, but an input field not always used), document reference, delivery note, or comments. Getting anyone to be held accountable for making bill of lading mandatory and entered in a consistent place required executive-level support and organizational change, neither of which was possible at the time. People refused to use the data warehouse because it was wrong. The data warehouse team refused to change the ETL process because it went against their principle of correcting data quality issues in the source systems. Stalemate.

> Learn from this company's lesson: You can only report on what is captured. For information to be trusted, data must be captured consistently and accurately.

Eventually, the data warehouse team made an exception, then another, then another. The ETL logic was changed repeatedly to check multiple fields and to trim erroneous text such as "BOL" from a comment field to derive a consistent bill of lading number. BI usage increased as users slowly gained confidence in the integrity of the data warehouse. Contrast the experience of this oil and gas company with that of Dow Chemical.

> "You can spend millions building the data warehouse, but if you don't have the back office under control, you are wasting money."
> —Mike Costa, former corporate director of quality process and architecture, The Dow Chemical Company

When Dow first began its business intelligence effort in 1993, SAP was a newly implemented ERP system that forced many of the work processes to change. Some of the work processes reengineered well and others did not. Using Six Sigma as a way of measuring data quality, Dow at the time was a 1.5 sigma level.[7] There were a number of hiccups from the reengineering efforts and bad data in the system as each business entered data into SAP slightly differently, based on their distinct requirements. Mike Costa, then a senior director in information systems and the main owner for business intelligence, had what he describes as an a-ha moment. "When we design work processes, we don't design governance around the work processes, and yet it impacts information management and delivery in the data warehouse. Managing all the stuff to the left of the architecture [see Figure 2-3, Chapter 2]—the process design, governance, security—if you miss any one, it impacts quality and the integrity of the data warehouse." Recognizing the importance of work processes and governance, the CEO and CIO promoted Costa to corporate director of quality process and architecture, continuing to give him control over the data warehouse, but in addition, giving him authority to change the operational processes that affect the full business intelligence life cycle. His role was separate from any individual function, work process, or business unit. Today, data quality in the back office is a 5.9 to 6.0 sigma level, and in the data warehouse, it is a 5.9.

Initially, having a single ERP system proved a competitive advantage to Dow. However, as the business environment changed to one with a greater emphasis on joint ventures, that differentiator has posed its

About Six Sigma

Six Sigma is a management strategy that focuses on product and service quality. Whereas many management strategies focus on quality by monitoring the number of defects after the fact, Six Sigma focuses on the processes that lead to the defects. "It provides specific methods to re-create the process so that defects and errors never arise in the first place."[8] The higher the sigma level, the less likely the process will lead to defects. For example, airlines in terms of safety operate at a sigma level higher than 6, whereas baggage handling is in the 3.5 to 4 range.[9] So for every million bags handled, between 6,000 and 23,000 are mishandled (or 7.92 per 1,000 as of June 2007[10]). Most companies operate at a 3.5 to 4 sigma level.

The Six Sigma proponents tie the sigma level or quality level directly to improved profitability, arguing that a large portion of higher product and service costs can be attributed to poor quality.

Sigma Level	Defects per Million Opportunities	Cost of Quality
2	308,537 (Noncompetitive companies)	Not applicable
3	66,807	25–40% of sales
4	6,210 (Industry average)	15–25% of sales
5	233	5–15% of sales
6	3.4 (World class)	<1% of sales

Each sigma shift provides a 10% net income improvement.

Source: Harry, Mikel and Schroeder, Richard. *Six Sigma: The Breakthrough Management Strategy Revolutionizing the World's Top Corporations*, Doubleday: 2000, page 17.

Six Sigma has been a key strategy at Dow Chemical. As the preceding table illustrates, the move in data quality in the data warehouse from a 1.5 sigma level to 5.9 is significant. Not only is the level of data quality noteworthy, but also that the company measures it!

own challenges, says CIO Dave Kepler.[11] When Dow acquired Rohm & Haas in 2009, Rohm & Haas was on a newer version of SAP ERP. The acquisition resulted in Dow having to manage two ERP systems while simultaneously moving on to the new version. Further, as Dow has become one of the last independent diversified chemical companies, it has expanded the number of joint ventures. For example, in 2011, Dow and Mitsui established a joint venture in Brazil to expand its products in plastics, hygiene, and medical products. Another joint venture, Sadara, is between Dow and Saudi Aramco, with manufacturing facilities in Saudi Arabia. Sadara is expected to bring $10 billion in annual revenues in chemicals and performance plastics used in automotive and consumer products.[12] With an expanding portfolio of joint ventures, Dow can no longer assume or establish a single ERP system. Explains Kepler, "The Rohm & Haas acquisition showed we needed more differentiation on ERP systems. In a culture of standardization, that's hard. The period of transition is hard and how you manage across different systems. It has to be architected to be the least disruptive as possible."

While Dow's business environment demanded more flexibility in its ERP systems, Medtronic meanwhile was looking to improve its processes and reporting by getting to a single system. Customer comments and complaints about medical devices are critical in tracking problems and identifying early warning indicators. With medical products such as pacemakers and spinal parts, any complaint is not just a matter of customer satisfaction; it could be a matter of life and death. Historically, Medtronic used custom-developed systems to capture customer comments and complaints. Each of the major business units (Cardiac Rhythm Disease Management, Cardiovascular, Neuromodulation, and Spine) had their own IT systems to support complaint handling Today, the company is moving to a single, global instance of SAP CRM to capture customer complaints. A single system and a single ERP instance will improve their ability to access relevant data to help ensure customer satisfaction and analyze potential impacts on patient safety. Going from multiple custom systems to a single global system has been a multiyear journey, with only two businesses remaining to be implemented.

When Medtronic first began its Global Complaint Handling (GCH) project in 2007, there were multiple and disparate systems in use for complaint management. Tracking complaints is critical to patient safety and ensuring compliance with the Food and Drug Administration (FDA). The system needs to handle not only complaints, but also any event related to one of their devices. Medtronic established a system based on requirements driven by the regulations that involved consolidating more than ten systems and converting over 100 million records. GCH is now used in 26 sites and processes more than 30,000 transactions per month. From a business process and reporting viewpoint, they are able to leverage standard and harmonized reporting across the organization, says Sara Rottunda, executive sponsor for Global Complaints Handling from 2009 to 2012.[13]

When Data Is Everywhere

Combining data from multiple disparate source systems also contributes to data quality problems. Norway Post, for example, initially had seven different general ledger systems.[14] Figure 8-4 shows how hard it was for users to get to any meaningful data from multiple systems. Prior to implementing a common data warehouse, users would do manual extracts into over 6,000 different Excel spreadsheets. If you struggle to discern the data access model in Figure 8-4, it is because it was *that* convoluted, a common situation for companies without an enterprise information architecture.

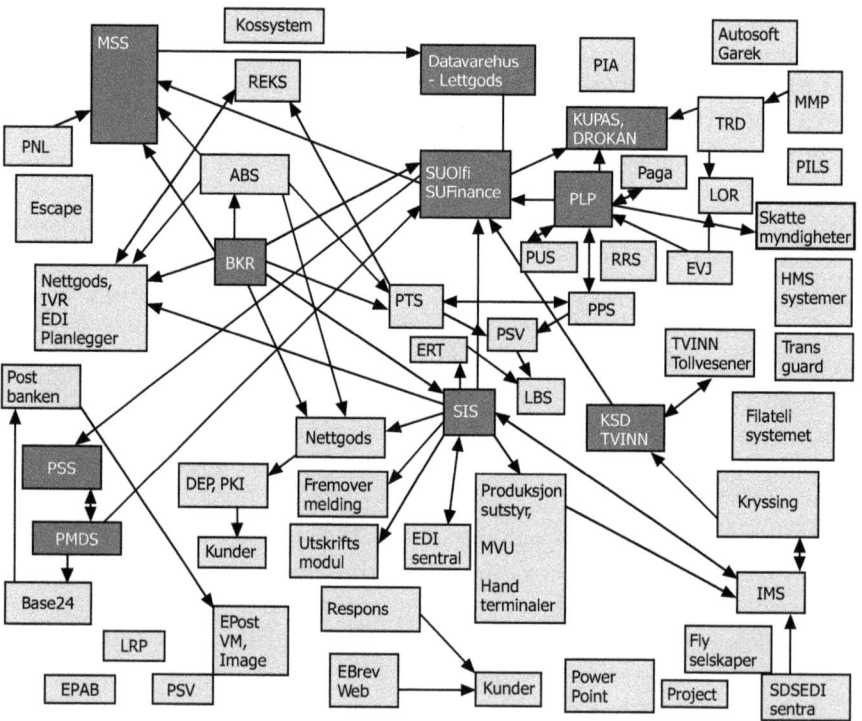

Figure 8-4   Norway Post's disparate data sources

About Norway Post

Norway Post is one of the country's biggest employers, with over 20,000 employees and revenues of just under 23 billion NOK (~$3.8 billion). The company privatized in 2002 but continues to be government owned. With privatization, Norway Post converted into a stock company and has implemented all the same steering and reporting standards as a publicly held stock company. It provides traditional mail and parcel delivery throughout the Nordic region along with express delivery, banking services, logistics, and electronic services. To provide some perspective, the distance from northern Norway to the southern part is similar in distance from New York City to Miami, Florida, in the United States, and yet 85 percent of the letters are delivered within one day. With changing laws of the European Union and changing consumer requirements, Norway Post's business model faces competitive and market pressures. Norway Post's vision is "to become the world's most future-oriented post and logistics group." Since privatizing in 2002, Norway Post has maintained profitability in nine of the years since, with only a small loss in 2008 (14 million NOK, or ~$2.3 million). (By comparison, the U.S. Postal Service had $65 billion in revenues in 2012 and $15 billion in losses.) In 2008, Norway Post acquired a number of companies and began delivering mail to Sweden under the Bring brand. Changes in mail and parcel delivery in Scandinavia and Europe have continued to force Norway Post to adapt and to respond to new competitive pressures. In 2008, the postal services of Denmark and Sweden merged,[15] and in 2011, European Union mail service was liberalized.[16]

About BI at Norway Post

- Start of BI efforts: 1995, refocused in 2001, rearchitected in 2013
- Executive-level sponsors: CFO and CIO
- Business intelligence competency center (BICC): Yes
- Number of users: 4,000, or 20 percent of all employees
- Number of source systems feeding the data warehouse: More than 30 systems from ERP, to delivery, and production systems
- ETL/EIM tools: SAS Data Integration Studio, Microsoft Integration Services, and IBM DB2 InfoSphere Change Data Delivery (CDD)
- Data warehouse platform: SAS SPD and Microsoft SQL Server
- Data warehouse size: 7TB, with portions updated every 15 minutes
- BI tools: Oracle Hyperion, SAS BI, SAS Enterprise Guide, and QlikView

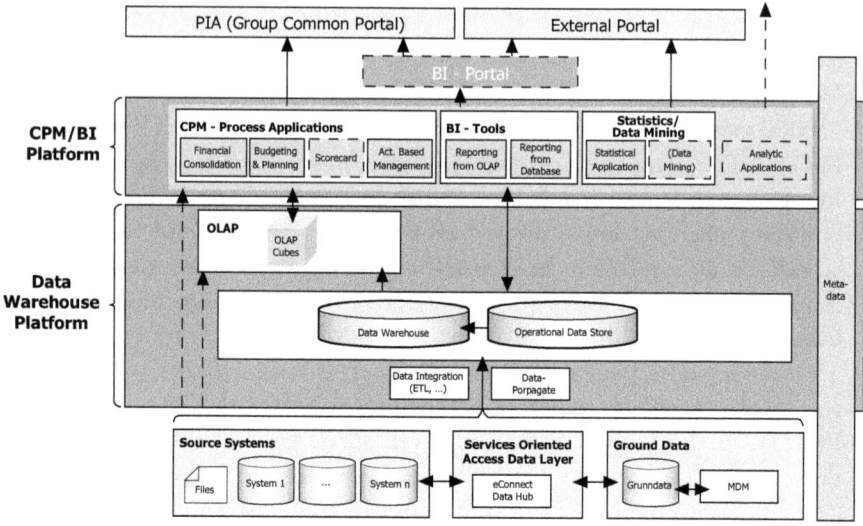

Figure 8-5   Norway Post's Integrated Performance Management System

As part of its performance management initiative, Norway Post phased out the manual, multiple extracts and made the common data warehouse the point of access for reports, plans, and statistical analysis (see Figure 8-5).[17] To further simplify the information architecture, the company began the process of phasing out multiple custom general-ledger systems to replace them with Oracle business applications.

Minimizing the number of source systems and related processes seems like the most straightforward approach to improving data quality. But not all companies have the luxury of standardizing on a packaged transaction system, particularly companies whose business models are based on external data, as is the case with FlightStats. FlightStats collects data from multiple data sources: government sources such as the Federal Aviation Administration (FAA); airports; and global distribution systems such as Sabre, Apollo, and Amadeus. Each data source provides flight information in a different format and often contains different information. For example, some data sources report aircraft positional information, while others report gate data or runway data. The data must be interpreted and normalized into a unified flight record that contains all information from all sources and then integrated to form a common flight history record. So, for example, if you are flying from New York to Australia, there may be two flight records: one that comes from United Airlines for the New York to Los Angeles route and a second one that comes from Qantas for the Los Angeles to Melbourne leg. In addition, the FAA provides positional and runway information. FlightStats will merge the information on these events that comes from multiple disparate data sources into a single flight history record for each leg. Every event has distinct nuances. For example, if a flight is delayed and crosses over the end of day, there are now two records for the same day, airline, and flight number. The data model has been refined to handle these types of events. It's been an iterative, ongoing process to understand the data nuances, achieve a high level of data quality, and apply consistent business definitions. Following the capture of real-time information, this detailed data is periodically extracted, transformed, and loaded into a data warehouse designed for historical reporting and statistical analysis. Customers can access both the real-time data warehouse and the historical data warehouse, depending on their information needs.

Common Business Definitions

FlightStats highlights another aspect to data quality, and that is the absence of and requirement for common business definitions. Even when data is correctly entered and accurate, differences in business definitions can cause problems. Whenever users access data and assume one business definition is being followed when, in fact, the BI platform follows a different definition, users will assume data in the BI platform is wrong. Instead, it's simply a matter of definition. A major U.S.-based telecommunication company said one of their barriers to success was different business definitions. They had more than 33 different definitions for "customer churn." Clearly, the rationalization of business definitions is a problem the business has to tackle. IT can only *implement* those business definitions.

Lack of common business definitions continues to be a challenge for many companies, with 35 percent of surveyed companies saying they lack common business definitions.

Successful Data Architectures

Beyond data quality, how best to store and model the data in the data warehouse is a matter of frequent debate. There are two predominant philosophies advocated by data warehouse visionaries, sometimes referred to as the fathers of data warehousing, Bill Inmon and Ralph Kimball. Their philosophies are similar in many respects, but where they differ most is in how to store the data. In simple terms, Inmon advocates storing the data in granular, normalized form once, with relevant data marts (whether a subset or aggregate of the detailed data) modeled off the normalized data model. Inmon's approach is often referred to as the "corporate information factory" or "hub and spoke" approach. Kimball, meanwhile, advocates using star schemas as a business presentation layer, referred to as the "data mart bus architecture." This star schema may or may not be built with extracts directly from the source systems or from data stored in a staging area. Research from professors Thilini Ariyachandra (University of Cincinnati) and Hugh Watson (University of Georgia) is one of the few studies that have looked at the degree to which approach is more successful.[18] According to their survey, 39 percent predominantly follow Inmon's corporate information factory or hub-and-spoke architecture, while 26 percent follow Kimball's data mart bus architecture. Both deployment approaches showed equal degrees of success. The only architecture that showed notably lower success rates was independent data marts.

The survey did not, however, look at who uses a combination of either approach, a model often used in large-scale data warehouses. Storing the data in third-normal form (in which repeating data values are stored in separate tables) is an approach often used in a data staging layer, with star schemas being used in subject areas accessible to business users via the BI tool (refer to Chapter 2 for explanations of these models). A poorly designed data model can prevent users from asking and answering their business questions with any degree of ease, and sometimes prevents them from answering them at all. Conversely, a data model optimized for business reporting and analysis facilitates insight and improves user adoption.

Replicating and modeling the data into one of these approaches is important for both performance reasons and for analytic reasons. A star schema is much more representative of how users want to access and analyze their data: There is a metric or fact, such as sales, that a user will want to analyze by various dimensions, such as time, product, and geography. However, in the age of big data, a number of technology solutions allow for sophisticated analysis without the data being modeled into a star schema. In-memory solutions, for example, may allow data to be stored as one big, flat table, with a myriad number of facts and thousands of dimensions and attributes. Because the data is held in-memory, queries are still fast.

When the data is stored in the Hadoop distributed file system, which may be the case with meter data, log files, social data, clicks, and so on, companies seem either to extract the raw data and load it into the traditional data warehouse in either third-normal form or star schemas, or they will load it directly into an in-memory system. Gaming company King.com, for example, captures 1.6 billion rows of user interactions per day in Hadoop. A subset of that data, 211 million rows, is loaded into a QlikView application to allow for analysis of players' interactions.[19]

Macy's has a traditional data warehouse for general reporting, but for rapid marketing analytics, the company uses a combination of Hadoop, Hbase, and Tableau. Web logs for www.Macys.com generate 5GB per day and hold important information about how the customer arrived at the site, which products they viewed, search terms, and ultimately, purchases. The company now has up to two years of web data, or approximately 2TB. The raw data will be accessed and explored by data scientists who write their own MapReduce jobs or via Tableau. Results of analyses are cached in Tableau's in-memory data engine.

Master Data Management

Master data management (MDM) is a set of technologies that improves the consistency of reference data. There are different types of master data: product, customer, region, facility location, patient, student, and chart of accounts, to name a few. In Chapter 2, Figure 2-1, master data existed in multiple transaction systems. The order entry system used a different set of customer codes from the invoice system. Ideally, these codes would be the same, regardless of the transaction system, and yet, that is rarely the case. Often, custom transaction systems will devise their own codes. ERP systems (shown in Chapter 2, Figure 2-2) will often share code tables across multiple modules, reducing the number of different codes for the same element. Data entry errors will continue to exist. In other words, you may still have multiple records for the same customer ("Howson" and "Howsin," for example), but those records are stored in one system.

As a fictitious example, assume customer "Preferred Purchasing" places an order. The customer number, 123, from the order entry system is used. When the product is shipped, the customer is invoiced. The customer number in the invoice system (I456) is different from that in the order system and includes an alphabetical character. This difference in codes can cause enormous data quality problems when information from the two different systems is combined. In the absence of common code files or a master data management system, the data warehouse team is left to define its own coding system (see Figure 8-6). Without

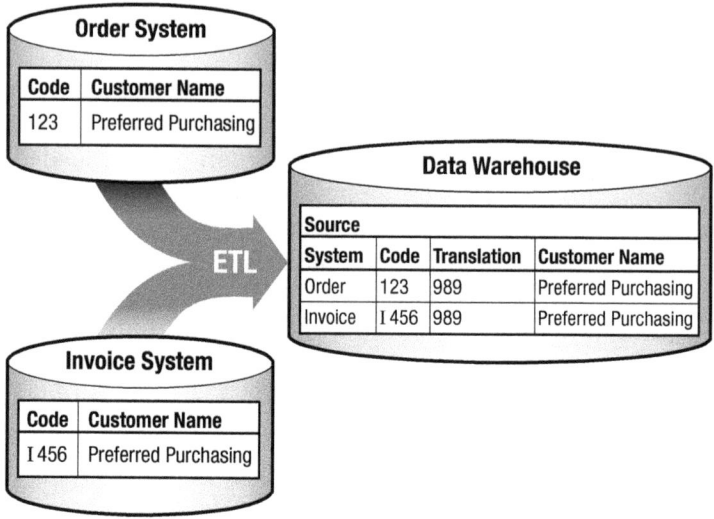

Figure 8-6   Customer master data

doing this, business users cannot create even the simplest reports such as customer order quantity and invoice amount.

In Figure 8-6, a centralized customer code—989—for Preferred Purchasing is implemented as part of the extract, transform, and load process to allow users to analyze data by customer, regardless of which transaction system the data originated in. The next issue, though, is when a business user wants to summarize data for this vendor and data needs to be aggregated. Preferred Purchasing may have hundreds of locations around the world. For each location, and sometimes even each contact person, there may be a unique customer code. If a user wants to understand global purchases by all the locations around the world, then these regional and global rollups must be maintained.

At question in the industry is whether these codes and customer hierarchies should be maintained in the ERP system, in the data warehouse, or in a separate master data management system. Increasingly, MDM experts advocate storing master data separately and allowing both the transaction systems and data warehouse to access it. This has been Dow's philosophy since the late 1980s, when it began implementing its own global code system, Infrastructure for Code Administration (INCA). As shown in Figure 8-7, master data is created in INCA. INCA then distributes data to SAP (the ERP system), Siebel (the CRM system), the Human Resources (HR) system, the Product Lifecycle Management (PLM), and other source systems, which can append

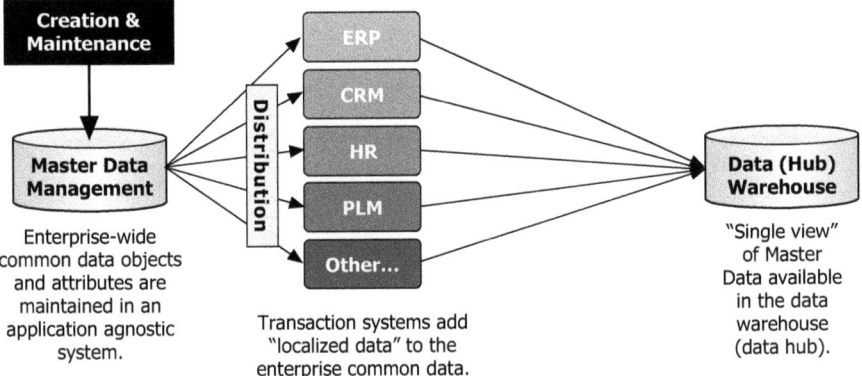

Figure 8-7   The Dow Chemical Company's original MDM strategy[20]

application-specific data as needed. Information is then extracted into the data warehouse.

Dow's global codes and approach to master data management were clearly ahead of the industry and continue to be so today. Dow recognizes its codes as an ingredient to its successful use of business intelligence, particularly on a global basis. Despite MDM's importance at Dow, even Costa recognizes the challenges of organizing for MDM and securing funding. "It is a lost child that nobody wants. Whenever resources get cut, MDM is sunset. It's so behind the scenes that nobody understands the value." Like much of the industry, the INCA system at Dow was custom developed. As the MDM market has matured, Dow is gradually moving to a packaged MDM solution.[21]

Phillip Russom, director of research at TDWI, advocates a bidirectional approach to MDM. As shown in Figure 8-8, master data will be created in either the source system or in the MDM system. If a new record is created in the MDM system, it is then sent back to the source system to be used. However, if master data does not exist in the transaction system, then users can still create new master data within the operational systems, but it is also sent to the MDM system to be resolved. In theory, it might seem ideal to set a policy that all new reference data should only be created in the MDM system. This might ensure a higher degree of consistency because there is only one version of that customer ID. However, imagine the situation if you are trying to enter an order for a new customer. A salesperson cannot wait for that customer ID first

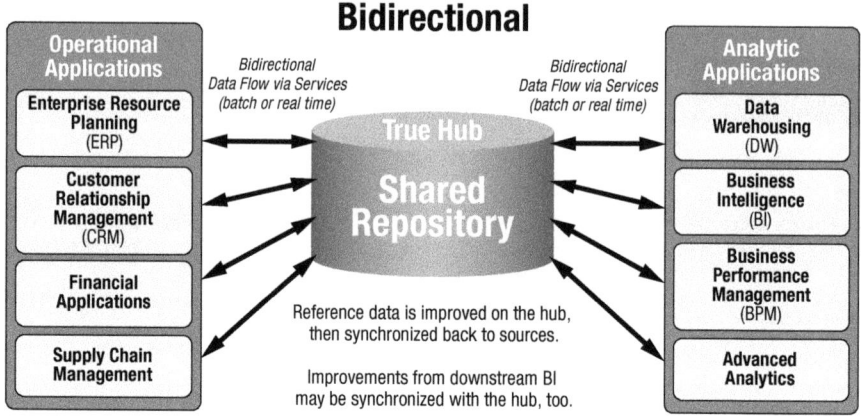

Figure 8-8   Bidirectional MDM system

to be entered in the MDM system, particularly if that is someone else's responsibility. Establishing such a policy can have a negative impact on customer service ("we can't process your order until your customer ID is established"), and therefore sales. In addition, making too much information mandatory can further erode data quality. As one customer confessed, "We have a lot of customers named Fred Flintstone," suggesting that people fill in fictitious customer names if they don't have all the supporting details.

Going from an approach where every process and source system creates its own master data to common master data requires time and clear organizational policies. Medtronic has been moving to a bidirectional MDM solution for several years. Experts recommend starting an MDM project by focusing on the reference data that is causing the most pain, and for Medtronic, that was the view of the customer.

Leon Wittmer, an IT director at Medtronic, emphasizes that the processes are more important than the technology.[22] As part of moving to improved master data, the company had to decide which source of data most often had the best quality. This "best source" data was then used as the single source in the MDM system that other applications can now consume. New data in the central instance has to go through a governance process before the data is entered. Wittmer suggests that there needs to be an incentive for people to enter data correctly and completely to maximize data quality.

Air travel data is a good example of a built-in incentive to ensure data quality for passenger information. In the days of paper tickets issued by a travel agent, my name might have appeared as Mr. C. Howson. When I began purchasing tickets online, I corrected it to Cindi Howson. However, with increased security, that profile was changed to Cynthia Howson, as it corresponds to my photo identification. The Transportation Security Administration (TSA) recently implemented a program called TSA Pre that allows travelers to go through a faster airport security line, without removing shoes or unpacking laptops. It can reduce the time to get through security from the usual 30+ minutes to just a few minutes. Getting into the TSA Pre program incentivized me to ensure my passenger details now also include my middle name as well.

Right-Time Data

In business intelligence's infancy, data warehouses were updated on a monthly, sometimes weekly, basis. As BI extends into operational applications, these data warehouses are increasingly updated in near real time. The update to the data warehouse may be seconds behind transaction system updates, or minutes, or hours, whatever best serves the business requirements. Industry expert Colin White, president of BI Research, refers to this as *right-time business intelligence*.[23]

With big data such as smart meters and patient vital signs, some information is streamed and analyzed in motion so that it can be acted upon in real time.

While much of right-time business intelligence is about supporting operational decision-making, the timeliness of updates also increasingly allows decision-makers to take swift action on strategic and tactical decisions. If, for example, a new product launch (strategy) is not performing as expected, it doesn't do executives much good to find this out three months into the launch based on monthly data warehouse updates. More timely updates allow for more timely insight and corrective action. 1-800 CONTACTS, for example, released its first data warehouse in spring 2005 with nightly loads from the source system.[24] It wasn't until six months later when the data warehouse moved to updates every 15 minutes that senior executives embraced the system. While the call center representatives may use the dashboard for operational purposes, the dashboard provides executives with a snapshot of how the business is doing in near real time. Spikes in the number of inbound calls to the call center act as an early warning system for an upcoming increased load in the distribution center.

Dr. Richard Hackathorn, founder of Bolder Technology, talks about three components of data latency that affect decision-making:[25]

- *Capture latency* is the time it takes between a business event happening and a piece of data being captured in a source system to when that data has been extracted into the business intelligence architecture.
- *Analysis latency* is the time it takes to disseminate, access, view, and analyze the updated information. Such dissemination and analysis may be in the form of a dashboard update, an alert, or a report refresh.
- *Decision latency* is the time to make a decision and take action based on the analysis.

Hackathorn suggests that reducing this data latency reduces the time to action. The reduced time to action has a corresponding business value, as shown in Figure 8-9. Assessing the business value is important in determining whether the cost to reduce data latency is justifiable. If the cost to update the data warehouse in near real time exceeds the business value gained, then it should not be done.

As an example, some of the data that FlightStats acquires is publicly available from the Department of Transportation. However, it is based on data and events two months prior and includes only a subset of routes and carriers. FlightStats collects other data in real time, allowing individual consumers and travel agents to act upon delays occurring at the moment. Travel agents who subscribe to FlightStats data will receive an alert for a delayed or canceled flight so that passengers with

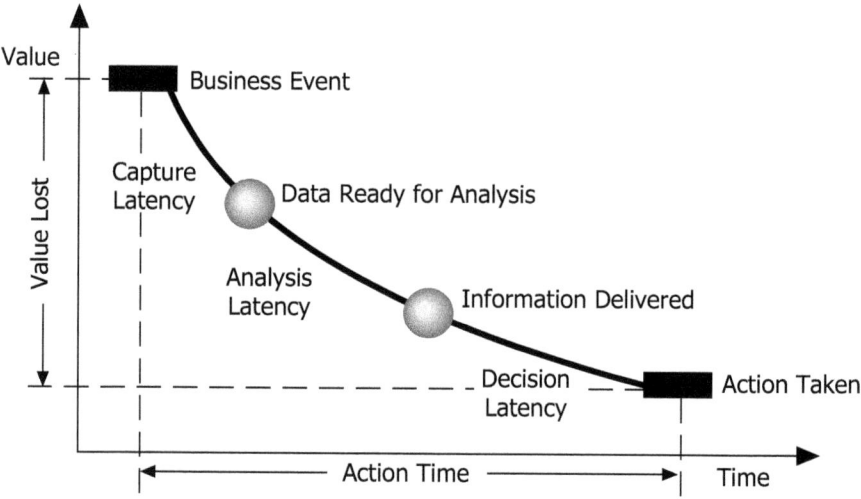

Figure 8-9 The benefit of reducing latency

connecting flights can be rebooked proactively while still mid-air on the delayed flight. The business value to the agent in providing this degree of service is a competitive differentiator and key in retaining customers. Therefore, FlightStats can charge for the access to the real-time flight information, as there is business value in reducing decision latency. As CEO Jeff Kennedy declares, "Building a smart, scalable, real-time data acquisition system has been key to our success."[26]

In the Successful BI survey, near real-time updates to the data warehouse were rated essential only by 10 percent of organizations (see earlier in Figure 8-2). As shown earlier in Figure 8-3, the majority of companies say the data is updated as often as is required, but 25 percent say it is not updated often enough.

Not all BI applications require real time, and the frequency of the data warehouse updates is something to evaluate for each data source and application. Mike Pekala, a finance director and power user at Dow, cautions, "Having even daily data at times is a burden versus a benefit. If a customer only orders twice a month, management panics when we get to the 14th of the month and daily sales velocity is looking bad because the customer has not placed their second large order. There are times when real-time data causes issues because people do not understand the underlying details. They are just looking at a highly summarized report."

Successful BI Company	Most Frequent Update
1-800 CONTACTS	Every 15 minutes
Constant Contact	Mostly daily, portions more frequent
The Dow Chemical Company	Daily
Emergency Medical Associates	Daily
FlightStats	Real time
The Learning Circle	Daily
Medtronic	Near real time, with portions every 3 seconds
Netflix	Near real time

Table 8-1   **Successful BI Case Studies Have Near Real-Time BI**

Data Quality's Chicken and Egg

Given just how difficult it is to achieve data quality and how far the industry is from addressing the root causes of data quality, it begs the question: What do you do first?

Fix the data and then strive for business intelligence.
or
Deliver business intelligence tools on top of messy data and later fix the data as you go.

This would sound like a no-brainer. Of course, nobody in their right mind would embark on a business intelligence initiative with bad data! In reality, however, many do because they have little choice. The business sponsors don't understand why the data quality is so bad and may not be in a position to address the root causes. Meanwhile, the BI team has to be responsive to deliver on the business's request to deliver BI capabilities. It would seem that the BI team is being set up for failure. In some respects, they are rather doomed. At issue is when is the data good enough? A second issue is that until the consequences of multiple disparate systems with messy codes, inconsistent business definitions, and incorrect data entry are exposed to the business via BI tools, there is little incentive to address the root causes. Given this chicken-and-egg situation, my recommendation is that if you have severe data quality issues, continue with the BI project, but with clear expectations and a limited scope.

Communicate where there are data quality problems and the associated risks with deploying BI tools on top of bad data. Also advise the different stakeholders on what can be done to address data quality problems—systematically and organizationally. Complaining without providing recommendations fixes nothing.

All too often, the BI team complains about bad data but provides no recommendations on how to improve data quality, which I often think is because their realm of responsibility doesn't allow them to get at the root causes of bad data. Use Figure 8-10 as a way of determining where your company is on the continuum of best practices for data quality.

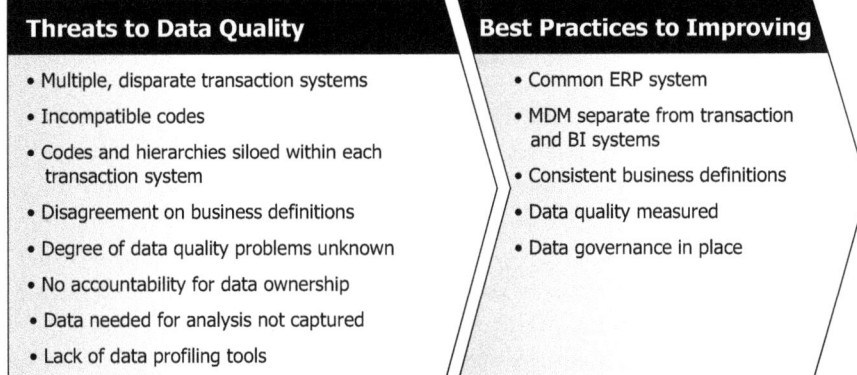

Threats to Data Quality	Best Practices to Improving
• Multiple, disparate transaction systems	• Common ERP system
• Incompatible codes	• MDM separate from transaction and BI systems
• Codes and hierarchies siloed within each transaction system	• Consistent business definitions
• Disagreement on business definitions	• Data quality measured
• Degree of data quality problems unknown	• Data governance in place
• No accountability for data ownership	
• Data needed for analysis not captured	
• Lack of data profiling tools	

Figure 8-10   A continuum toward data quality

Depending on the extent of the data quality issues, be careful about where you deploy BI. Without a reasonable degree of confidence in the data quality, BI should be kept in the hands of knowledge workers and not extended to frontline workers, and certainly not to customers and suppliers. Deploy BI in this limited fashion as data quality issues are gradually exposed, understood, and ultimately addressed. Don't wait for every last data quality issue to be resolved; if you do, you will never deliver any BI capabilities, business users will never see the problem, and quality will never improve.

Also recognize that the requisite data quality will vary depending upon its purpose. A financial or regulatory report, patient treatment plan, or student's report card all must have high data quality. Various people, whether accountants or administrators, will have had a role in transforming, vetting, and redefining data elements to ensure consistency and quality.

With big data, on the other hand, more granular, unscrubbed data may have less consistency. Outliers in the form of erroneous data may in fact be what the analyst is looking for. For example, in one failure of a smart meter, a customer showed zero water consumption for a three-month period. Perhaps the customer was out of town for the winter and traveling, so no activity is theoretically valid data, but it turned out the meter had stopped transmitting. It was bad data but not data that should have been corrected in an ETL process, because it required corrective action elsewhere—on the device.

Best Practices for Successful Business Intelligence

The data architecture is the most important technical aspect of your business intelligence initiative. Fail to build an information architecture that is flexible, with consistent, timely, quality data, and decision makers will not rely on BI. Business users will not trust the information, no matter how powerful and pretty the BI tools. However, sometimes it takes displaying that messy data to get business users to understand the importance of data quality and to take ownership of a problem that extends beyond business intelligence, to the source systems and to the organizational structures that govern a company's data. To build an information architecture that decision makers can trust, do the following:

- Assess the degree to which your source systems and BI applications have data quality problems, and recognize the role it plays in business intelligence success.
- Ensure the source systems capture what you want to report and analyze.
- Understand the role of operational processes in ensuring data quality and the degree to which disparate transaction systems challenge data quality.
- Separate master data from transactional and business intelligence systems, evolving to a bidirectional approach for master data.
- Agree on consistent business definitions. Expose those business definitions to users via the BI tools or an internal dictionary or Wikipedia page.
- Review organizational structures to determine who owns the data and can ensure its integrity.
- Make continuous improvement in data quality part of a company-wide initiative.
- Evaluate the timeliness of data warehouse updates against the business value provided.

Chapter 9

Relevance

Sociologists have declared Millenials the "me" generation, a market segment of one. Shopping experiences are personalized, and consumers, who only decades ago could only order a car in black or black, are in control. The same, however, cannot be said for BI. Some industry experts have referred to the consumerization of IT as a gradual shift from central IT dictating standards to one in which business users make their own choices. The consumerization of IT, for example, has led from IT once dictating BlackBerry as the only supported mobile device, to a policy of Bring Your Own Device (BYOD).

The consumerization of IT and a stronger push toward self-service BI is making BI more relevant to more users. But if BI is to be relevant beyond power users, IT needs to shift the mindset from a reactive approach to a proactive one.

Webster's dictionary defines relevance as "1. Pertinence to the matter at hand. 2. The capability of an information retrieval system to select and retrieve data suitable for a user's needs." The most successful BI deployments go beyond delivering a massive repository of data with unconstrained, sometimes overwhelming, data access. Instead, they deliver tailored applications relevant to the intended user. Some would describe this as personalization, but *relevance* goes beyond personalization to provide not only a personalized view of data a user requested, but also to consider other data that may improve the work flow, the decisions, and even the life of the BI user.

In most companies, inside staff such as call center agents don't use business intelligence (as shown in Chapter 4, Figure 4-6, 46 percent of inside staff use BI). If you think of BI as synonymous with business query tools for power users only, then inside staff would not need such capabilities. Their information requirements are somewhat predictable. And yet, dozens of times every day they make decisions and take actions, many of which can be supported by *relevant* business intelligence.

Relevance Brings Clearer Vision

At 1-800 CONTACTS, prior to the BI application, call center agents were frustrated with inadequate information access (see the section on frustration in Chapter 5). Agent turnover was high, and on exit interviews, agents complained that they were compensated based on things beyond their control. Agents were paid commissions on a number of performance measures, but these measures were only available via a piece of paper posted on the wall the next day—too late, too aggregated, too inaccessible to be actionable. As 1-800 CONTACTS began designing their first BI application, they studied what motivated call center agents and what information could help them do their jobs better. The BI team worked side by side with the agents to the point that BI team members would be able to handle an incoming call—they understood the job responsibilities and work flow that well. In the initial prototype, the BI application showed agents their daily performance. Call center managers thought this would be a big win for the agents. In debating the dynamics of the call center, senior executives noted that there was a degree of healthy competition among the agents. Executives wanted to tap into their competitive nature to drive better performance. They thought that showing agents what percentile they were performing in would create a kind of horse race among the agents.[1] By increasing the dashboard update to refresh every 15 minutes, it would allow agents to take action that same day.

For example, Figure 9-1 shows multiple performance indicators, such as closing ratio, revenue per call (RPC), and quality (confidential information is intentionally blurred). The quality is assessed by a team of auditors who sample and listen to inbound calls, giving a score, much like a grade, with the maximum quality score of 4. The top left blue bars show the agent's month-to-date performance and the relationship of variable bonus pay to quality levels; call center representatives receive a bonus per hour and per metric, as long as both the revenue per call and quality score minimum levels are met. The table at the right shows how well the agent is performing versus the agent's team and the entire call center. Any key performance indicators (KPIs) above target are colored in green, and below target, in red. For example, this agent had higher sales than his department, but a slightly lower closing ratio and quality score. Finally, the bottom bar chart and trend line show how the agent has performed compared to the department for the last 30 days. Prior to 2006, agents didn't have timely access to this information and not in such a visual way. The very week that the new dashboard went live, there was a measurable lift in sales.

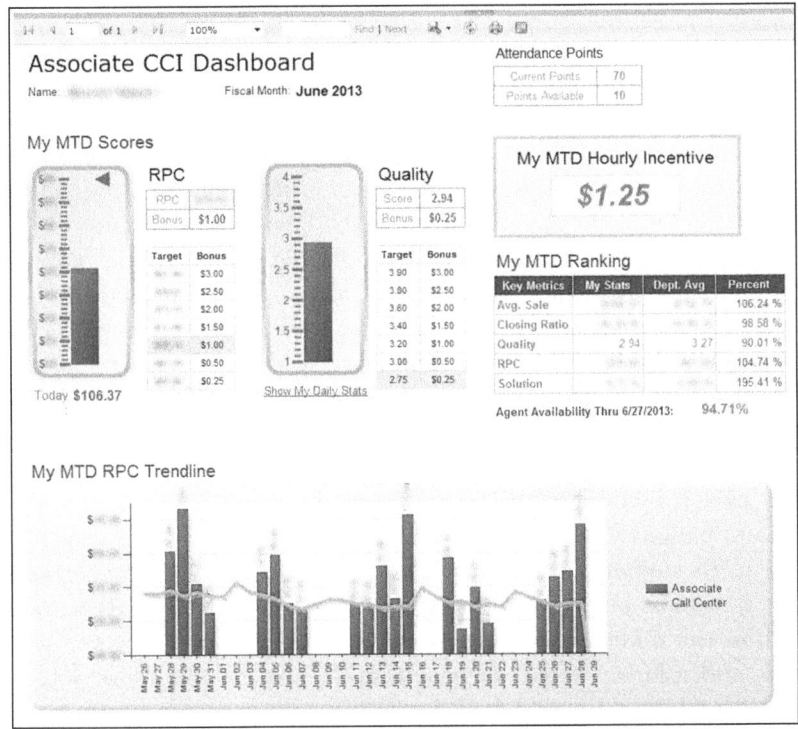

Figure 9-1   1-800 CONTACTS agent key performance indicators

Data about an individual agent's performance is certainly relevant to the agent, but the other piece that gave agents greater control was a customer snapshot. Over the years, the company has amassed a lot of information on how customers behave, such as when they are most likely to need a prescription refill, how often they return, and their lifetime value. When a customer calls 1-800 CONTACTS, the agent now gets a snapshot of this information. This enables the representative both to provide better customer service and to influence their sales levels.

Relevance Improves Patient Care

Emergency Medical Associates (EMA) described a similar story of relevance. Biosurveillance is the use of data to try to predict where there may be disease outbreaks or signs of bioterrorist attacks. Some of this data originates in emergency rooms. As patients check into an emergency room, their symptoms and complaints are coded to allow for analysis. In fall 2004, the United States faced a shortage of flu vaccine after one of the main vaccine manufacturers in Britain was forced to suspend manufacturing due to contamination issues at the plant.[2] A few months later, EMA made mainstream news headlines at NBC News with its unique ability to predict a severe flu outbreak in the New York–New Jersey area. While EMA routinely sends such data to a number of reporting authorities, including local health officials and the Centers for Disease Control and Prevention,[3] the ability to analyze the data, predict the outbreak, and graphically show the most affected areas at the hospital level was exceptional. The ability to improve patient care is *relevant* to physicians; that business intelligence tools allow improved care is what makes BI attractive to a group of users who otherwise lag the industry in adoption of information technology.

Another way that doctors use business intelligence to improve patient care is by improving emergency room operations so that staffing levels and patient wait times are optimal. In much the same way 1-800 CONTACTS studied the drivers of call center agents, EMA looked at the factors that most affected emergency room operations. The BI team did not follow the traditional requirements-gathering process of going to the doctors and asking, "What do you want?" Doctors, like most potential business intelligence users, don't know what they want until they see it and may not know what is even possible with information technology. Jonathan Rothman, then director of data management at EMA and now a principal at EMBI, had a healthcare background but no experience with emergency room care. So he learned the business by interviewing and collaborating with doctors, hospital administrators, and other stakeholders on the dynamics of the emergency room.[4] Rothman kept thinking, "How can we exploit this technology to provide more services at less cost?" Wait time is a key indicator for emergency rooms (ERs). For some patients, it's a matter of life and death. For others, it is a matter of patient dissatisfaction. In the United States, average ER wait times have been reported as high as 3 hours and 42 minutes.[5] In 2009, the Government Accounting Office (GAO) studied data from a number of hospitals and found the average wait time to be 56 minutes.[6] However, the GAO report analyzed wait times by acuity level, and even for patients who should have been seen immediately (i.e., the patient is choking, having a heart attack, etc.), the average wait time was 28 to 37 minutes and exceeded recommended time frames for care. For non-life-threatening issues, when ER wait times are high, patients walk out and either go to another emergency room or wait to see their regular physician. While patient walk-outs was acknowledged by all the stakeholders at EMA as being important, it was not one that was routinely tracked or that could be proven to impact care and finances.[7] Rothman prototyped some reports to demonstrate that when wait times went up, walk-outs went up, and care and income went down. The reports evolved into a series of dashboards and now a commercial product shown in Figures 9-2 and 9-3.

As shown in the top left, the dashboard user can select which key performance indicators they want to view. In Figure 9-2, the following KPIs are shown: time from arrival to room assignment, patients left without being seen (LWBS), time from entering the ER to a decision on whether to admit or treat in the ER, whether a patient had visited the ER in the last 72 hours, doctor staffing levels, and patient satisfaction. The trend line in the top right shows the relationship between wait times and the rate of patients leaving the ER without being seen. Wait times seem to be within a reasonable range for this hospital, ranging from 12 to 20 minutes. Appropriate staffing levels in emergency rooms are particularly difficult to determine: By definition, emergencies are not scheduled events, and yet, with all the data available, EMA and EMBI can discern trends to be more proactive. Weekends are peak periods, so staffing levels can be adjusted for this. Changing registration procedures and the layout of the emergency room can also bring faster treatment.

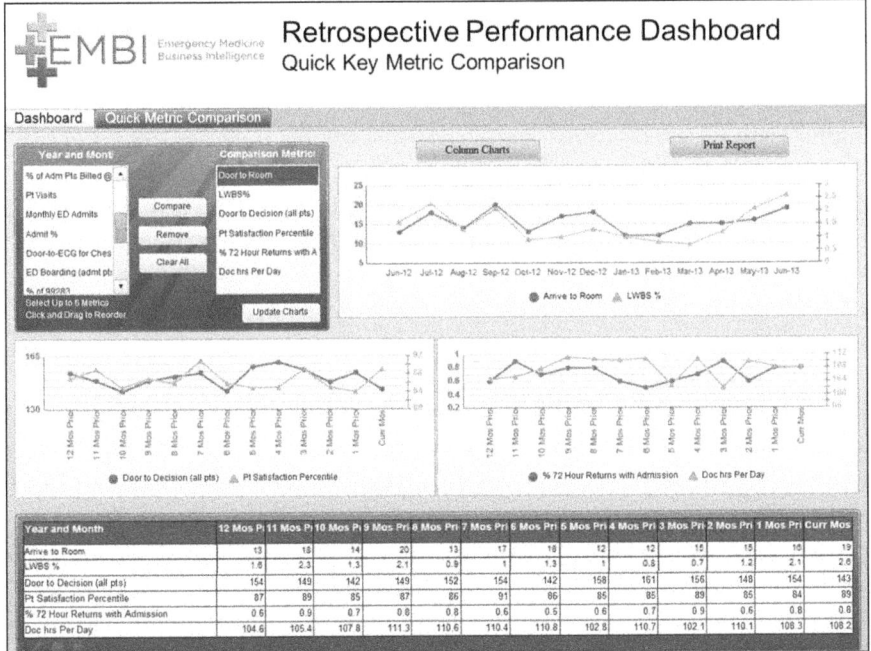

Year and Month	12 Mos Pri	11 Mos Pri	10 Mos Pri	9 Mos Pri	8 Mos Pri	7 Mos Pri	6 Mos Pri	5 Mos Pri	4 Mos Pri	3 Mos Pri	2 Mos Pri	1 Mos Pri	Curr Mos
Arrive to Room	13	18	14	20	13	17	18	12	12	15	15	16	19
LWBS %	1.6	2.3	1.3	2.1	0.9	1	1.3	1	0.8	0.7	1.2	2.1	2.6
Door to Decision (all pts)	154	149	142	149	152	154	142	158	161	156	148	154	143
Pt Satisfaction Percentile	87	89	85	87	86	91	86	85	88	89	85	84	89
% 72 Hour Returns with Admission	0.6	0.9	0.7	0.6	0.8	0.6	0.5	0.6	0.7	0.9	0.6	0.8	0.8
Doc hrs Per Day	104.6	105.4	107.8	111.3	110.6	110.4	110.8	102.8	110.7	102.1	110.1	108.3	108.2

Figure 9-2 EMBI Performance Dashboard

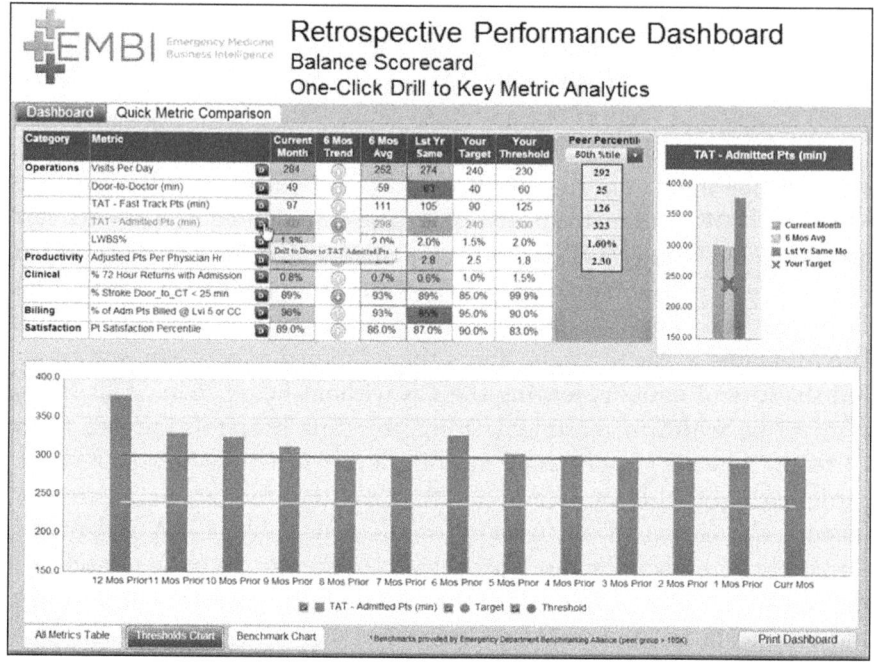

Figure 9-3   EMBI Performance Dashboard

Simply treating patients faster does not always result in better care and higher patient satisfaction, though. Also shown is how the more doctors on duty reduces the rate of patients retreated within 72 hours, presumably as doctors are less rushed in their diagnoses and treatments.

Because EMBI collects data from multiple hospitals, it also can provide benchmarking information. Figure 9-3 shows a scorecard of KPIs for an individual hospital relative to its peer group. Traffic lights and trend indicators provide an at-a-glance view of how well the hospital is doing. For example, in this hospital, a year ago the patient wait time to see a doctor was 63 minutes (red traffic light), but this month it is averaging 49 minutes, so a positive trend (green upward-pointing arrow). For stroke patients where time to see a doctor is a matter of life and death, the target is to have 85 percent of patients seen by a doctor within less than 25 minutes after entering the ER. At this hospital, 93 percent were seen that quickly, but for the current month, the rate is 85 percent, so the trend arrow is colored in red to show a negative trend.

Using some of the same techniques that 1-800 CONTACTS applied, the doctors within a given hospital are allowed to see other doctors' metrics so that a degree of professional competitiveness further contributes to performance. By giving hospital administrators and doctors access to this information, EMA has been able to reduce the ER wait time by 50 percent in some cases.[8]

When EMA first shared their story of BI success with me, I couldn't help thinking, "In an emergency, patients have no choice. You go to whichever hospital is nearest." While the reduced ER wait times clearly affect patient satisfaction and care, I was skeptical that there was any connection to ER financials. (Recall from the section on threats in Chapter 5 some of the extreme financial pressures facing hospitals today.) A friend, who just happens to be a somewhat frequent visitor of emergency rooms, enlightened me. Dale has three children, one with asthma and another with unexplained high fevers. Her nearest emergency room is about 20 minutes away. And yet, in an emergency Dale will travel to an EMA-operated emergency room at Saint Barnabas Health Care System, about 45 minutes away. She has visited at least three other area ERs. When once visiting a closer hospital (not EMA operated), her son was sent home after waiting hours and being told his arm was only bruised. Two days later, when the pain would not subside, Dale took her son to a specialist. Looking at the X-ray herself, Dale could see it was a full break. "I would rather drive farther, get seen faster, and have my children better sooner than go to one of these other hospitals." Dale's experiences do not mean that only EMA-operated hospitals provide excellent emergency room care, but they do confirm that my assumptions about emergency rooms were wrong: Proximity is not the only deciding factor in which hospital a patient chooses. Instead, for non-life-threatening emergencies, patients will indeed go to the most efficient hospital with the best reputation for quality care.

In many companies, finance and marketing departments often are early adopters of business intelligence. At EMA, business intelligence has wide support at senior levels and across the company. The BI team has been proactive in focusing its efforts on the opportunities that most drive the business: information to support physicians and emergency room operations. While BI is still important to the finance department, EMA prioritized finance users as one of the later adopters. Contrast this approach with many BI teams who are more reactive, delivering applications first to those departments who shout the loudest.

Relevance for Teachers

Teachers are perhaps not the face of a typical BI user. I can clearly picture our school district's business manager as a BI user, but not the teacher. "Most teachers got into teaching to make a difference. Data is not part of that," says Barb Boyd, President of Learning Circle.[9] "They are skeptical of data."

And yet, data can show who is making a difference and who is not. With urban schools, many teachers are pedaling as fast as they can to keep up, explains Boyd. In one school, there was a shooting near the school, so students live in a tough environment. At another school in the district, student turnover in a classroom can be as a high as 50 percent as families move in and out of a neighborhood based on employment or family care. Children may be going home to an empty house, with little parental supervision or homework assistance. Under such difficult conditions, a teacher can only do so much to ensure a child is learning. However, in Learning Circle's work with one school, there was a noticeable difference in higher math and lower reading scores for the same students. "The data was not used to place blame on the reading teacher. It was used to start a conversation, to ask the next question—what was the math teacher doing differently from the reading teacher?" As discussed in Chapter 6, the right culture enables such a conversation, but it is the *relevance* of the data that allows a teacher to fulfill the ultimate goal of making a difference in that student's life.

Parents also have an incentive to help their children succeed. In this way, a number of schools across the United States are now providing access to student test data. Providing test results and individual grades is an important first step, but what is generally lacking is the appropriate context, as well as easy-to-use BI tools. As a parent, raw test scores are not relevant unless I can compare how my child performed relative to his or her peers and over time. In New Jersey, where I reside, I can download multiple flat files of annual standardized tests. I have on occasion downloaded them into a BI tool to see what the trend is, but clearly, a typical parent would not go through such a convoluted process. Other states, including Ohio, use a commercial BI tool with a set of dashboards and reports to allow parents to more readily access such data.

Learning Circle is also looking at data in a longitudinal way, as well as looking beyond the classroom to the social environment such as recreational and fitness activities. Parents have given permission for social data from local Boys and Girls Clubs and the YMCAs to be correlated with educational data. The project is currently in a pilot, but will give a more holistic view of a student.

The Role of Incentives

As I pieced together the common threads of each of these examples, it initially seemed to me that financial incentives were at the heart of relevance. The authors of *Freakonomics* write, "Experts are humans, and humans respond to incentives."[10] The authors provide case after case to show that misaligned incentives often produce undesirable results. For example, real estate agents may not always sell a house for the highest price (the seller's desired result), but rather in a way that maximizes their net commission (the real estate agent's incentive).

I began asking interviewees what role incentives played in their use of business intelligence. One responded, quite seriously, "Just using business intelligence is its own reward!" (He is one of the enthusiastic users of BI who was previously starved for data and BI tools.) He felt that perhaps the relationship between business intelligence and compensation is one of "six degrees of separation," so somewhat related but not obvious enough to be a motivator. Financial compensation, however, is only one form of incentive, and other forms of incentives in this idea of relevance are

- A desire to win or to outperform their colleagues
- A desire to do a better job, whether to improve patient care or customer satisfaction or student performance
- A sense of happiness or removal of frustration that information they struggled to access and compile before has been made significantly easier to access

There are a number of barriers to BI success, and individual resistance to change is one of them. When this is the case, then incentives—whether financial or other—can play a role in encouraging people to use business intelligence effectively. While I have encountered companies that use specific incentives to encourage BI use (for example, attending a BI training class or proof of logging into the BI application), a better approach is to integrate business intelligence into achieving a level of performance that is tied to existing compensation.

Leaders need to be careful, though, that the incentives are aligned with the goals of the organization and that there are no disincentives. For example, with teacher performance and school funding now tied so heavily to test scores, there have been a number of reported cheating scandals in Washington, D.C., and Atlanta school districts to produce the desired test results, as well as the data scrubbing investigation in Ohio. An opinion piece in *USA Today* by an Advanced Placement (AP) teacher told how he actively encouraged students to drop his class who he didn't think could achieve a good grade on the AP test.[11] In this way, he manipulated class enrollment to produce better test results.

Personalization

Personalizing business intelligence has a role in relevance. Personalization goes beyond simply matching the BI tool with the user segment, as discussed in Chapter 12. Personalization involves tailoring the software interface, such as the menus and capabilities, as well as ensuring each individual only sees the data relevant to him or her.

Row-level security is one approach to personalizing the data. With row-level security, each user is granted permission to see certain rows within the database. For example, at 1-800 CONTACTS, a given call center agent can see only his or her individual performance in the dashboard shown earlier in Figure 9-1. Each customer phone call and order record is associated to the agent so that in the dashboard, the information is personalized for that agent. This kind of personalization can be a challenge to implement when data is extracted from multiple systems and aggregated. For example, while it may be straightforward to associate the call and order records, and therefore the detailed rows in a database, with a single call agent, the process is complicated when you want to personalize aggregated information for a call center manager. Somewhere the relationship between call center managers and the particular agents has to be established to provide personalization on this aggregated data. Increasingly within the industry, enterprise resource planning (ERP) vendors are enhancing the transaction systems to ensure personalization implemented in the source systems can later be leveraged in the business intelligence environment. As this is still an emerging capability, many BI administrators are forced to develop their own personalization approaches, whether in the physical data warehouse or in the BI tools.

It's important to note that personalization is not synonymous with security. The former emphasizes data restrictions for the purposes of improving relevancy; the latter is about preventing people from seeing information not pertinent to their jobs. Unfortunately, sometimes in the desire to personalize and the need to secure information, access to data in a BI environment can be overly restrictive. Neil Raden, founder of Hired Brains, has written about the issues that unnecessary data restrictions can cause. He argues that when data is restricted based on outdated hierarchical management structures, it may remove valuable context for the information. "In many BI implementations, every user of the system is restricted to the data they are allowed to see. With respect to confidential information, privacy regulations, or other mandated restrictions, this seems like a reasonable approach, but in most organizations, the 'need-to-know' restrictions are the result of the pyramid, not logic. The eastern region sales manager is unable to see how the western region sales manager is doing with respect to a certain kind of sale and thus, deprived of potentially valuable insight."[12] It's noteworthy then that the 1-800 CONTACTS dashboard in Figure 9-1 provides context in a way that preserves security: Agents can see their performance relative to the team and call center, but cannot see details for other agents.

Personalization is also apparent in the way that Netflix optimizes which movies and TV shows appear on a customer's initial screen. The algorithms work similar to Google's search ranking or Amazon's recommendations. Modifications to the algorithms are tested with A/B testing and are rolled out when the company is sure the modification brings a better experience.[13]

Requirements-Driven BI

A commonly held opinion for successful business intelligence is that it should be requirements driven: The users define their requirements, and the BI team builds a solution according to those specifications. And yet, these stories of relevance show a very different model. The requirements were not explicitly defined by the users at all. They were deduced by the business intelligence experts. These BI experts didn't have a "build it and they will come" mentality, nor did they "build what was asked for"; instead, they studied the activities of these potential users and delivered something that would benefit the individuals.

It is this model of development that is most required for extending BI beyond traditional information workers. Knowledge workers may have a better idea of what data and tools they need to do their jobs, so a traditional requirements-driven development model may work for this segment. For others, though, it is up to the BI experts to study people's jobs, daily decisions, and performance incentives to discover these requirements. In short, relevance is about finding a way to use business intelligence to simplify their work and make it better.

What to Do with Big Data

To date, so much of business intelligence has been about accessing and analyzing data captured through transactional systems. Finding the relevance in BI for such data seems more straightforward. Did the company achieve its goals? How am I performing? How do measures compare to other time periods, products, and so on? With big data, on the other hand, companies are capturing more and more data, but with uncertain uses. Progressive Insurance and Travelers, for example, have gadgets to capture driving distance and speeds, offering insurance discounts for drivers who drive fewer miles in a year. However, the devices also capture driver behavior such as acceleration and sudden braking, so customers are concerned that such data can be used against them to increase premiums. Teens are worried that the data could be used to track their whereabouts.

In mid-2013, a number of U.S. police departments revealed that they routinely capture images of license plates as cars enter states or cities. Law enforcement may use the data for locating a stolen vehicle or a criminal. The data is captured, unbeknownst to most citizens, and it is used when needed, left dormant and unmined when not.

Starbucks, too, with its loyalty key cards, noted the company was capturing a lot of data on consumer behavior, but as of yet was unsure what else they would do with that data.[14] It doesn't make sense to offer a loyal customer a coupon for a beverage that they are willing to pay full price for. For now, the data has primarily been used for customer segmentation and profiling. In some respects, lack of a clear application for newly captured data is not surprising. However, I find the contrast about views on data from the CEOs at Starbucks and Constant Contact noteworthy. Joe LaCugna, director of analytics and business intelligence at Starbucks, described his CEO at the annual National Retail Federation convention: "He has absolutely no head for data." Meanwhile, the Constant Contact CEO clearly values data and is proactive about leveraging it.[15]

With smart meters, a lot of detailed data can be generated on energy consumption. The main benefits touted have been that utility companies no longer need people to manually read an analog meter, and consumers no longer need to pay an estimated bill. The long-term vision is that energy companies can better predict and align supply and demand. I was shocked (gobsmacked, really) that in the United Kingdom, where adoption of smart meters was mandated in 2008,[16] several utilities said they were unsure what precisely they would do with these new levels of detailed data. Some citizens are worried the collected data will be used for surveillance and see such collection as an invasion of privacy.[17] Call me too trusting of Big Brother (or a data geek), but the benefits of having this data seem to outweigh the concerns. As a consumer with an electric bill that tops $700 in summer (a poorly insulated house atop a hill, direct sunlight, with cathedral ceilings), I would love a dashboard of our electricity consumption. Tell me if the energy hog is really the dehumidifier running in our damp basement or the 20-year-old refrig-erator. And just how much extra energy do Xbox Live and the TV con-sume, particularly when played during summer school break until the early hours of the morning? Like a frustrated business manager trying to make decisions about which products will have the most market adop-tion, I am a consumer flying blind on why my electric bill is so darn high. The relevance for this big data seems obvious to me, but with any new data, the generators and custodians of that data need to think first about its usefulness and beneficiaries, but then also how that data might be used in a negative way, with unintended consequences. Through my data-centric lens, I like that data is captured, even if its application is not yet clear. The relevance may be something that needs to be devel-oped over time.

Best Practices for Successful Business Intelligence

When it comes to extending the reach of business intelligence, rel-evance is a key secret to success. Relevance is business intelligence with an "it's all about me" mindset. To make BI more relevant to all workers in your company

- Study the drivers of company performance to determine which deci-sions and people will have the biggest impact. Don't let BI priorities be driven only by those individuals who shout the loudest.
- Look at your current BI deployment rates by roles and understand where there is the biggest room for improvement. (Refer to Figure 4-6, Chapter 4, for current industry averages.)
- Personalize the content of BI applications—whether reports, dash-boards, alerts, or scorecards—so that users have information in a context and in a way that facilitates insight.
- Don't rely exclusively on the traditional requirements-gathering pro-cess of asking people what they want; instead, study the way people work, incentives that influence them, decisions they make, and the information that supports those decisions to derive requirements.

Chapter 10

Agile Development

The role of agile development in BI success is one of those secrets that emerged only from a study of common themes in the successful BI case studies. When the first edition of this book was published in 2007, few companies were using agile software development, and even fewer were using it in BI. Since then, agile for BI is more widely accepted, and, advocating it as a best practice, The Data Warehousing Institute (TDWI) now focuses a number of conferences on agile. Despite broader awareness of agile development, awareness of it is not required for newly certified project management professionals.[1] Instead, certification in agile development techniques are more often provided separately by organizations who offer consulting and education on agile.

Waterfall Development Process

Traditional systems development projects often follow a waterfall project approach: A set of tasks is completed, and then another set, until several months or years later, you have a working piece of software (see Figure 10-1). The waterfall approach is heavy on defining requirements precisely up front. The thinking goes that if you get your requirements right up front, then you save development costs later in the process. The waterfall approach is also preferred when a development project is outsourced and a systems provider must build a solution to a specification.

Such a project approach is reasonable for *portions* of a business intelligence solution and as long as the time frames are reasonable, but it is less effective for business-facing solutions when requirements are difficult to articulate and frequently change and processes are fluid. With business intelligence, the project is never-ending and the focus is not on finishing, but rather, on delivering a certain set of capabilities

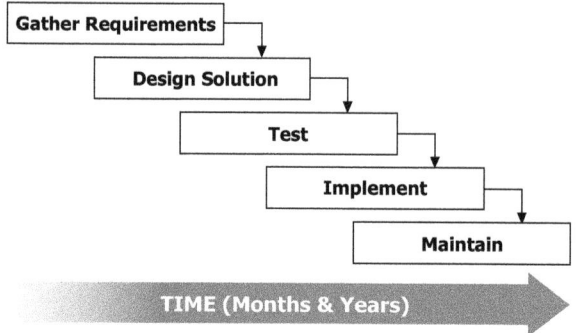

Figure 10-1   Waterfall project methodology

within a defined period. Recall from Chapter 1 that one of the ways in which business intelligence is used is to uncover opportunities. Requirements for discovery-style applications, then, are not precisely known. Instead of a fixed report or dashboard, the BI application has to facilitate exploration of a broad set of data. As well, consider in Chapter 9 that in finding out how BI can be most relevant to front-line workers, the requirements-definition process is much more collaborative versus the traditional, somewhat rigid process of "define requirements precisely and build to the specification." These fundamental aspects of business intelligence make the waterfall approach to project management inappropriate to much of the BI initiative. I suspect some of the early failures of data warehouse projects can be attributed to the use of a waterfall approach in which the data warehouse team spent a year or more building out enterprise architecture, later delivering a system not at all useful to the business.

A key principle to ensuring BI has the biggest business impact is to provide a business intelligence environment that is flexible enough to adapt to a changing business environment *at the pace* of the business environment—fast and with frequent change.

Within the BI architecture (see Figure 10-2 here, discussed in detail in Chapter 2), making changes to items on the far left (source

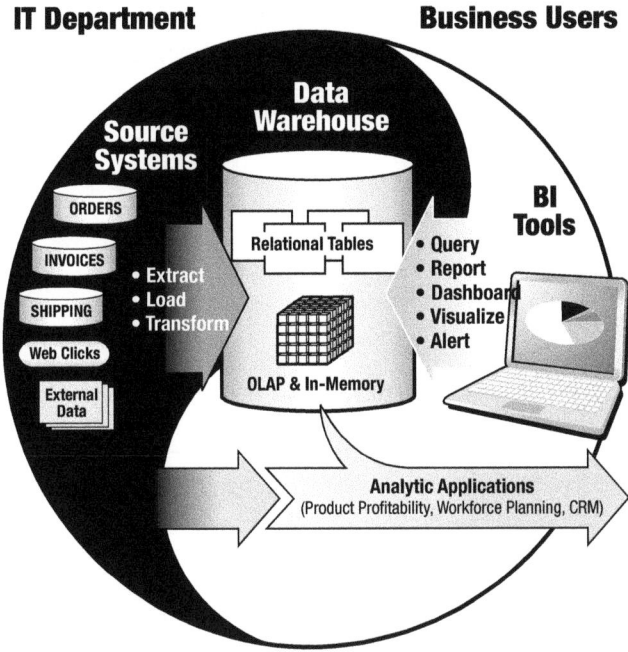

Figure 10-2   Major components in the business intelligence life cycle

systems and extract, transform, and load [ETL] processes) is often more costly to do, requires more time, has a greater risk, and may have less of an immediate value-add to the business. Items farther on the right (dashboards, reports, alerts) are less time-consuming to change and therefore more adaptable to changing business requirements. Specific elements are listed in Table 10-1. For each portion of the BI architecture, you may want to adopt a periodic release schedule, but a schedule that balances the need for stability with responsiveness. Items on the far left may only change every few years; those in the middle, once a quarter; and items on the further right, on an as-needed basis (daily, weekly, or monthly). The frequency for change varies due to the cost of change, the degree of difficulty to change, the number of people and related components affected by the change, risk, and the corresponding business value provided by the change. Using the car analogy again, you may change the oil frequently, the tires periodically, and the actual car every five years.

Less Frequent Change/Higher Risk and Cost	Periodic Change	Frequent Change/ Lower Risk and Cost
Hardware	Physical tables	Business views
Software	Custom-coded applications	Reports
Source systems	ETL processes	Dashboards
	Code files and hierarchy definitions	Calculation of key performance indicators within the business view, scorecard, or dashboard
	OLAP database structure	

Table 10-1   Specific elements requiring change in the BI architecture

As an example, getting various stakeholders and individual lines of business to agree on consistent business definitions is difficult and time-consuming. Important metrics such as "customer churn" or "product profitability" can be calculated in a myriad of ways. Once everyone agrees on a definition, however, implementing a consistent calculation of such business metrics within a business view or scorecard is something that can be implemented rapidly. If, however, the definition or calculation logic has been hard-coded into ETL processes or into physical tables in the data warehouse, then consolidating and changing these business rules can mean a major overhaul to multiple programs. Sometimes developers will hard-code business definitions into individual reports or dashboards: Stakeholders can't agree, so a report is the "easiest" and fastest place to define an element. This has some short-term value until there is a new business rule. Now those hundreds of instances of "customer churn" or "product profitability" have to be changed in hundreds of individual reports, as opposed to in one business view. Such business-facing capabilities demand flexibility. Other components, such as the hardware for the BI server or data warehouse, may only need to be changed when a company wants to update the infrastructure, add capacity, or exploit a new technology.

For every BI element, consider carefully where to place the capability and what promotes the most reusability and flexibility while balancing the trade-offs in risk, cost, and business benefit. Figure 10-3 provides a

Summary of Alternatives and Trade-offs
on Where to Put Intelligence

Consistent Business Terms	●	●	●	⬡
Fast Queries	●	●	▲	▲
Flexibility / Implementation Time	⬡	▲	▲	●
User Autonomy	⬡	▲	▲	●
Scalability	●	●	▲	⬡
Politics	⬡	▲	▲	●
Consistent Business Terms	▲	▲	●	⬡
Skills Required	⬡	▲	▲	●
Robustness	●	●	Varies by Vendor	▲

● Good   ▲ Use with Caution   ⬡ Problematic

Figure 10-3   Alternatives and trade-offs in where to put the intelligence

summary of trade-offs in cost, benefit, and flexibility of where to put the intelligence in various parts of the BI life cycle.

For example, if your requirement is to calculate customer churn, you may write the logic to do this in

- The ETL or ELT script that then populates the data warehouse
- An Online Analytical Processing (OLAP) cube or in-memory application that an OLAP viewer, visual discovery tool, or dashboard may access
- The business view or business meta data layer of a BI tool
- As a calculation within an individual report or dashboard

At one end of the spectrum in which IT is strongly involved in developing the solution, logic inside an ETL or ELT script provides the following benefits:

- Consistency of business terms across all applications and reports that would use this metric

- Fast performance, as queries that use the calculation would access data physically stored in the relational data warehouse or loaded into memory
- Good scalability, as large volumes of data and large numbers of users can reuse this
- Low cost to maintain after the initial implementation, but frequent changes can be expensive
- Robust modeling and calculation logic that can handle multiple data passes, if-then-else logic, and so on

However, building intelligence in the ETL script provides the following disadvantages:

- Less flexibility and a longer implementation time up front.
- No business user autonomy to change the way something is calculated.
- Political challenges to establish how to calculate the metric, requiring consensus from all business units and stakeholders. If marketing defines churn differently from finance, such differences in definitions need to be resolved before the ETL process can be written.
- Highly skilled ETL developers are required to understand distinct data sources, data integration tools, and programming, so there may be a bottleneck or additional cost.

At the other end of the BI life cycle, an individual business power user may calculate customer churn inside a dashboard or report. This approach provides the following advantages:

- Strong flexibility and a fast implementation time.
- Strong business user autonomy to change the way something is calculated.
- Minimal to no political obstacles. Only the requirements of the individual business unit are considered in defining the calculation logic. The needs of the larger organization do not need to be considered.
- Business users can implement the design and only need limited training in a BI tool.

When a business user implements intelligence inside a report or dashboard, it poses the following disadvantages:

- Inconsistent business terms when other report authors or dashboard developers want to use a similar metric that they may inadvertently or intentionally calculate differently.

- Variable performance, depending on if the back-end source is an in-memory application or relational database. Query performance may suffer when there is complex SQL generated at query run time.
- Poor scalability when there are large volumes of data or large numbers of users accessing the calculation.
- Higher cost to maintain because, when there is a change, each individual report or dashboard needs to be modified.
- Less robust calculation logic than with other points in the BI life cycle, but capabilities vary widely.

Agile Development Techniques

The concept of agile software development emerged from an informal gathering of software engineers in 2001.[2] The group published a manifesto, some of whose principles aptly apply to business intelligence.

Upon first reading the Agile Manifesto, I had to chuckle at "Welcome changing requirements…" In truth, changing requirements are typically something IT people dread because they mean rework, which leads to a project deliverable that is over budget and late. However, with agile development, BI developers do not work from a precise list of requirements, in stark contrast to the waterfall approach. Instead, they work from a broad requirement, with specific capabilities that are identified and narrowed down through a prototyping process. This prototyping process may involve sample screens mocked up within an Excel spreadsheet, or reports and dashboards built within a BI tool. When using packaged BI software, building a report or dashboard takes a matter of minutes and hours, not days and weeks of custom-coded solutions. Discarding a prototype after a collaborative session is more expeditious than asking the business users to list precisely their requirements, having someone build a solution to those requirements, and then discovering that the requirements have changed or that there was a misinterpretation.

A project plan for a BI solution using agile development techniques is illustrated in Figure 10-4. A specific task is iterated and recycled until the project team is satisfied with the capabilities, within a defined time frame, and in adherence to the resource constraints (time and people) agreed upon in the planning stage. Time frames are usually measured in weeks (as opposed to months and years in waterfall-style projects). In this way, there is not a concept of a project being late. Instead, requirements and deliverables are time boxed. So the question is not whether or not the project was late, but rather, were the requirements met and of an appropriate quality.

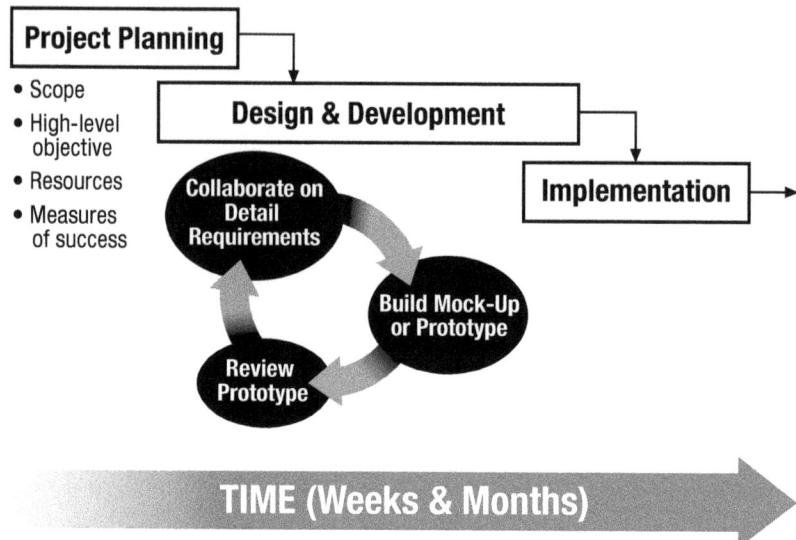

Figure 10-4   Iterative approach to delivering BI capabilities

A Subset of Principles from the Agile Manifesto

- Our highest priority is to satisfy the customer through early and continuous delivery of valuable software.
- Welcome changing requirements, even late in development. Agile processes harness change for the customer's competitive advantage.
- Businesspeople and developers must work together daily throughout the project.
- The most efficient and effective method of conveying information to and within a development team is face-to-face conversation.
- The sponsors, developers, and users should be able to maintain a constant pace indefinitely.
- Continuous attention to technical excellence and good design enhances agility.
- Simplicity—the art of maximizing the amount of work not done—is essential.
- The best architectures, requirements, and designs emerge from self-organizing teams.

For this iterative process to be successful, the business users and the IT developers must work closely together in a collaborative fashion. Some BI project teams will establish "war rooms" to facilitate collaboration in which business users and IT developers routinely meet to review prototypes and hash out requirements. In addition to logistical issues such as co-location in war rooms, in order for such collaborative development to be successful, the business and IT must have a strong partnership, as described in Chapter 7.

The State of Agile Software Development

According to the Successful BI survey, 15 percent of respondents strongly agree that they are using agile development techniques, and 44 percent are using them to some extent. A sizable minority (41 percent) are not using agile at all. The influence on business impact, though, is significant. As shown in Figure 10-5, those that strongly agree they use agile, 46 percent, report significant business impact, 12 percentage points higher than the industry average of 34 percent.

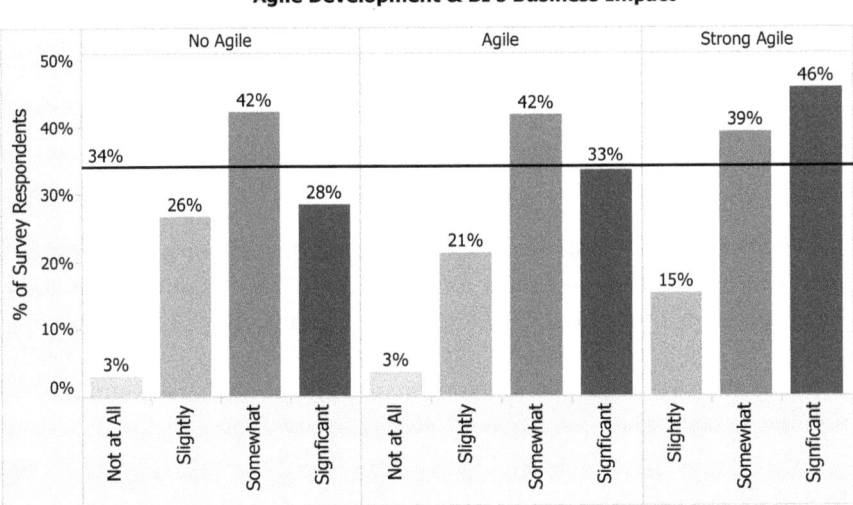

Figure 10-5   Use of agile development relates to greater business impact.

Industry literature suggests that some of the barriers to adoption of agile development are concerns about higher costs, loss of control, and inability for the business and IT to partner together. Scott Ambler, an author of several books on agile software development, conducted a broad survey in March 2007 (781 respondents)[3] with an updated version in July 2010 (233 respondents).[4] Some key findings in support of agile software development include the following:

- Small teams of one to ten people report the highest success rates (83 percent).
- Co-located agile projects are more successful on average than non-co-located, which in turn, are more successful than projects involving off-shoring.
- Regardless of team size, agile showed higher success rates than traditional waterfall development.

A Recognized Need for Agile

With the frenetic pace of business, business intelligence needs to be able to adapt at an equally rapid pace to new requirements and changes. Agile development can help achieve flexibility and rapid delivery, but it requires the right culture, business–IT partnership, and an understanding of new development approaches. A number of Successful BI survey respondents wrote of the need for more agility in delivering BI solutions. A senior systems accountant voiced frustration at the disconnect: "IT is very reluctant to get involved with business requirements and manages projects in a very linear, waterfall approach, which turns quite basic data warehousing and BI requests into long, drawn-out process which fail to deliver what is needed as an end output. The business goes back to workarounds and Excel." A supply chain manager in manufacturing blames their lack of BI success on slow delivery times. "Lack of a lean IT deployment process; it takes too much time; is too costly, and is not prepared to anticipate future needs and developments."

Conversely, a systems developer who has been using agile development credits their BI success to this development approach. "A good relationship with business is essential, and we have a good experience of scrum with the business BI-manager as the product owner."

Basic Concepts of Scrum

Some of the terminology in agile development draws from the sport of rugby. There are different approaches to agile development, but scrum seems to be the most widely used. In rugby, a scrum is a method used to restart play when a ball goes out of bounds or there's been some penalty. The scrum is like a huddle of players, locked arm in arm, who try to move the ball forward. It requires significant team work, with all players moving in the same direction. (My husband's broken shoulder shows the consequences of not moving in the same direction when locked in a scrum.)

Scrum.org publishes a guide on scrum development techniques and provides training and certifications. It uses self-organizing teams to develop capabilities within a specific time frame.[5] Following are some of the key terms that anyone involved with a BI team using agile should be familiar with:

- **Product owner** A single person responsible for the completed product and for deciding what's in scope and what's out of scope, setting priorities, and managing the list of requirements or product backlog.
- **Scrum master** The team leader who ensures scrum theories and practices are being followed.
- **Sprints** A development time, usually a month, in which a set of product capabilities is delivered. A release cycle may be composed of multiple sprints.
- **Product backlog** A list of requirements or capabilities needed in the deliverable. These may be captured as user stories.
- **Co-location** IT developers and business users will be located in the same physical room to facilitate collaborative development.
- **Task board** A wall or chart that shows the progress of each story (Figure 10-6 is an example of a task board). It usually consists of the following columns: Story by Priority, Tasks Waiting, Tests Written, Under Development, Waiting Validation, and Ready to Demo.[6] The last step, Ready to Demo, is when the development team confirms with the product owner that all requirements for that sprint have been met.
- **Swim lanes** Because the task board has been organized into columns that appear as swim lanes in a lap pool. Items can be reshuffled in priority and phase within the task board.

Ralph Hughes of Ceregenics and author of *Agile Data Warehousing* (iUniverse, 2008) cautions, though, that generic scrum doesn't work for data warehousing and that organizations need to adapt the model.[7] In particular, he recommends including a solutions architect that is responsible for the long-term integration and vision. "The solutions architect is the hero of the project, driving requirements, quality assurance, and design."

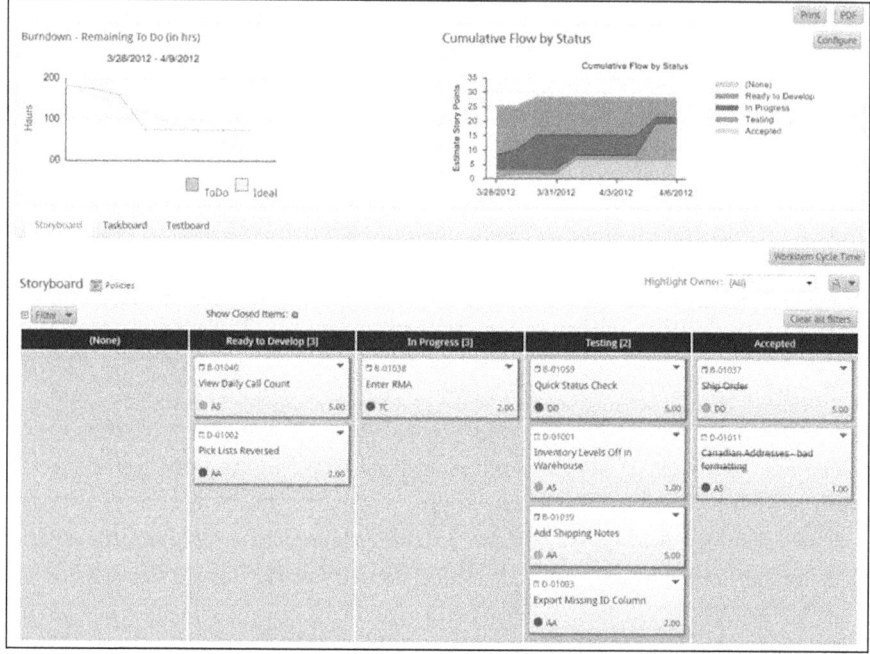

Figure 10-6   Sample task board from VersionOne agile project management tool. (Source: VersionOne, http://www.versionone.com/product/agile-project-management-tool-overview/)

Basic Concepts of Kanban

Kanban is another agile development approach. In Japanese, kanban means "signal card" and is an approach that Toyota uses in its production system to signal when a phase of work has completed decentralized manufacturing.[8] Where scrum is time boxed, Kanban is focused on continuous development. Both approaches rely heavily on the concept of teams.[9] Several of the Successful BI case study companies use a combination of kanban and scrum.

Kanban includes four main principles:[10]

- Assess current development processes
- Pursue incremental, evolutionary change
- Respect the current process, roles, responsibilities, and titles
- Leadership at all levels

With Kanban, the focus is on reducing work in progress and continuing to move outstanding requests through the development process.

How Well Are BI Projects Managed?

Agile development processes may require different and perhaps stronger project management skills than a waterfall approach. Collaborative design sessions that are characteristic of agile development can too easily slip into never-ending tweaks to the system. Without a detailed requirement document, it's harder for project personnel to declare a particular item is out of scope. In fact, Hughes attributes some of the fear about agile to this loss of control. "In the industrial era, the thinking was that management knows better and should control what workers do. With agile, the thinking is that workers know best. So let them self-organize, give them performance measures, and let them achieve the results."

According to the Successful BI survey results, having a well-managed BI program ranked sixth in importance for organizational factors (refer back to Figure 6-1, Chapter 6), with 24 percent rating this as essential to a successful business intelligence deployment. It seems that data warehouse failures, wasted investments, and late projects were reported more often in the mid-1990s, when the concepts of data warehousing and business intelligence were still new. Nonetheless, the stigma of project failures still seems to linger and is perhaps exaggerated. I continue to hear new vendors and consulting companies saying most BI projects fail, which the survey results clearly show is not true. Research by Professor Hugh Watson of the Terry College of Business at the University of Georgia in 2005 showed that only a slight majority of data warehouse projects then were on time and on budget.[11] A sizable portion of data warehouse projects, 44 percent on average, were late.

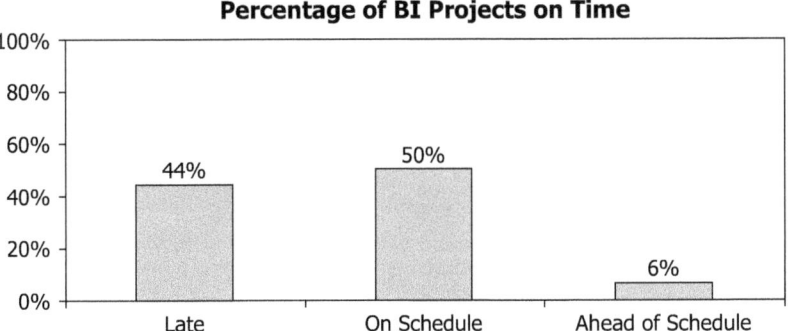

The degree to which data warehouse projects were over budget was also sizable at 37 percent.

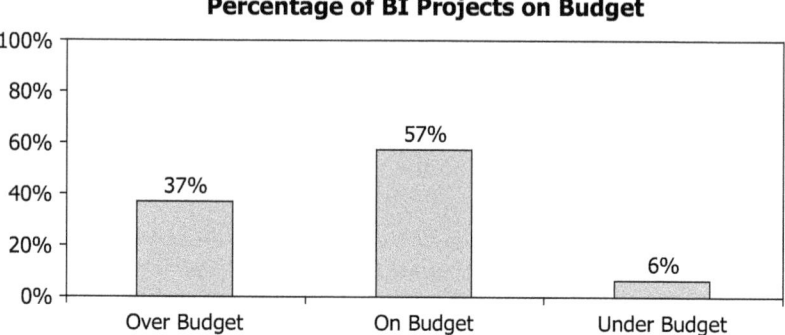

More recent data shows improvement in productivity, customer satisfaction, and quality when agile development methodologies are used. As shown in Figure 10-7, a joint survey conducted by Ralph Hughes of Ceregenics and TDWI in 2012 (204 respondents) found that 80 percent had better productivity, 81 percent had better customer satisfaction, and 60 percent had better quality when using agile over traditional waterfall development. The only project performance indicator that did not have a major improvement was cost, for which 40 percent said the cost was worse.

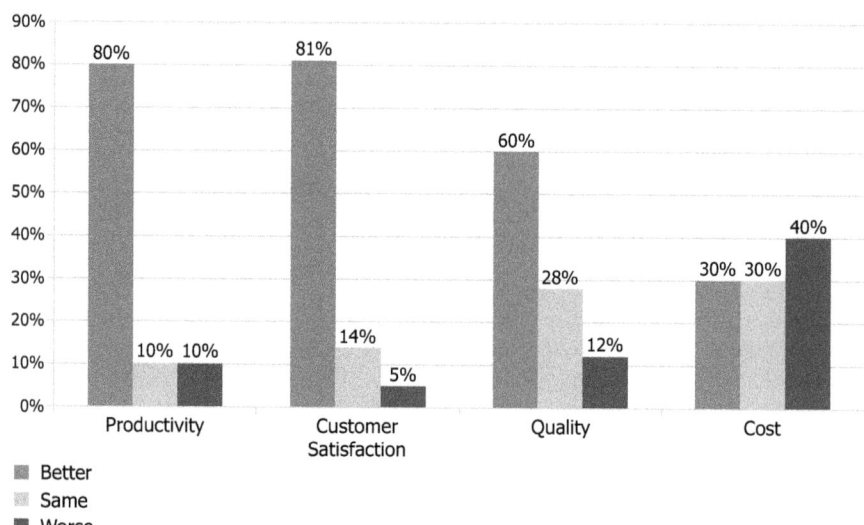

Figure 10-7 Ralph Hughes and TDWI: Agile's impact on BI project key performance indicators

There are three key variables in managing a BI project effectively:

- **Scope**   For example, the subject areas and data accessible for analysis, the underlying infrastructure, the BI tool capabilities, and the quality
- **Resources**   The amount of money and number of people you have available to invest in the project
- **Time**   The deadline for delivering a set of capabilities

Like a three-legged stool, when any one of these variables changes, it affects the other variables.

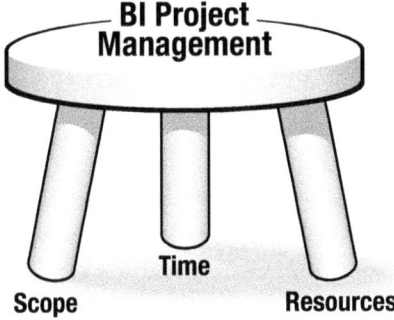

So when the business asks for more data than originally agreed upon in the scope, either

- You need more *resources* or better productivity to deliver the changed scope on time.

or

- The resources will stay fixed and the project *timeline* must be renegotiated.

Unfortunately, 44 percent of the Successful BI survey respondents said they do not have adequate time and funding to be successful.

Quality is part of the project scope, and this is an aspect that can sabotage the timeliness of any project, no matter how well planned. When the severity of data quality problems is not known, allowing appropriate time to handle such issues is guesswork. In an ideal world, data would be 100 percent accurate, software would be bug-free, and functionality would be as expected. That's not reality. One of the most challenging aspects to project management, then, is delivering a solution whose quality is good enough within the agreed-upon time constraints and available resources.

> To manage a BI project effectively, repeat the project manager's mantra, frequently, and to anyone who requests a change: *There's scope, time, and resources. Scope, time, and resources. Scope, time, and resources.* If there is a budget cut, plan to cut the scope. If new capabilities are requested, communicate the corresponding increase in resources and time.

Agile Culture at Netflix

Agile is not just a development approach at Netflix; it is part of the company culture. The company actively recruits people who are willing to take risks, think out of the box, and work with a great deal of freedom as a team member.[12] One of the major differences in waterfall development versus agile development is the idea of control and individual freedom. With waterfall development, a developer is assigned a task by a supervisor. It is much more suited to a hierarchical organization and culture. With agile development, the team will agree on who works on which tasks for maximum value and efficiency. Team members are free to make decisions and voice concerns or alternatives. In fact, normally a daily stand up is part of the agile development process. This type of work style requires the right people and culture.

To a certain extent, that Netflix is in the entertainment industry and is an innovator allows and requires agility, so they actively recruit top performers able to work in such an environment. Netflix CEO Reed Hastings says, "In procedural work, the best are two times better than the average. In creative/inventive work, the best are ten times better than the average, so there is a huge premium on creating effective teams of the best."[13]

Across the industry, IT often has been criticized for moving too slowly, but conversely, what happens when the business moves too fast? For example, in 2011, Netflix announced changes to its subscription plans, initially trying to separate DVD and streaming customers. There was a big customer backlash that sent the share price plunging. Later in the fall, CEO Reed Hastings announced that a separate company, Qwikster, would handle DVD subscribers, and a month later, the company back-tracked. In explaining these changes, CEO Hastings said, "There is a difference between moving quickly—which Netflix has done very well for years—and moving too fast, which is what we did in this case."[14]

IT has to keep pace with such changing business priorities. Andrew Dempsey, director of DVD BI and analytics, says the speed of the business can sometimes be a challenge in ensuring BI success.[15]

> Sometimes the business is too fast. The Netflix culture is faster than agile. There is a lot of freedom and responsibility so you need a higher level of communication. Changes in one system impact another, and they are done without really checking. For example, we'll get a new data feed in [the] morning, it will have something new in the afternoon, and it's impacted basic reporting. Whilst the rate of change of data does impact standard reporting, we also have the agility to react to it quickly and can thus stay in sync with all the changes going on around us.

The culture and right people have enabled Netflix to be agile, but so have rapid changes in technology. The use of public cloud and open source have been pivotal in allowing Netflix to launch streaming in new markets, such as to Europe in 2012. Ariel Tseitlin, director of cloud solutions, explains, "Every engineer who needed cloud resources was able to procure them at the click of a button. The elastic nature of the cloud makes capacity planning less crucial, and teams can simply add resources as needed."[16]

While agile is part of Netflix, the company clarifies that they can adopt this approach because they "are in a creative-inventive market, not a safety-critical market like medicine or nuclear power." This is an important point of contrast for a company such as Medtronic.

Medtronic: Agile for the Right Projects

I would probably be alarmed to envision the use of agile development in something like pacemakers. I wouldn't want the requirements for a medical device design jotted on the back of an index card. Truly, I want the specifications for that pacemaker well documented and reviewed and cross-reviewed by engineers, medical professionals, and the Food and Drug Administration (FDA), at a minimum.

The same, however, should not be true when developing a report or dashboard, but adopting agile development approaches in an otherwise waterfall environment clearly goes against the norm. For Medtronic, one of the keys to success was using agile development techniques when and where it made sense rather than adopting the methodology in its entirety. Collaborative development is a fundamental concept of agile, and to this end, Medtronic had three full-time business analysts dedicated to the reporting aspect of the Global Complaint Handling (GCH) system. These business analysts teamed up with individuals in the business who knew the details on what had to go into FDA audit needs, weekly scorecards, or quarterly metrics for senior management. "They worked side by side in flushing out the requirements," explains IT Director Sarah Nieters, who acted as the IT sponsor for GCH.[17] Co-developing reports was new to Medtronic, and the team set up war rooms for individual businesses. The agile concept of a "task board" was used, with the status of various reports posted on the wall: Design, Complete, Written, Validated.

Another concept of agile is voicing alternatives to ensure maximum quality, value, and expediency. Sara Rottunda, business lead on the project, suggests there needs to be more of this mindset. "Don't just take the order. BI developers should push back and engage critical thinking. Tell us: Did you know that another business unit just asked for the same thing?"

Rottunda makes a valid point, but this is where company culture and adequate resources have to be in place before BI specialists or IT developers in general will challenge or probe business requirements. If a developer fears for his job or is perceived as being a second-guesser, such critical thinking and dialogue will rarely happen.

Similar to Netflix, changes in technology also played a role in allowing Medtronic to be more agile, but at the same time, use of agile development on the vendor's part presented its own set of challenges. Medtronic was the fourth live customer in the United States on a new technology, SAP Hana, an in-memory appliance. Medtronic selected the technology for its performance, but also, because it could handle long text fields. In the past, Medtronic couldn't readily search or analyze comments because its relational data warehouse had a 60-character limit. Kiran Musunuru, the SAP HANA architect at Medtronic, recalls, "Bleeding edge technology had some challenges. We got a new vendor release every two weeks." Despite these challenges, Nieters says, "When you look at what we have now and the capability, it's a huge leap forward in capability. It's been worth the pain."

Sharper BI at 1-800 CONTACTS

1-800 Contacts implemented agile software development methodology early in its BI journey in 2005.[18] Prior to this, users had to define their requirements in advance and formally submit them to the IT group. Now the BI team meets with various businesspeople on a weekly basis to plan the week's iterations. Dave Walker, the vice president of operations at 1-800 Contacts, describes the dynamics of agile development as one of the reasons for their success. "We are virtually one team. The IT people in the data warehouse team understand the call center so well, they could probably take some calls. There is partnership, high trust, and it's collaborative. It's not 'make a list, send it over.' It's very iterative. It takes lot of time and effort on both sides, but the end product is well worth it."

The team still works within a high-level roadmap with yearly deliverables, and Jim Hill, director of data management, says these weekly planning sessions could not work without that roadmap. Disagreements about prioritizations and resource allocation are resolved by a finance director who reports to the executive sponsor.

In many respects, the BI technology itself allows for agile development because the business users themselves may be building the solution. If users are building or customizing their own reports and dashboards, they most likely are not working from a documented list of requirements, but rather working from, at most, needs and thoughts jotted in an e-mail request. Chris Coon, a senior analyst at 1-800 CONTACTS, says the Microsoft Analysis Services OLAP cube allows for exploration. "Before the data warehouse and these cubes, we always had to go to the IT group who produced something static. It always took a long time. It didn't facilitate a rapid response to change in sales volume or other business event." Now Coon estimates 80 percent of his requirements can be fulfilled by the OLAP database, allowing him to explore sales by new customers, by repeat customers, or by different products.

Best Practices for Successful Business Intelligence

Project managers should recognize that because of the ways in which business intelligence is used, solutions must be flexible and modifiable in response to changing business requirements. Given the lack of understanding of what is possible with BI and that users often don't know what they want until they see it, agile development techniques are preferable to traditional waterfall development process for BI applications.

- Be prepared to change the business-facing parts of BI on a more rapid basis than the behind-the-scenes infrastructure.
- Use collaborative development and rapid prototyping.
- Repeat the project manager's mantra: There is scope, resources, and time. When you change one aspect, expect it to affect the others.
- Understand how quality and the desire for perfection can sabotage a project's timeline. Manage expectations about quality early on, and agree upon acceptable quality levels.
- Recognize the role of culture and the right people in adopting agile development techniques.

Chapter 11

Organizing for Success

Given the myriad ways that business intelligence reaches across an entire organization, attention to organizational issues can accelerate BI success; failure to address organizational issues hinders success. In each of the successful BI case studies, how the BI team was organized and evolved played a pivotal role in ensuring greater success.

Enterprise vs. Departmental BI

If your company is new to business intelligence, it may be difficult to pursue an enterprise solution. Some of the best ideas may incubate within individual departments or business units, and this may be the ideal place to test the BI waters. However, even if you begin with BI at the department level, keep your view on the enterprise.

> "We started small to avoid enterprise data governance issues and be able to get the foundation right. We are ready to grow from a solid foundation."
> —Database administrator from a state agency who describes their BI deployment as very successful

Some of the same challenges in establishing a strong business–IT partnership also affect whether business intelligence is approached as an enterprise solution or as a departmental initiative. When a particular business unit is under time pressure to perform better, to identify an opportunity, and so on, that business unit may not have the luxury of waiting on decisions and solutions from a central organization. The consequences of underperforming at a departmental or business unit level can be severe. Underperformance of a business unit can have the following consequences:

- The business unit may be sold off, or if it involves a new product launch, a new way of doing business, or a new location, the unit may be shut down.
- Job layoffs may follow the underperformance.
- The service function may be outsourced.

When business intelligence is deployed departmentally or at the business unit level and is pivotal in ensuring the success of that department or business unit, then the BI team is usually at liberty to do whatever it takes to be successful. The goals, requirements, and constraints for one business unit are often at odds with the goals of the enterprise:

Departmental BI	Enterprise BI
Focus on the individual business unit needs	Focus on the needs of the company and all business units and departments
Use whatever technology works	Adhere to corporate standards
Short-term success	Long-term viability
Dedicated resources	Shared resources

Asking people and business units to consider the greater good of the company when their jobs and livelihoods are at risk seems a preposterous proposition. And yet, for greater company success, business intelligence must be treated as a strategic asset managed at the enterprise level. Treating BI as a departmental resource seems a best practice only when

- That department is a self-contained business unit.
- The business unit does not derive any added value from synergies with other business units in the company.
- The department or business unit does not leverage shared services (whether IT-related, accounting, human resources, purchasing, and so on).
- Employee compensation at the business unit level is not tied to any total company performance objectives.

Rarely, then, is treating BI strictly as a departmental resource a best practice.

In looking at how BI is typically delivered according to survey respondents, it is fairly mixed, with 29 percent describing their BI deployment as a departmental or business unit initiative, 40 percent as enterprise-wide, and 31 percent as a hybrid in which the business unit relies on some centralized components such as an enterprise data warehouse (see Figure 11-1).

However, as Figure 11-2 shows, the percentage that describes their deployments as having significant business impact is double for enterprise-wide deployments (43 percent) as for departmental (21 percent). This pattern is similar to the 2007 survey results. Conversely, the percentage of those who describe their project for departmental BI with no or only a slight impact is double that for the enterprise solution.

As discussed in Chapter 4, one measure of BI success is the percentage of employees who routinely use business intelligence. Here, too, enterprise-wide deployments report a higher rate of users, at 27 percent of employees, versus departmental at 20 percent of employees, and hybrid at 24 percent, in line with the survey average.

What was surprising to me was that the size of the company did not have much relationship as to whether BI was treated as a departmental or enterprise solution. Roughly the same percentage of small companies (fewer than 100 employees or less than $100 million in annual revenues) delivered BI departmentally as did large companies (more than 5,000 employees or greater than $1 billion in revenues). The age of the BI deployment did show differences in approaches. In newer

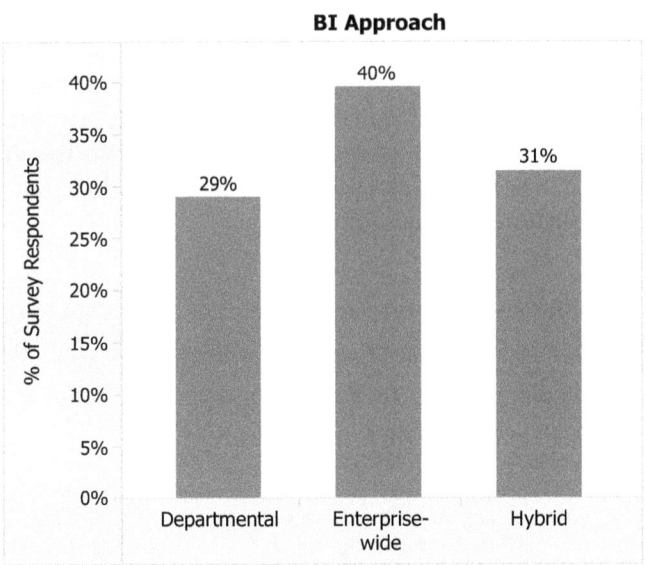

Figure 11-1 BI deployments use a mix of approaches.

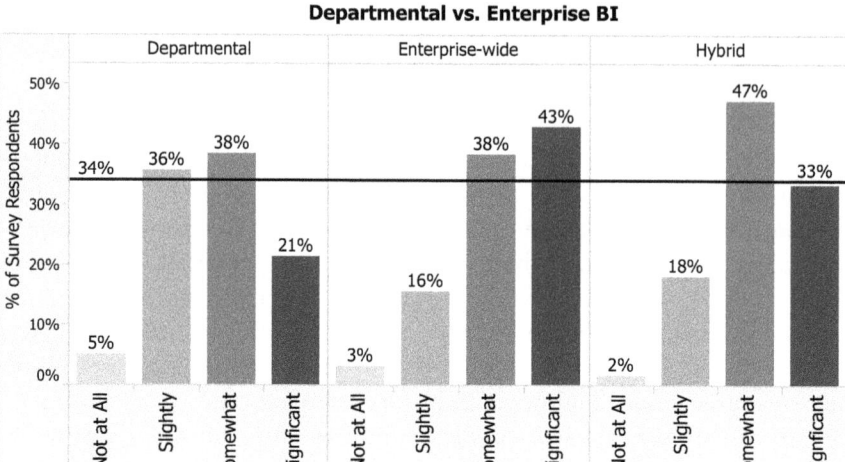

Figure 11-2 Enterprise-wide deployments have a higher percentage of deployments with significant business impact than do departmental solutions.

deployments, there is a greater rate of a departmental approach (43 percent less than a year, and 37 percent if one to three years old). However, for BI deployments that are more than 10 years old, the percentage of departmental deployments drops to 12 percent. This pattern suggests that companies new to BI start small before growing to the enterprise. Conversely, as BI expands, a departmental approach does not continue to provide the optimum value and impact.

> Departmental BI may allow for a faster solution, tailored to the specific needs of a business or department, but enterprise-wide BI allows for greater sustainable impact. The key is in ensuring a shift to the enterprise does not become inflexible and monolithic.

Departmental BI may show success faster because the BI team is dealing with less diverse requirements, requiring less buy-in, and with less consideration to an enterprise-class infrastructure. As discussed in

Chapter 5, the Dow SUCCESS solution was built so quickly, in less than a year, because only one business unit was involved and they had a dedicated programmer. With only one programmer, there was not even a project plan! Meanwhile, the Global Reporting Project was trying to understand, prioritize, and meld requirements from 15 different business units, with developers spread around the world. The project was a multiyear project, with capabilities delivered incrementally each quarter. Despite these differences, there is no excuse for a BI project, enterprise or otherwise, to take years before there are visible benefits. Use the agile development techniques described in Chapter 10 to deliver enterprise capabilities in time frames that mirror those of departmental solutions, ideally every 90 days.

All too often when BI success is shown in an isolated department, other departments subsequently demand similar capabilities, and IT is forced to try to replicate that departmental success for the enterprise. Often, this success can't be replicated. The software, processes, and approach break under the strains of increased demand, more diverse requirements, limited funding, and so on. Whatever was initially built at the departmental level may have to be scrapped and an enterprise solution built from scratch. Despite whatever technology, code, or software that may have to be replaced, there is enormous value in expertise and business understanding gained from departmental developments.

"The customer can have any color he wants so long as it's black."

—Henry Ford[1]

While the enterprise solution may have to focus on commonality, this is not to say that enterprise solutions should neglect the unique requirements of a business unit or department. The goal with BI is to deliver what is common to all departments in a way that provides economies of scale. If ever a department or business unit perceives critical requirements are being neglected by a central BI team, they will be forced to develop their own solutions. The BI infrastructure (see Chapter 2), such as server hardware; a data warehouse; extract, transform, and load (ETL) tools; a metadata repository; and policies and procedures, is typically common for all departments and business units. Some components of the BI front end (see Chapter 3), in particular the business views, dashboards, and reports, will be specific to each individual department. The decision on which components should be

BI and Tragedy of the Commons

The tragedy of the commons "involves a conflict over resources between individual interests and the common good."[2] This concept has been used to describe a number of social and economic problems where individuals pursue their own gain at the expense of the group. Herders, for example, who have to share pasture for sheep will continue to add sheep to the property when the products from the sheep (wool production) exceed the cost in degrading the common pasture. Global warming problems have been explained by the tragedy of the commons in that individual countries and people don't inherently want to cut emissions or drive smaller cars, not wanting to trade national or personal sacrifices for the greater good of the world.

The tragedy of the commons was first introduced to me in business school. In truth, I was a skeptic, thinking people, countries, and businesses are not *that* self-interested. I believed that if the negative impact on the common good were better understood, we'd behave differently. Yet several professors did "tests" to illustrate how often the tragedy plays out. One professor would offer an A or one less assignment if the group acted in unison. The individuals always won out. Another professor resorted to cold, hard cash as the common resource. Everyone contributed a couple of dollars that either a few individuals would win or we would all get back our small contribution if as a class we made decisions that benefited the entire class. A few made out like bandits, while the more naïve of us were left mouths agape at how greedily some behaved.

It seems to me that a similar tragedy exists with business intelligence. In 2005, a sizeable 42 percent of companies bought BI tools at a departmental level.[3] From the 2012 Successful BI survey results, only 25 percent of companies now buy BI tools departmentally. Funds for technology investments are limited and so are the resources and expertise to deploy them. It would make sense to build an enterprise solution once, rather than build multiple islands of solutions that end up costing the company more. Yet when the department buying the BI tool derives all the benefit (whether in time to implement BI capabilities or in software that meets a high portion of their requirements), their BI success is sometimes at the expense of other departments who would also benefit from business intelligence. Individual departments are forced to fight for their own solutions rather than working together to share resources, data, and expertise. The more important question, then, is not whether BI is deployed only departmentally, but rather *why*.

Departmental BI is most justifiable when BI is new and is a starting point, or when the central BI resources are not responsive.

tailored for a particular business unit or department should be based on whether the differentiation adds business value. Sometimes, that business value might be in time-to-market.

"There are many levels of BI initiatives in a company as large as the one in which I work. There are rogue initiatives started by people with a need that cannot convince the official corporate program to undertake since the corporate program has bigger projects in mind. These rogue programs can be much more effective since the people with the need are designing the system. Some of the data I need for my business is owned by another department, and I cannot get my hands on it because they are too busy with other projects to work on my request. However, they refuse to allow me access to the database because they own it."
            —Business user in customer service in the computer industry

Table 11-1 lists items and responsibilities that are either best centralized at an enterprise level or optimized at a business unit or departmental level. In comparing this table to the BI life cycle (see Figure 2-3 in Chapter 2), the farther left on the BI life cycle, the greater the likelihood it can be treated as an enterprise resource; the farther right on the diagram, the more likely it will be optimized by or for a business unit or department.

As an example, fraud detection is a type of software used by a number of banks. Within a bank, there may be a credit card business unit, a mortgage unit, and a consumer checking account unit. Fraud detection capabilities may be most important to the credit card unit (which has a higher volume and more anonymous transactions) and might be of less importance to the mortgage unit (which has lower volume and more

Centralized or Enterprise Resource	Optimized by/for Department or Business Unit
▪ Technical infrastructure (servers, backup servers)	▪ Business views
▪ Data warehouse infrastructure (ETL processes, modeling, cleansing)	▪ Reports
	▪ Dashboards
▪ Software standards, acquisition, deployment	▪ Definition of roles for role-based security
▪ Policies and procedures	▪ Analytic applications
▪ Best practices and quality assurance	▪ Statistical and predictive models
▪ Project management services	
▪ Training services	
▪ Company-wide business views and reports	
▪ User ID definition and authentication (ideally integrated with HR records)	

Table 11-1 Components to share across the enterprise or optimize by department

personalized transactions). Here, then, the credit card business unit may decide to buy its own fraud detection solution. This solution may or may not run on hardware supported at the enterprise level (the left-hand column of Table 11-1); ideally, it would use a common technical infrastructure, just as ideally it would use a common approach to setting up development, test, and production environments (policies and procedures); a consistent set of user IDs for authentication; and so on.

One of the items in the right-hand column in Table 11-1 that seems to generate the most debate is the responsibility for the business views (see the section on a business view of the data in Chapter 3). In companies with enterprise-wide BI deployments, these business views are collaboratively developed with the business units and departments. In some cases, though, responsibility for building the business views gravitates to the individual departments. A central organization continues to quality assure the business view, ensuring adherence to naming conventions, SQL optimization, and other best practices. The ability to do this and whether it's in the best interest of the company and the business unit will depend greatly on

- Availability of technical resources within the business unit or department
- Responsiveness of the central BI group
- Business or domain expertise of the central BI group
- Degree to which a business unit–specific business view must be reused by other departments and business units
- Ease of use to create a business view in the particular BI tool

All of these best practices, however, are only possible when other aspects of the company and the business intelligence initiative are working well. If, for example, the business and IT are not working in partnership, then the business has to pursue solutions on their own. When personal agendas, politics, or analysis-paralysis prevail, then an enterprise-wide approach to business intelligence also becomes less viable.

The BI Steering Committee

A BI steering committee includes senior representatives from the various businesses and functions who set priorities on both the data and functional capabilities of the BI portfolio. The BI program manager is also an active member of the steering committee. Other IT directors that have integration points with BI, such as the enterprise resource planning (ERP) owner, should also be on the steering committee. Steering committee members will meet on a regular basis, as often as weekly, to resolve conflicting priorities, identify new opportunities, and resolve issues escalated from the project team. The steering committee is an important forum for the BI project leader to understand the business context for BI, ensure business alignment, and keep business leaders abreast of new project developments.

In establishing any steering committee, it's important to consider both buy-in and size of the committee. Sometimes working with such large committees can make progress more difficult than smaller committees. I found in working with a biotechnology client that they had a large steering committee but one whose effectiveness I would question. In many respects, it was necessary to include all functions and business units to ensure buy-in to the BI initiative. However, cultural and political issues that existed outside the BI steering committee impacted the dynamics of the committee. Trying to schedule face-to-face meetings with larger groups became a logistical nightmare. When key committee members failed to participate in such meetings, they would later second-guess priorities and decisions agreed upon by those present. In this regard, the ideal size of the committee balances the trade-offs of being able to perform with the needs of ensuring buy-in and alignment with the business.

At 1-800 CONTACTS, an IT steering committee initially determined the priorities of the overall data warehouse activities. With the infrastructure established, the BI team meets with the director of treasury, financial planning, and analysis on a weekly basis to coordinate and prioritize activities. The BI team meets with the executive sponsor, the CFO, only on an as-needed basis, such as to review major milestones or prototypes.[4]

Business Intelligence Competency Centers (BICC)

Gartner Research defines a BICC as a "cross-functional team with specific tasks, roles, responsibilities, and processes for supporting and promoting the effective use of BI across the organization."[5] BICCs may also be referred to as "BI Centers of Excellence." While the terminology for BICCs may vary, their existence has become more mainstream.

The desire to implement a BICC will be influenced by the degree to which your company uses a shared services model. If you are trying to transform your BI focus from a departmental resource to an enterprise solution, a BICC is an effective organizational model that will facilitate this. A major difference between a BICC and a BI project is that a BICC is a permanent organization, whereas a BI project has a clear scope, set of deliverables, and time line. A BI project may be partially or fully staffed by BICC personnel. When there are no available BICC resources to staff a new project, then the BICC may act as an advisor and quality assurer to the BI project. The BICC can either be a virtual team or a dedicated team with permanent resources and a formal budget. Figure 11-3 shows an organizational model for the BICC, steering committee, and executive sponsor.

Some of the roles within the BICC may be dedicated resources or they may be shared with other groups. For example, the BICC may have a dedicated database administrator who creates the physical tables, optimizes indexes, and so on. Alternatively, a DBA (database administrator) from a central IT department may allocate a percentage of his or her time to the BICC. Similarly, the business subject matter experts may be part-time resources that the business allocates to their BI efforts, or they may be full-time BICC staff. When to staff a person as a full-time member of the BICC will depend on how much of a full-time resource you need, the possibility for career advancement, and funding.

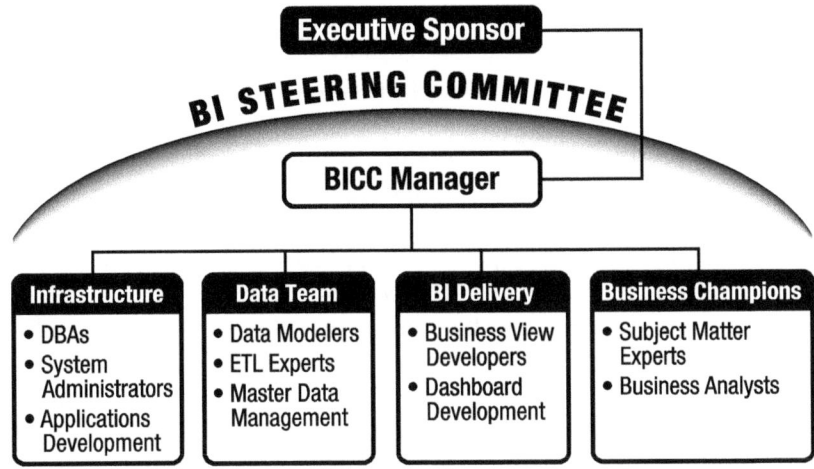

Figure 11-3   BI organizational model

Physical or Virtual, Centralized or Decentralized

Just as there are debates about how to physically architect your BI environment, there are debates and pros and cons on how to organize personnel to build out and support a BI environment. A BICC may be a central group of people who physically work near one another, with reporting lines into a BI director, and the BICC its own cost center. A BICC may also be virtual, where BI experts are geographically dispersed and have multiple reporting lines into either IT or a business unit. The cost for BI resources may be allocated to various departments based on time spent working on various tasks, or absorbed by the individual business units where the BI experts report into.

In considering personnel, it is a challenge to develop technical expertise while also maximizing business value. For example, BI experts may physically sit within a business unit and report into that manager or director. In this example, the business unit gets maximum BI support and business alignment, but there may not be a clear career path or development of BI and IT expertise. Do the BI experts get promoted within the business or to more senior position with IT? Conversely, if the BI expert resides within IT, there may be clearer career development and progression, but less alignment to and understanding of the business.

For example, at Netflix, the BI organizations within DVD and streaming are separate organizations. Each BI group is aligned to the goals of the respective business units and exploits the appropriate technologies. DVD relies more on traditional data warehousing and BI tools, whereas streaming is exploiting more cloud and Hadoop.[6]

Facebook Director of Analytics Ken Rudin describes how, organizationally, they began with a decentralized approach in which BI analysts worked directly for individual product teams (like a business unit).[7] This allowed individual teams to move quickly, but resulted in silos of Hadoop. Now, Facebook has a hybrid approach in which there is a limited pool of central BI experts but also BI experts who sit with the product teams four days a week. The centralization allows for efficiency, collaboration, and career development, while the product focus allows for greater alignment and the ability to be proactive.

National Instruments is a TDWI Best Practices award winner for its organizational model. (National Instruments provides an integrated hardware and software platform for engineers and scientists to develop systems and products that require measurement. For example, the automotive industry in developing fuel cells, transportation departments in measuring bridge fatigue, and NASA for Space Shuttle testing. The company had $1.14 billion in revenues in 2012.)[8] Early in its BI initiative, there was not a clear approach to implementing BI capabilities.[9] In 2009, the company moved to a virtual team approach that included five key areas (see Figure 11-4):

- **Business client services**   A client services program manager works within a particular business or functional area (the term "client" refers to an internal client). These program managers will prioritize requests based on business value and potential return on investment.
- **Data management**   Data modelers identify source systems and process improvements to improve data quality, DBAs tune the data warehouse, and ETL developers create and optimize load processes.
- **Business analysts**   Business analysts translate business needs into technical requirements and specifications or business process improvement, manage projects, and oversee quality assurance and support.
- **Complex analytics**   Data scientists and statisticians use statistical tools to create predictive models and to perform more advanced analytics.
- **Information delivery**   BI experts include people who create reports and dashboards and model metadata in their BI tool.

Drake Botello, BI/DW program manager at National Instruments, says that with this virtual team approach, the roles are clearer on who does what. It's also allowed them to evolve from a primarily reporting focus to a more sophisticated use of data and analytics.

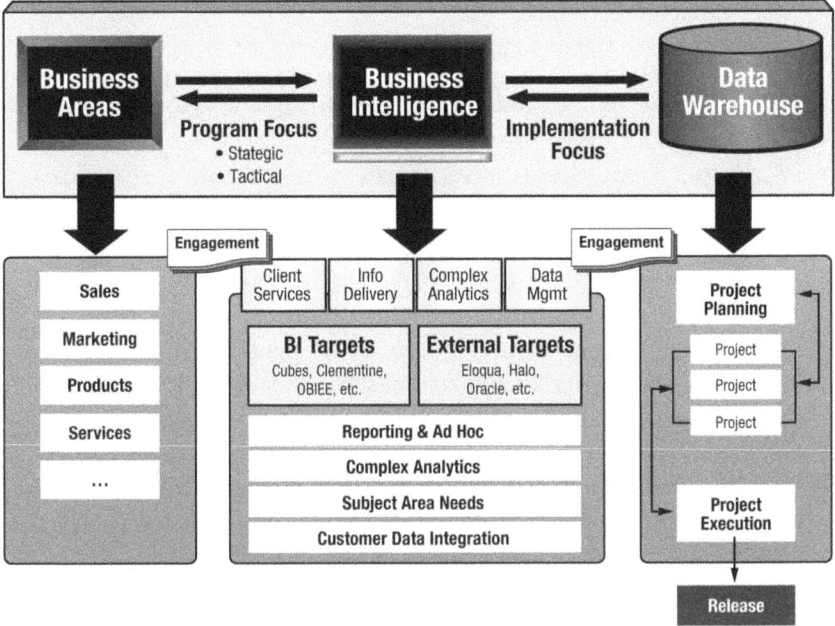

Figure 11-4 National Instruments virtual teams

Does the BICC Belong in IT?

A majority of the centralized BI teams report into IT, and whether or not this is a good fit organizationally depends on some of the discussion in Chapter 6 about the type of CIO your company has— technology focused or business minded. I've encountered some BI teams that report into another shared service such as finance or marketing. When the BI team reports directly into the CEO, then there is a higher degree of impact. Few companies are organized this way, though, with only 9 percent of Successful BI survey respondents having BI teams report directly to the CEO.

BICC Guiding Principles

Develop a vision for BI and establish guiding principles that all the stakeholders, steering committee members, project teams, and BICC can refer to. Use the following list as inspiration for developing your own principles:

(Continued)

- Business intelligence is a strategic asset that provides a competitive differentiator.
- The business will establish the priorities, and IT will deliver according to those priorities.
- Issues that cannot be resolved by the project team will be escalated to the steering committee.
- The BI team will strive to focus on the business value of business intelligence and not get sidetracked by technology for technology's sake.
- BI experts will borrow great ideas from people who have gone before us, garnering the best ideas from departmental innovations (otherwise known as no "not invented here" attitude).
- Data errors will be corrected at the source.
- Success will be measured according to perceived business impact, number of active users, and return on investment. These successes will be communicated and actively promoted.
- The BI team will build a portfolio of business anecdotes on how BI and big data have had an impact on the business.
- Services that can be shared and that provide economies of scale will be centralized, including hardware, software, policies and procedures, data acquisition, cleansing, and modeling. Customize those items in which there is a major difference in requirements and fulfilling those requirements adds value to the business.
- The BICC will promote a buy versus build mentality.
- Technology adoption will fall into the leading edge, not bleeding edge, category.

Funding for a BICC can be a point of contention. For example, a large aerospace manufacturer began moving to a BICC model in 2004. While there are 34 employees in the BICC, there is only a budget for 11 resources. The remaining staff get billed to specific BI projects. The leader of the BICC says, "It's an ongoing process of trying to strike the right balance of teaching people to fish versus doing the projects for them. Our goal is to help our IT counterparts within the businesses to succeed."[10]

Organizationally, support for BI training often comes from the BICC. The BICC may develop common training materials and select a vendor to deliver the training. Business subject matter experts may facilitate the data-specific training. In larger organizations, training may be coordinated via the human resources department.

The Best People

Organizing the BI team in a way that enables agile development (see Chapter 10) and stronger business alignment (Chapter 8) is important for a successful BI initiative. It's also important to ensure that the team is composed of the best people.

This may sound obvious. With the best people, a clear vision, and empowerment, you can accomplish anything, not just successful business intelligence! It's not that anyone sets out to hire mediocre people, right? In reality, though, attracting and keeping the best people is no small task. The job market for BI experts is extremely tight; employee turnover can be high, and sometimes the best people simply go to the highest bidder, or to whichever organization will most value their talents.

Having a successful BI initiative and a culture that fosters information sharing and fact-based decisions can further help companies attract the best people. Eric Bachenheimer, director of client account management at Emergency Medical Associates (EMA), joined EMA in 2004 and was previously an administrator at a New York hospital. Bachenheimer describes his initial reaction to EMA's BI application: "When first interviewing here, I saw a report and drooled! My hospital was struggling with this stuff. So I wanted to work for a company that is leading edge."

Professor Rosabeth Kanter of the Harvard Business School describes three mechanisms companies can use to ensure greater commitment in a tight labor market: meaning, membership, and mastery.[11]

- **Meaning** Ensuring the work has meaning to the company and to the world at large. This is one reason why it's important for technical experts to understand the business value of what they are building and that success stories are actively promoted (see Chapter 13).
- **Membership** Demonstrate concern for the individual and ensure they feel they are an integral part of the team. One way companies can foster a greater sense of membership is to celebrate major BI milestones, whether it's by giving out silver dollars or throwing a party.
- **Mastery** The ability for employees to enjoy challenging work, gain new skills, and contribute to the future. This last dimension of ensuring commitment can be a challenge with BI when an overemphasis on the latest technology can distract from the business focus of the BI project. New expertise, though, can come from working with different business units and ensuring a clear career path.

Attracting the best people and keeping the BI team motivated are only possible when the importance of BI is recognized by senior management. When it's not, the best BI people will leave.

BI Team Leaders as Level 5 Leaders

Some of the organizational concepts covered in this chapter become increasingly important with larger companies and more complex deployments. The BI director plays a pivotal role in evangelizing BI to business leaders, maintaining positive team morale, and ensuring a steady flow of deliverables. (Note: The precise title for this person will vary company to company. I am referring to data warehouse managers, directors of business analysis, data managers, and so on, collectively as "BI director.") In small to mid-size businesses, the BI director is even more important because this may be the whole team or the director may have only a couple of full-time resources. Data modelers, report designers, and so on, may all be outsourced or supplemented with interim consulting services.

As I interviewed sponsors, users, and BI directors from multiple companies, people often attributed their BI success to the BI director, particularly in the smaller firms. What I found most interesting is the way these smaller companies described their BI directors; it was not an autocratic leadership style that led them to adopt business intelligence, nor do these directors want too much credit for their contribution. Instead, there is a degree of humility about the role they have played in their company's BI success. I started to think of these BI directors as what author Jim Collins describes as level 5 leaders in *Good to Great* (HarperBusiness, 2001).

Collins describes a level 5 leader as "an individual who blends extreme personal humility with intense professional will . . . Level 5 leaders channel their ego needs away from themselves and into the larger goal of building a great company. It's not that level 5 leaders have no ego or self-interest. Indeed they are incredibly ambitious—but their ambition is first and foremost for the institution, not for themselves."[12] In the case of level 5 BI leaders, the ambition is for the success of the BI project and the vision for how it can add value to the company.

At one point, I was concerned my admiration for Collins's work was skewing my perception, that this phenomenon was perhaps not as big a driver of success as I was making it. But then I spoke to Dave Walker, the vice president of operations at 1-800 CONTACTS, who declared that one of the three key reasons for their BI success rests with their data warehouse manager, Jim Hill.[13] "Before Jim joined the company, everything was just queries. You might take cookies with you to the IT group depending on how badly you needed something. Jim established a discipline and vision." I challenged Walker, arguing that anyone can come in and establish a greater sense of discipline. Walker was insistent that not all leaders are like Jim Hill. "He has an air of approachability, an air of competency, but he's very humble. He just wants to dig in and has an amazing service attitude. Jim will take our ideas and amplify them. He interjects energy into all these projects and is so engaging in meetings. His attitude has trickled down to his team." Walker then concluded, "He really is one of those leaders in that book . . . that book . . ." I waited, not wanting to put words in his mouth. Finally, I asked, "You don't mean a level 5 leader in *Good to Great*, do you?" He did! So there you have it:

> The most successful BI deployments, particularly in small to mid-sized companies, have BI directors who exhibit the characteristics of level 5 leaders, those who blend personal humility with professional will to focus not on their personal gain, but rather, on ensuring the success of the BI efforts for the value of the company.

Best Practices for Successful Business Intelligence

Organizational issues can hinder or accelerate successful business intelligence. To accelerate success

- Use departmental BI initiatives for inspiration and innovations when your company first embarks on business intelligence. Even in the early stages, keep a view on the future and consider how the departmental initiative will evolve into an enterprise effort. Recognize the reasons that departments want to do their own BI projects and address them; remove the arguments against an enterprise solution, the prime one being the time it takes to deliver capabilities.
- Establish a BI steering committee composed of senior executives from all major business units and functions who use business intelligence.
- Share resources and best practices in a central way that provides economies of scale. Establish a Business Intelligence Competency Center, whether virtual or physical.

- Embed business people within the BICC, or embed BI experts within individual business units while ensuring a pool of common expertise.
- Don't underestimate the job protection issues and personal agendas you will encounter in changing organizational structures.
- Hire, motivate, and retain the best people.
- In small and mid-sized companies, look for BI directors who exemplify the characteristics of level 5 leaders.

Chapter 12

The Right BI Tool for the Right User

It was 1994, the early days of the BI market, and the Dow BI tool selection process was contentious from the start. One of the main justifications for the Global Reporting Project was to reduce the cost of multiple regional homegrown systems. We had a "buy not build" strategy and agreed to be "leading edge, not bleeding edge." And yet, everything about BI and data warehousing in the early 1990s was bleeding edge. The market was highly fragmented, with no clear market leader and solutions mainly from start-ups. The current market for big data analytic tools is reminiscent of those early years in BI.

Within the Global Reporting Project, we formed a BI tool selection team that was charged with gathering and ranking requirements, conducting proof of concepts, and recommending standards. Technical experts and end users were jointly involved in the process, a best practice by today's standards but a somewhat novel approach then. We consulted leading analyst firms, one of which suggested that we take a "throwaway" mentality, as whatever we selected would be superseded within two years by solutions from Microsoft. Having gotten burned by the IBM OS/2 demise beneath Microsoft Windows, we did not want to underestimate Microsoft's force in the BI market. (At the time, Microsoft BI or modules like Analysis Services, Reporting Services, and PowerPivot did not exist.)

We attended software industry conferences, such as CeBIT in Germany and Business Intelligence Forum in England (TDWI—The Data Warehousing Institute—also did not yet exist), searching for solutions. Many of the leading products today were not available then or were in 1.0 releases. A solution installed in Dow Elanco (a subsidiary of Dow Chemical in Indiana, now Dow AgroSciences) caught our attention. That was another guiding principle—"not invented here" mentality was not allowed. We would borrow great ideas from any region or subsidiary who had come before us. Dow Elanco had BusinessObjects installed for a couple hundred users. At the time, Business Objects was a privately held company that few had heard of and was viewed as a risky investment.

We gave preference to solutions from vendors with whom we had relationships, which included Oracle, our database standard, and SAP, our enterprise resource planning (ERP) standard. After a few months of research, demos, and prototypes, we ultimately recommended two standards: BusinessObjects for query and reporting to answer "what" was going on in the business and Cognos PowerPlay for OLAP to discover "why" performance appeared a certain way. We had intended BusinessObjects to be for power users for self-service BI and Cognos PowerPlay for managers who were accustomed to guided screens and drill-downs of the decision support systems. At the time, the difference between these two products and vendors was quite distinct, an easy positioning that no longer exists today.

As soon as we published our recommendations, they met with resistance on all sides. The commercial users declared Cognos PowerPlay was too hard for them. They wanted a custom solution like SUCCESS (see Chapter 5). The finance users wanted to know what our transition plans were for their thousands of FOCEXECs (files created with Information Builders Focus, a fourth-generation programming language, or 4GL, that was then the primary method for creating ad hoc reports). Our explanation that these FOCEXEC reports would have to be rewritten anyway as the regional systems were being phased out didn't offset user outrage. Further inciting dissatisfaction, the Global Reporting Project manager said we only had time and resources to deploy one of the two tools recommended. PowerPlay's MOLAP architecture (see Chapter 3) made IT balk: IT could not guarantee data integrity if data had to be replicated into a proprietary storage mechanism. As discussed in Chapter 10, the manager might have been right in trying to manage scope to stay on time and within budget, but it didn't satisfy requirements for some very important and vocal stakeholders. It seemed the only adequate buy-in we got was from the database and ERP standard leaders.

As with politics, BI selections require consensus building along the way. No matter how sound your recommendations or that they may be in the best interests of the company, if you fail to build consensus with a *wider* constituency along the way, your recommendations will be rejected out of fear, uncertainty, job protection, and other political reasons.

As the marketing users were not satisfied with the Global Reporting Project's decision to support only one tool, they did what many lines of business continue to do today: They went out and bought their own BI solution and proceeded to deploy Cognos PowerPlay on their own. Germany and the polyurethane's business unit followed a similar path and continued to develop a custom solution with SUCCESS. This departmental initiative was highly successful—until the lead programmer left Dow. Employee departures and the inherent risk of an all-knowing, irreplaceable programmer are reasons I continue to have a strong "buy" mentality for BI software.

In 1996, just two years after our initial recommendations, when the arguments about which BI tool or tools to use would not subside, we embarked on yet another BI tool selection. The prediction that Microsoft would have a dominating solution had not yet come true, but one prediction had: Oracle had just acquired the OLAP vendor and product IRI Express. Yes! We really could have a single standard with both the relational database management system (RDBMS) and BI tool coming from the same vendor. We never got beyond the prototype. Ultimately, this second selection team reinforced the initial recommendation: The company needed multiple tools based on different user requirements and use cases. What was initially a backroom deployment of Cognos PowerPlay became an officially supported solution from the Global Reporting Project, in addition to BusinessObjects.

With the acquisition of Business Objects by SAP in 2008 and Dow's use of SAP as the ERP system, it has continued to invest more in SAP's BI technologies, including SAP BW for the packaged data warehouse and SAP BW Accelerator for an in-memory appliance. When Dow acquired Rohm and Haas in 2009, that company primarily used SAP BW and BEx as the company standards, so the BI platforms were compatible and brought additional expertise to Dow. More often with mergers and acquisitions, I've seen incompatible BI platforms brought together, and a company has to make hard decisions about running multiple BI platforms or disrupting what may have otherwise been a satisfied group of users.

Dow's BI tool strategy continues to be based on aligning the tool capabilities with the corresponding user requirements and use cases. SAS JMP has since been added to Dow's portfolio to provide users with visual predictive analysis capabilities, and Tableau for visual data discovery. Although Dow's BI tool decisions took place when the BI market was first emerging, the challenges Dow faced still hold true for many organizations. Market leadership and tool capabilities are in a constant state of flux. Where Dow has excelled is in ensuring the business value these tools provide remains the first priority.

The dynamics and decisions I face today with many BI teams are remarkably similar to my first major tool selection at Dow. Companies debate if they should deploy QlikView or Tableau, or ask why they need those tools in addition to their BI platform. Since they are upgrading major component X, they want to know the impact on BI tool strategy. The importance of the BI tool in turning data into insight has not waned in the last 30 years. Nor have the desire and angst to come up with a perfect, one-size-fits-all solution. However, with a greater realization of the business impact of BI, BI tool purchases are now treated more strategically. In addition, many companies are realizing that ease of use trumps sophisticated features in bringing BI to new classes of users.

The Importance of BI Tools

BI front-end tools seem to get the lion's share of attention from business users. IT may happily choose a data integration platform or analytic appliance, involving only technical experts in the evaluation, but when it comes to the front end, business users are at the forefront in defining requirements. These joint business–IT evaluations are less contentious than they once were, with both sides wanting the best tool: Easy to use, but scalable. Flexible, but ensuring consistent results. Visually appealing, but secure.

Providing users with a BI tool that facilitates data access, insight, and action is essential to successful business intelligence. Fail to do this and your data warehouse is a wasteland of bits and bytes. (See Chapter 2 for an explanation of technical components and Chapter 3 for BI front-end tools.) Contrary to widely held opinion, business users do not care *only* about BI front-end tools. In fact, on average, both IT personnel and business users alike agree that the information architecture and underlying data quality are important technical aspects in successful BI. However, the ability to access multiple data sources and easy-to-use BI tools are now considered slightly more important than data quality (see Figure 8-2 in Chapter 8).

I suspect the increase in importance of the BI tool is both a reflection of frustration with some BI tools and an acceptable level of satisfaction with other components in the information life cycle. When data quality and system stability are hugely problematic, a BI tool is not useful. When the data quality and system stability are good enough, then business users need to be able to get to the data, easily, and with flexibility. It's a little like Maslow's hierarchy of needs and air travel: Passengers may gripe about flight delays the most, but only after we have trusted that air travel is safe. As BI tools have matured, some have become more complex and less flexible. This is only in part due to software complexity, but also, to how IT and central BI teams organize around developing and deploying them. For example, if the BI team sets a policy stating that changes to a business view can only be implemented monthly, that is an organizational decision, not a software constraint.

In developing your company's BI tool portfolio, it's important to involve both business users and IT in the process. Consider your current needs as well as how you wish to evolve your capabilities.

"We let the user group select the tool, and the process was only facilitated by IT. When it came time to sign, it was the user selection team that signed the agreement, not IT. Total buy-in resulted."
—Karen Larson, senior director, IT, Lawson Products, Inc.

The Role of BI Standardization

With the plethora of BI tools now on the market and the degree to which individual departments and business units buy BI solutions, multiple front-end tools have only added to data chaos and multiple versions of the truth. A single, consistent data element in a data warehouse, say, revenue, can get further transformed, manipulated, massaged, and displayed in spreadsheets, report-based calculations, OLAP databases, dashboards, and so on. Revenue in one instance may be calculated on gross invoice amount; in another it could include adjustments for returns and discounts; and in another it may include bad debts. While lower cost of ownership is the main criterion for BI standardization, the ability to deliver a single version of truth is another important criterion. A single version of the truth requires consistent representation in BI tools, in addition to a common data architecture. As BI demand continues to outpace resources, standardization also means IT can provide better support for fewer tools, an aspect that benefits both IT and the business users.

BI standardization should not be confused with a one-size-fits-all approach. A business analyst who is a power user does not have the same functionality requirements as a front-line worker who may only need a visual gadget of a smaller amount of information.

Historically, companies had to buy multiple BI front-end tools from multiple vendors because no single vendor offered the full spectrum of tools described in Chapter 3. Increasingly, vendors do offer a spectrum of tools in a complete suite or BI platform. These integrated suites provide IT the benefit of having one business view to maintain, on a common set of servers, with common security. It offers users the benefit of seamlessly navigating from a dashboard, through to a report, to a business query. That's the theory! Some products and vendors are already there; for others, it's an ongoing vision.

When you think of BI standardization, also recognize that consulting companies and vendors may advocate standardizing beyond just the front-end components to include the back-end components such as the extract, transform, and load (ETL) tool, data quality tool, data warehouse platform, and big data solutions (as shown in Figure 12-1 and discussed in Chapters 2 and 3). How much you pursue this broader standardization effort depends largely on where you are in your BI deployment, in which vendors you have already made investments, and if your company pursues a "best-of-breed" strategy versus a single-vendor solution.

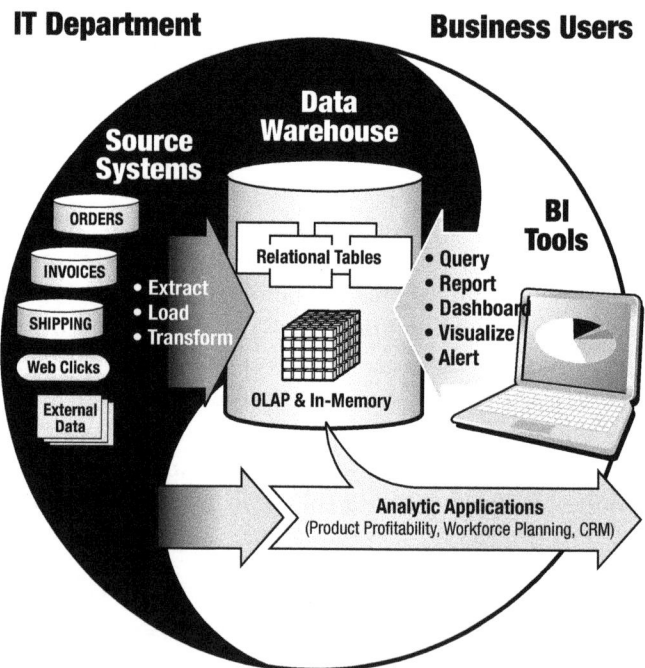

Figure 12-1   Major components in the business intelligence life cycle

At this time, I more often see a multivendor approach across the entire BI life cycle, particularly in larger companies, but a greater degree of standardization within the BI tools space. In other words, companies may buy multiple modules within a BI suite or platform that is composed of business query, production reporting, dashboards, and so on, but will buy from a different vendor for ETL, the data warehouse platform, or the source systems. For example, Netflix DVD business unit uses Ab Initio for ETL, Teradata for its data warehouse, and MicroStrategy for its BI platform. Likewise, Medtronic uses a combination of ETL tools with Informatica and SAP Data Services, for the data warehouse Oracle, for big data SAP Hana, and the BI platform SAP BusinessObjects.

While companies will mix and match components across the BI lifecycle, within the BI front-end tools, there is a greater degree of standardization toward a predominant standard. This is a change since 2007, before significant industry consolidation and a greater BI prominence from mega vendors. If you have multiple tools in any single sub-BI tool segment, such as multiple production reporting tools (such as Microsoft Reporting Services and Crystal Reports), rationalizing some of this duplication should be your first standardization priority.

NOTE I refer to a BI *tool* as any front-end component, as some people refer to the whole BI infrastructure as "BI." Vendors may refer to their product(s) as a BI platform, suite, or toolset. I use the term *module* to refer to a distinct set of capabilities. A module may be a component within the BI platform, or it may be a stand-alone tool, with a distinct interface and user license. Which modules are part of a BI platform or stand-alone vary from one vendor to the next.

When you read of companies having seemingly outrageous numbers—as many as 13 BI tools—such numbers often reflect an overstatement, as they are talking about the number of individual modules or components of what might be a single BI platform. If you consider all the modules described in Chapter 3, then you have potentially ten tools right there. The question, then, is how many of those ten modules can you buy from a single BI vendor?

Table 12-1 shows a slight majority of companies (56 percent) use multiple BI front-end modules from a *single* vendor versus multiple modules from *multiple* vendors. This is an increase from the number of companies with a predominant standard in 2007 (42 percent). If the company has standardized on a single vendor by department or line of business (15 percent), then in total 71 percent of companies are proactively managing

BI Tool Approach	Percentage of Survey Respondents	
	2007	2012
Mostly custom BI front ends	17%	5%
No standard—multiple modules from multiple vendors	41%	15%
Standard by tool module		9%
Standard by business unit or department		15%
Predominant BI standard, primarily from a single vendor	42%	56%

Table 12-1   How Companies Manage Their BI Tools *(In the 2007 survey, we did not ask if BI tool standards were by business unit or tool module.)*

their BI tool portfolios. A minority of survey respondents deploy custom front ends as their primary tool approach (5 percent), which is a decline from 2007.

For a while, it seemed that companies were trying to pursue exclusive standards, but this approach seems to have subsided in response to sometimes better solutions from specialty vendors or distinct requirements for particular business units. Of those that have a predominant standard, 38 percent of the survey respondents say it's an exclusive standard. The successful BI case studies reflect a similar pattern to the survey results (see Table 12-2); some of the case study companies have standardized on a single BI vendor, and some have partnered with multiple BI vendors.

While it is clearly harder to switch standardization strategies and vendors mid-deployment, the survey results indicate the BI tool approach plays a role in successful business intelligence. As shown in Figure 12-2, 68 percent of the respondents who describe their deployment as having significant business impact have a predominant BI standard. Contrast this with those who classify their deployment as a failure, where the percentage standardizing is much lower (31 percent). In addition, for customers who said their BI deployment had little to no impact, there was a greater reliance on custom development.

Figure 12-3 shows an alternative view of the survey results according to the approach used to manage the BI tool portfolio. Those with a predominant standard have the highest portion of significant impact, whereas those who have no standard at all or rely on custom development have the highest failure or only slight impact.

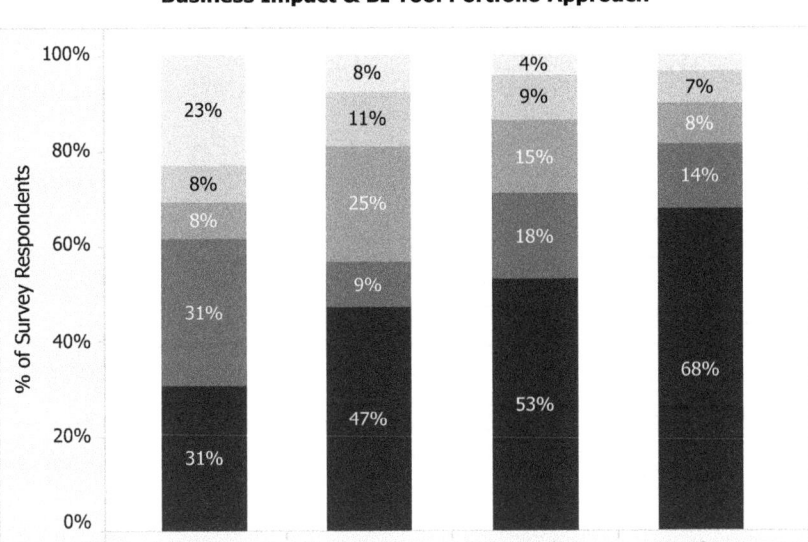

Business Impact & BI Tool Portfolio Approach

Approach

⬚ Custom
▒ Standard per major tool category
▨ No standard
▦ Departmental or business unit standard
■ Predominant standard

Figure 12-2   Companies deriving greater impact from BI also have a predominant BI standard.

> Failed BI deployments have a higher rate of primarily custom applications. The operative word here is *primarily*. Custom applications can complement a purchased BI solution, but they should not be the primary or exclusive way of delivering business intelligence.

In assessing the BI tool portfolio approach at Successful BI Case Studies, several companies have solutions from multiple BI vendors, but none reported overlapping functionality. Another interesting aspect was that several of the companies changed their preferred BI tool early in the course of their BI deployment and attributed greater BI success to that change. The reasons for the change varied, including licensing costs, vendor complacency, and need for a more flexible solution. Fortunately, such changes were made early in the BI life cycle, when adoption was limited.

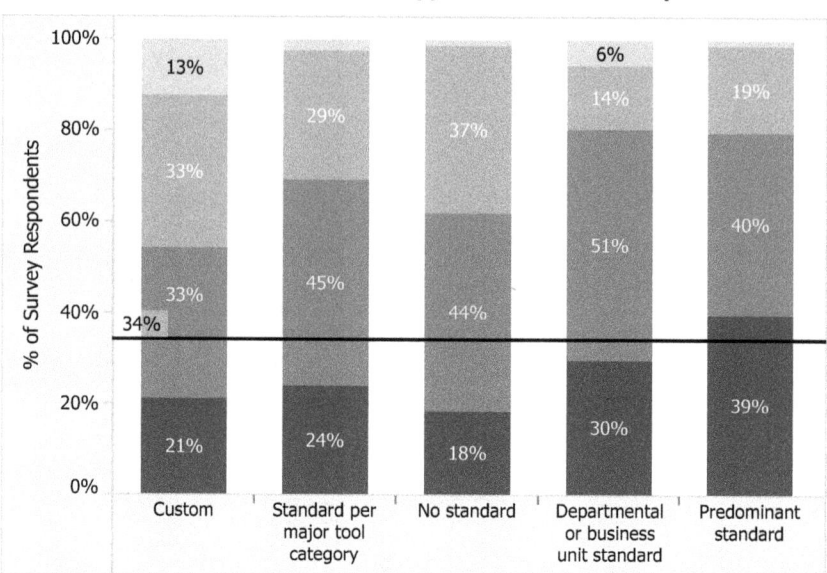

BI Tool Portfolio Approach & Business Impact

Business impact
- Not at all
- Slightly
- Somewhat
- Signficant

Figure 12-3 Companies with no BI standard have less business impact.

The only BI module where companies seem to consistently use multiple tools from different vendors is for advanced analytics. In this regard, the role of the data scientist requires an arsenal of capabilities. I also think that companies can handle multiple standards in this segment because they are investing in and recruiting existing expertise, where available talent is in short supply. For example, if a company hires a statistician with deep expertise in SAS, they will not insist that the statistician relearn IBM SPSS simply because that is the company standard.

Some other important themes to consider from each of the case study companies:

- As the scale of a deployment increases, switching BI platform vendors is hard. This is rarely undertaken unless there has been a major change in technology or business environment, such as a merger and acquisition or extreme dissatisfaction with an incumbent vendor.
- As BI tool capabilities evolve, successful case study companies have expanded their portfolios. The expansion has been primarily in newer

BI tool segment areas, such as visual data discovery, Software as a Service, and big data analytics.

- Custom development is used on a limited basis to supplement out-of-the-box capabilities. Rarely are all capabilities coded from scratch.
- Even though companies have standardized on BI platforms and tools, they continue to stay abreast of new releases from other vendors, both from direct competitors and start-ups. Continued market awareness ensures their BI environment continues to evolve in robustness and encourages the incumbent BI vendor to be responsive and innovative.

The Right Tool for the Right User

A common misconception about BI standardization is the assumption that all users must use the same tool. It would be a mistake to pursue this strategy. Instead, successful BI companies use the *right tool for the right user—and the right use case.* For a senior executive, the right tool might be a dashboard. For a power user, it might be a business query tool. For a call center agent, it might be a custom application or a BI gadget embedded in an operational application. A salesperson or store manager will want the gadget or dashboard on a tablet or smartphone.

Use the marketing concept of customer segmentation to identify and understand the various user groups within your company. A simple starting point of classifying your users is recognizing that there are two main groups: information consumers and information producers. Figure 12-4 shows various spectrums of users.

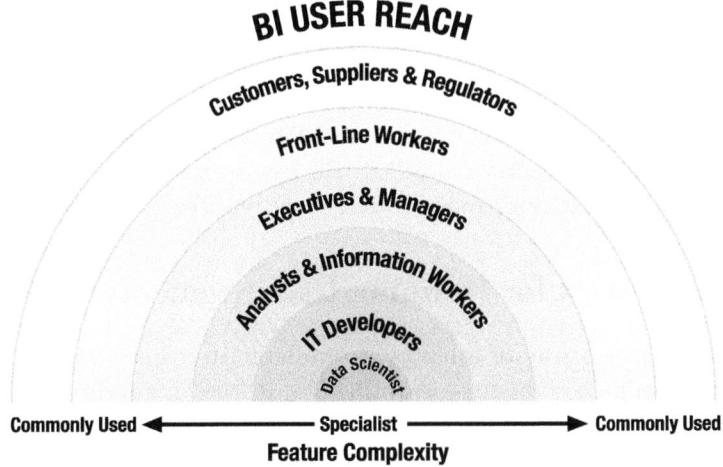

Figure 12-4   Range of BI users

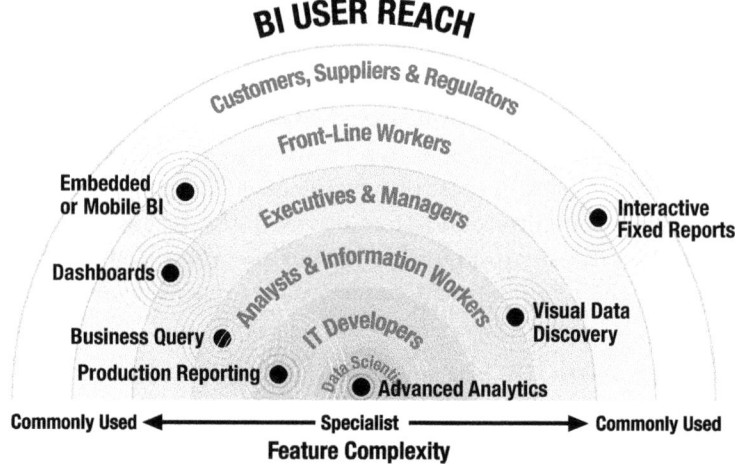

Figure 12-5 Different users require different tool capabilities.

Once you have refined your user segments, you can match the BI tool module with the appropriate user group. Figure 12-5 shows how different user segments require different tool capabilities. For clarity's sake, I have not listed all the potential BI modules in Figure 12-5 and have only included the most frequently used ones. (Visit www. BIScorecard.com for a complimentary PowerPoint version of the spectrum with modules listed for each leading BI vendor.)

Each module has its "sweet spot" as indicated by the dark dot, but the positioning can certainly span into other user segments as conveyed by the concentric circles. Users also may require different tools for a particular use case or application. For example, as a small business owner, I may use a visual data discovery tool when I am trying to explore and discover from where my customers are learning about us—through TDWI, Google, a conference, or a book. However, as a consumer, when I want to view my credit card bill, I will use an interactive fixed report to compare spending this month versus last month.

Characteristics for Defining User Segments

Segmentation is a way of looking at one large user base—for example, all employees in a company—and dividing it into smaller groups. Each segment, or smaller group, has similar characteristics, needs, and desired benefits. Segmentation provides a way of better understanding your users and why their requirements are different. Following are some characteristics that will help you segment potential business intelligence users. Use the self-assessment worksheet in the following table to develop your own user segments.

Business Unit, Department, or Function						
	Executives	Managers	Inside Staff	Field Staff	Customers	Suppliers
Percentage or number of users per segment						
Frequency and nature of decision-making						
Predictability of information requirements						
Analytic job content						
Need for detailed data (vs. aggregated)						
Need for multiple data sources and subject areas						
Data literacy						
Familiarity with source systems						
Technical literacy						
Spreadsheet expertise						
Web knowledge						
Use of smartphones for data access						
Use of tablet devices for data access						
Degree of travel						

H = High, M = Medium, L = Low

Frequency and Nature of Fact-Based Decisions

The types of decisions supported by business intelligence can be classified into the following:

- **Strategic decisions** of longer-term consequences with broader implications. Such decisions are made on a less frequent basis, perhaps yearly or longer. Some strategic decisions include whether to acquire a particular company, launch a new product, change suppliers, or enter a new market.
- **Tactical** decisions are made on a more frequent basis, weekly or monthly. They may include planning for a plant outage, increasing capacity, changing distribution routes, and optimizing pricing policies. Historically, many of the business intelligence initiatives have focused on tactical decision-makers.
- **Operational** decisions are more detailed in nature and may affect a smaller number of people than strategic decisions. Can an order be sourced from a particular warehouse? Should a loan application be approved or denied? A student shows an excessive number of absences—should we meet with the parents? A larger number of people make many more operational decisions on a daily basis than people who make strategic decisions. Brenda Jansen, director of information systems at Energizer Holdings (maker of Energizer batteries, Schick razors, Banana Boat suntan lotion, and other consumer products), refers to this group of users as the "difference makers" because of the big impact these thousands of individual decisions have in aggregate.[1]

In *Smart Enough Systems,* authors Neil Raden and James Taylor use the chart in Figure 12-6 to describe the relationship between the value of the decisions made and the frequency of those decisions.[2] Figure 12-6 clearly shows that any individual operational decision taken in isolation does not have a major impact on a company's performance in aggregate. Yet as the case study companies demonstrate and as the *Smart Enough Systems* authors advocate, these "difference makers" have a profound impact when viewed in total. As 1-800 CONTACTS explained in Chapter 9, they saw an immediate lift in sales when they enabled the call center dashboard. Prior to the call center dashboard, it might have been all too easy to assume that the decisions of a single call center agent didn't have such a big impact. They do!

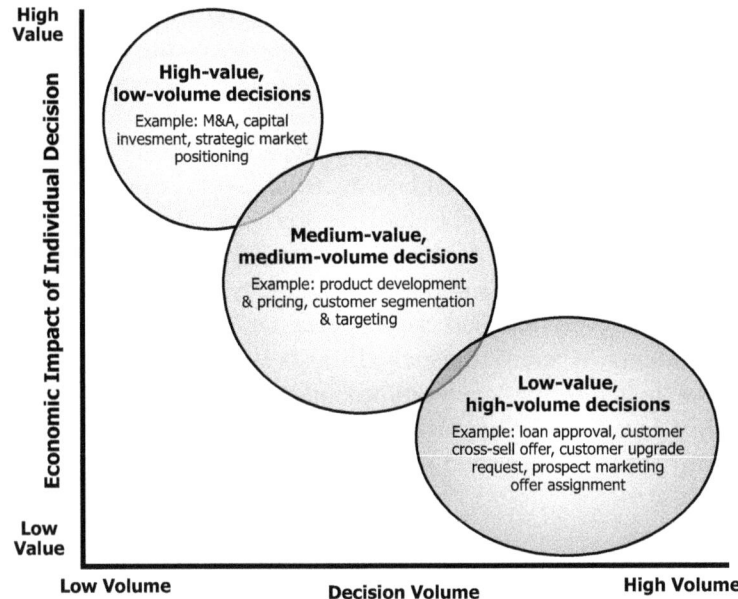

High Value

Economic Impact of Individual Decision

High-value, low-volume decisions
Example: M&A, capital invesment, strategic market positioning

Medium-value, medium-volume decisions
Example: product development & pricing, customer segmentation & targeting

Low-value, high-volume decisions
Example: loan approval, customer cross-sell offer, customer upgrade request, prospect marketing offer assignment

Low Value

Low Volume   Decision Volume   High Volume

Figure 12-6   The value and volume of different kinds of decisions

Predictability of Information Requirements

The degree to which information requirements are predictable is somewhat related to the type of decision (strategic, tactical, operational), but also to the application. When business intelligence is used for management and control purposes, information needs may be static. The BI application (whether an individual report, dashboard, or widget) should provide an overview as to the health of the business or organization, efficiency, or progress toward a goal. When something is trending in a negative direction, then the information requirements will change and demand more exploratory capabilities. Big data applications often start out exploratory and then may get instantiated in a fixed report or dashboard. Information needs for operational BI users also may be relatively predictable. When the requirements are predictable, modules such as dashboards, standard reports, or custom-built applications are ideal.

Job Level

A user's job level will affect the breadth of data the user wants to access and the level of detail. Executive-level jobs may need a broad set of data but without a lot of detail. *Access* to information may be critical, but *analyzing* the data is a minor aspect of these jobs, making this segment of users ideal candidates for dashboards with key performance indicators. Mid-level jobs may still need a broad set of data but with more detail. The combination of broad data requirements and more detailed data may make it hard to deliver only dashboards. Such workers may need access to multiple dashboards and standard reports with slice-and-dice ability, what-if analysis, and so on. At the other end of the spectrum, office staff such as accounts payable clerks or customer service representatives may want to see only very detailed data. A teacher may want detailed data on their students, whereas a principal wants the summary view, at least initially. As their information requirements are narrow, these users may need only a few standard reports with interactive prompts or a custom application, perhaps integrated within an operational application.

Job Function

You also can segment users according to job function. For example, supply chain users will all have similar information needs, which will be different from the information needs of users in the finance department. Requirements for particular features also may vary by function: Consider how many spreadsheet power users there are in any finance department. This group of users then may not care about dashboards as much as they care about spreadsheet integration. Marketing personnel will have different information requirements, and with respect to functionality, they may ask for things such as predictive analysis or Microsoft PowerPoint integration that other groups have not requested. Sales personnel may put a higher priority on support for mobile and tablet devices.

Degree of Analytic Job Content

Some jobs require a significant amount of data analysis. The analytic component also may relate to either the job level or the job function, or sometimes to both. For example, financial analysts and economic evaluators may be fairly senior in a business; these jobs have a high analytic component. These are the number crunchers who will work intensely with business intelligence tools. They understand the different data nuances and even the potential data sources. Statisticians and data scientists are even more sophisticated users, able to create their own queries in SQL, MapReduce, MDX, or whatever language is required.

It's easy to assume that these people are your only users, since they may have solutions implemented first, complain loudest when something is wrong, live and die by access to information, and control the information flow to secondary users. According to the Successful BI survey, this user segment shows the highest BI usage rate. Remember, though, that not everyone can spend all day collecting, manipulating, and exploring data. Some users, such as managers and supervisors, need access to standard reports and dashboards simply to know what is going on at a glance. They may only log in to a BI tool for ten minutes a day (or week) just to make sure the business is running smoothly. When the information indicates a problem area, it may not be their job to sift through the data to identify the underlying cause. Instead, they may call the business or financial analyst to figure out why there is a problem.

In BI, there has sometimes been the tendency to assume all users should become BI experts. It's a profound difference to *empower* a user—to provide them with easy tools to access and explore information when they need to—and an altogether different scenario to assume accessing and analyzing data is their primary job.

Users whose job content requires a fair bit of data analysis often demand more features and functions. Do not let their demands fool you into thinking all your users need these advanced capabilities. As you segment your users, recognize these differences in analytic abilities and job requirements.

Level of Data Literacy

Data literacy and technical literacy are two entirely different things. I may be technically literate, but if you ask me to decipher the meaning of baseball statistics, I'm clueless, much to my technical editor's chagrin (RBIs maybe, but ERA and WHIP, forget it!); I don't know the data! Corporate data also has its nuances with varying definitions depending on the context. Source system users and users whose jobs have a high analytic content may understand the data well and have a high level of data literacy. Certain users may understand the finer points of "revenue" (is it invoiced amount, net of returns, and so on?). Other users may not understand these nuances. In this regard, how you deploy particular BI modules will influence your success. If you give users with low data literacy access to a business query tool and they create incorrect queries because they didn't understand the different ways revenue could be calculated, the BI tool will be perceived as delivering bad data.

ERP or Source System Use

Some of your users may also enter data into the transaction or ERP system. Regardless of whether your company uses a BI tool directly against the transaction system or an ERP-populated data warehouse, these users will be more familiar with the precise meanings of individual data elements. At the same time, dimensional groupings and hierarchies that don't exist in the source system may be a completely new concept. These users may need additional explanation as to why there is a data warehouse, a BI platform, and how the data has been transformed.

Technical Literacy

As technology has become more prevalent in everyday life, from smartphones, to tablets, to streaming movies and TV shows, to the Web, the level of technical literacy has increased. Despite technology's prevalence, there are still some users who are less technically proficient. This can be dependent on age, education, and socioeconomic factors. Potential BI users who have worked with personal computers and the Internet since their inception will greet business intelligence differently than those who did not. Users who primarily surf the Web or access mobile apps but who are not proficient with spreadsheets fall somewhere in the middle. As discussed in Chapter 1, the changing workforce demographics mean that technical literacy today is much higher than in the early 1990s, when business intelligence as an industry first emerged. Information sharing is much more prevalent, yet boundaries still exist, and less tech-savvy employees may greet BI either with a degree of trepidation or a view that BI doesn't benefit them. As discussed in Chapter 9, you need to find BI's relevance, the "What's in it for me (WIFM)?" Recognize that such users may need information to do their jobs, yet they may not see a BI application as their primary resource. These users may use only scheduled, e-mailed reports. In certain roles, such as a nurse in an emergency room, a teacher in a classroom, or a transportation manager in the warehouse, there is reliance on handwritten documents that have not been automated. Until such documents are digitized, such users will synthesize data manually, often at a glance, and may rely more on gut-feel decision-making when trying to aggregate information.

Even if you have previously tried to engage tech-wary users and were met with a lackluster response, try again. Technical and information literacy is evolutionary. BI tools have gotten significantly easier to use with more interface options to suit diverse user requirements, even for users with less affinity for information technology.

Level of Spreadsheet Usage

Spreadsheet users deserve their own segment and, thus, sometimes their own BI interface. These users are spreadsheet enthusiasts and think everything should be delivered in a spreadsheet. There are a number of reasons why users want all their data delivered via spreadsheets; some reasons are valid, and others less so (for more discussion on this, see www.BIScorecard.com, "Spreadsheet Integration Criteria"). If spreadsheet usage is high for a particular user segment, then you may deploy spreadsheet-based BI interfaces to this segment. These spreadsheet-based BI interfaces are a far cry from the far too prevalent approach of exporting data into a spreadsheet and the ensuing data chaos. Instead, users work within a spreadsheet and refresh the data live from the BI platform into the spreadsheet, preserving data integrity. For users who are not as savvy with spreadsheets, such an interface is not optimal for that segment.

Amount of Travel

Certain job types require more travel than others. Some users may access BI tools only from their desktop or a corporate browser; users who travel may want access via a smartphone, tablet device such as an iPad, or a notebook computer. Support for mobile capabilities within the BI tool will be important for this user segment.

Internal vs. External Users

Consider the different needs of employees of the company and regulators, suppliers, and customers that you may provide information to via an extranet. Internal employees may be allowed to access whatever software module you have licensed, whereas external customers and suppliers often will have more restrictions on content and functionality. External users have different requirements from your internal users. Authentication in large extranets can be one challenge if you will have thousands of potential extranet users.

The Most Successful BI Module

Figure 12-7 shows which front-end modules of a BI deployment survey respondents considered most successful. Within the survey, the list of available options was randomly ordered for each respondent to ensure that the order did not skew the rankings.

In some respects, the survey results did not surprise me in that standard reports and business query tools are some of the more mature BI interfaces. However, some vendors in emerging markets such as SaaS, visual data discovery, and advanced analytics will say that BI has failed—that these older tools are too inflexible. The survey results don't support those claims entirely. I see the difference in evolving BI beyond just straightforward access to solutions that provide greater insight and action, with less IT support. Compared to four other annual and bian- nual surveys I've run on this topic, 2012 was the first year that fixed reports was ranked number one. Arguably, not by a very large margin, but the movement is still noteworthy. It suggests to me that uncon- trolled access to data is not what users most want; they just want their data when they need it. If someone—whether central IT, central BICC, or a power user—is doing a better job of creating that fixed report, the business user is satisfied. Further, if that "fixed" report has some inter- activity, such as a sort or filter, that allows the information consumer to tweak it, then that is an acceptable degree of self-service.

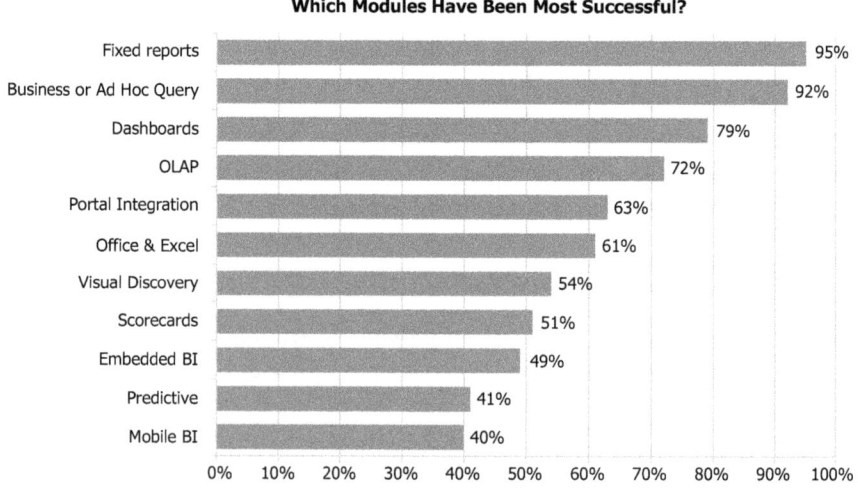

Figure 12-7 Overall, interactive fixed reports and business query tools are con- sidered the most successful aspect of a BI deployment.

The survey results for visual data discovery, with a total of 54 percent of companies having successful deployed these modules, seems high. This may be due to the fact that some survey respondents interpreted the module as any tool that supports creating charts, which is not how I define this market segment.

However, it's important to remember that the ranking of which BI modules have been most successful is according to user perception and not according to a consistent measure of the business contribution any given BI tool module has provided. In further exploring which modules were successfully deployed and which companies had the most significant business impact, there is a correlation with the use of scorecards, as shown in Figure 12-8. The survey did not distinguish between strategic scorecards that include strategy maps and business objects (refer to Chapter 3 for definitions) and scorecards that only include a list of key performance indicators. I suspect that the greater business impact from

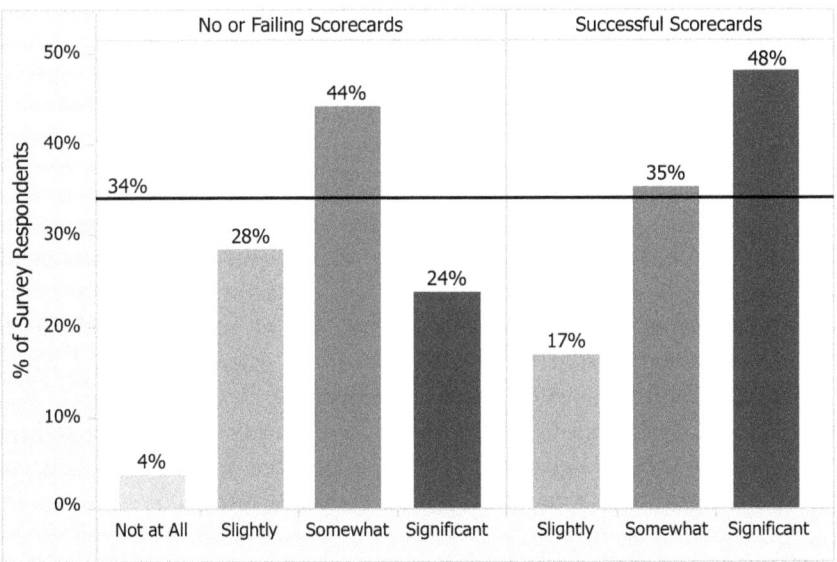

Figure 12-8   Companies that use scorecards have a high degree of business impact from BI.

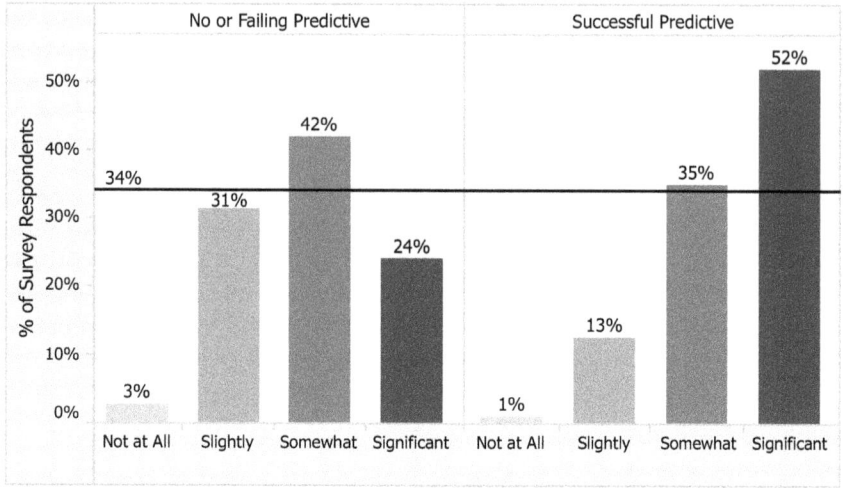

Figure 12-9   Companies who successfully deploy predictive analytics have the highest degree of significant business impact.

scorecards comes in part from ensuring the greatest business alignment. All of the Successful BI case study companies were using scorecards with key performance indicators (KPIs) but not strategy maps.

In evaluating the business impact and use of particular tool modules, it's noteworthy that the highest business impact occurred when predictive analytics was successfully deployed, as shown in Figure 12-9. And yet, this tool module had both limited adoption and high failure rates. Part of these challenges can be attributed to limited talent to exploit advanced analytics and the higher skillset required.

A Word about Microsoft Office Integration

Microsoft Excel is sometimes referred to as the leading BI tool, and yet, it ranked in the middle of tool modules, with only 61 percent of respondents selecting Microsoft Office integration and Excel as the most successful part of the BI deployment. I suspect this is in part because of the chaos that disconnected spreadsheets have wreaked on business intelligence efforts. The problem is not with spreadsheets per se, but rather with how they are used and not managed. Some of the biggest problems from spreadsheet errors include the following:

- Kodak had to restate earnings because of an incorrect number of 0's being entered into a spreadsheet.[3]
- Shares of RedEnvelope, a catalog gift company, fell 25 percent when cost of goods sold was incorrectly reported due to a spreadsheet error.[4]
- Utah Department of Education had a $25 million school funding error that led to the resignation of two officials.[5]
- The global financial crisis has in part been blamed on a spreadsheet formula that suggests that when debt exceeds 90 percent of gross domestic product (GDP), it threatens economic growth.[6] High debt levels in Europe and the United States have led to a number of austerity measures that some economists now think were too excessive, exacerbating the financial crisis.
- A number of companies have reported security breaches when laptops containing unencrypted spreadsheet data were stolen. This problem can also arise for any BI content, but better BI tools that support offline access also require an authentication process.

Despite these problems, BI users consistently say that a large percentage of ad hoc and standard BI reports are routinely exported to Excel. Of the successful BI case studies, Excel is widely used, but for routine reports, spreadsheets are used in a managed way in which data is updated from the BI platform rather than manually exported. The ability to integrate with Excel in this managed way has been an area of continuous improvement for many BI vendors.

Microsoft Office and BI integration has extended beyond spreadsheets to include PowerPoint and e-mail.

Best Practices for Successful Business Intelligence

For business users, the BI tool is the face of the entire business intelligence architecture. Fail to select an appealing and intuitive BI tool, and your technical architecture will remain unused. Deploy a good BI tool on top of messy data or an unreliable system, and the tool will be blamed for underlying difficulties. To ensure the BI tool facilitates rather than impedes your success

- Standardize on a BI platform to provide users with seamless navigation between BI modules. Supplement the BI platform with specialty products and custom applications on a limited basis only where the BI platform is lacking or has inferior capabilities.

- Be prepared to change BI platforms as you undergo mergers and acquisitions, requirements changes, or you gain a greater understanding of which capabilities and vendors meet your company's needs.
- Do not constantly change products and vendors only for technology's sake, as BI vendors innovate at different rates, and vendors may leapfrog each other in capabilities for any individual module. *Do* switch vendors if your BI tool is largely shelfware and if the lack of capabilities or the right interface have been a deterrent to greater BI success.
- Segment your users to understand their unique requirements, and deploy the correct BI module for that group of users.
- Evolve your BI tool portfolio as technology changes and new modules emerge.

Chapter 13

Other Secrets to Success

The preceding chapters highlight the nine most important organization-al and technical aspects that catapult companies to greater BI success and bigger business impact. Aspects in this chapter are not as significant but they are common themes that warrant attention: innovation, pro-moting the BI application, training, and smart use of graphics.

Innovation

Technology is constantly changing. When the first edition of this book was published in 2007, cloud computing had little to no presence in the BI space, big data was not a mainstream concept, and Hadoop had only just been created at Yahoo!. The iPad had not yet been invented, and mobile BI, at best, was an e-mail alert on a BlackBerry, perhaps with a static image of a report.

BI capabilities and user requirements will evolve over time, with technology and analytic maturity. The more successful companies will ensure that their BI teams will innovate to leverage these new capabili-ties. This can be a challenge, though, when BI teams are more project focused and when BI teams are underfunded and understaffed, a prob-lem in 44 percent of companies surveyed.

Most often, a BI innovation is funded by a particular business unit or project that sees value in the technology. For example, this was the case with Medtronic's use of SAP Hana for the Global Complaint Handling System. Likewise, when Dow wanted its sales force to use mobile BI and mobile apps were immature, the company turned to custom-developed HTML5 apps.

Some companies tend to be more innovative than others. This is due partly to the company culture (discussed in Chapter 6) and partly to the industry in which the company operates. Netflix, for example, operates in an industry with new and rapidly changing delivery models, as does

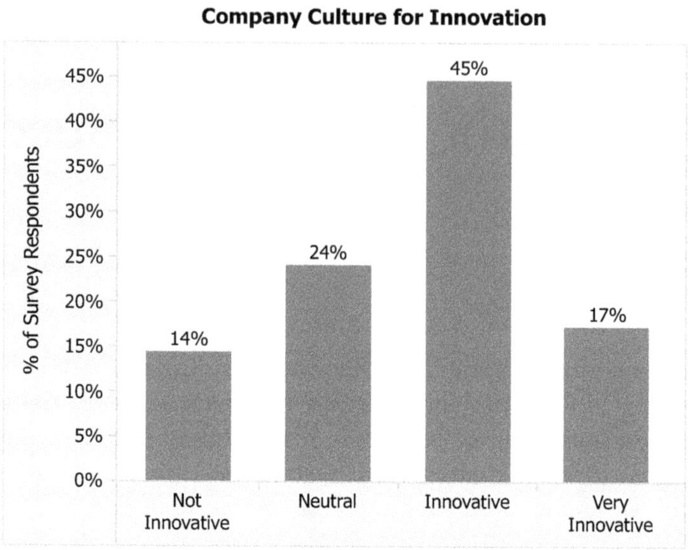

Company Culture for Innovation

Figure 13-1   The majority of companies say they are innovative.

gaming company King.com. As shown in Figure 13-1, the majority of companies surveyed describe themselves as innovative and constantly looking for ways to do things better, with 17 percent saying they are *very* innovative. The not innovative companies are in the minority at 14 percent, and those who were neutral in their self-assessment are 24 percent. There were some interesting trends by world region and company size. Canadian respondents were less innovative (26 percent were not innovative, and only 4 percent were very innovative). In Latin America, only 8 percent of respondents described their companies as very innovative. In terms of company size, smaller companies are the most innovative, with 28 percent of companies with fewer than 100 employees describing themselves as very innovative.

Innovation and business impact have a strong relationship, as shown in Figure 13-2. Of the companies who described their culture as very innovative, 59 percent also have a significant business impact from BI (versus the industry average of 34 percent). Meanwhile, companies that described themselves as not at all innovative had the lowest BI impact.

Beyond a "first project to use" approach to innovation, companies can foster BI innovation by establishing a BI lab. The BI lab is charged with investigating new technologies and conducting proofs of concept (POCs). Some of the POCs may never materialize into real applications, and it's important that such POCs be allowed also to fail. One company

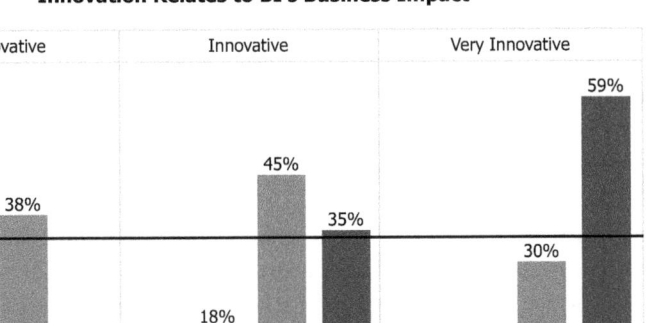

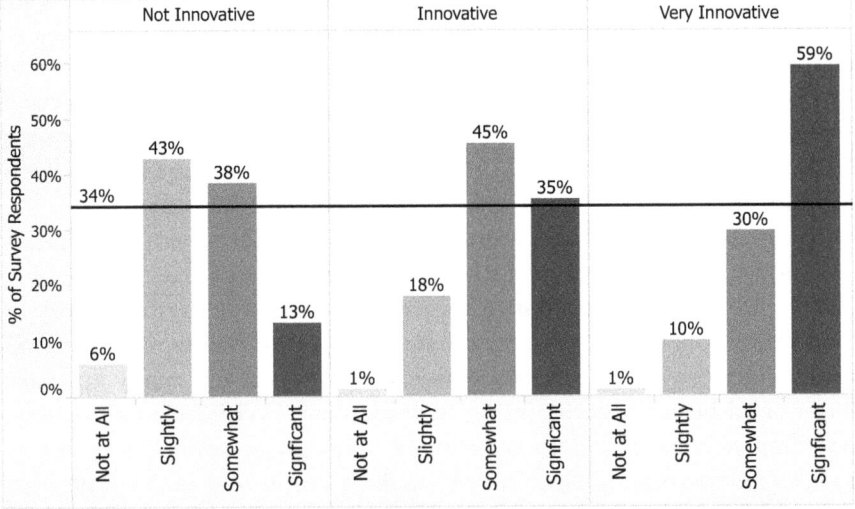

Figure 13-2   Innovation and BI business impact are related.

that uses the concept of a BI lab is USAA, a $22 billion financial services and insurance firm that serves military families. It consistently receives *Computerworld's* annual awards for the best places to work in IT and is a TDWI Best Practices award winner. For every dollar spent in IT, 50 percent is spent on new functionality.[1] The BI Lab brings together the concepts of agile development and co-location (discussed in Chapter 10), using subsets of data to prototype new applications and technologies. According to CTO Rickey Burks and Charles Thomas, vice president of research and analytics, the concept of the BI lab has strengthened the business–IT relationship, improved time to value, and resulted in better BI solutions.[2]

Medtronic also has the concept of an innovation group that is more broadly focused than BI. One of the projects out of the innovation group is a concept of The Hospital of the Future that combines technology, data, and customer partnerships to improve care, increase efficiencies, and ultimately reduce the cost of care. In discussing obtaining funding for the innovation group, CIO Mike Hedges acknowledges that if he had asked the line-of-business leaders to fund it up front as only a conceptual idea, it's unlikely he would have gotten the approval. Sometimes it's necessary to show the idea and the possible business value before getting broader funding, explains Hedges. With The Hospital of the Future, doctors, patients, and Medtronic device experts can collaborate in real time via video conferencing to determine the best device or medical approach. Doctors explain a procedure to a patient via a touchscreen device that is the size of a desk. Hedges considers bringing IT innovation to Medtronic as one of his biggest career accomplishments.[3]

Innovation starts with inquisitive people, and research hospitals are known for a culture of learning and inquisitiveness. So in 2011, Charles Boicey,[4] an informatics solutions architect at the University of California Irvine Health, was fascinated with social media. He saw similarities between Facebook and patient records that are really episodes of care and began experimenting with Hadoop. "With medical records, modeling a relational data warehouse takes an enormous amount of time," explains Boicey. "You have to make a lot of decisions about what data to bring in. With Hadoop, you can bring it all in without a rigid data model." By loading all 22 years of historical medical records into Hadoop rather than a proprietary medical records system, Boicey estimates they have saved $500,000 per year in software fees. In addition, he can now explore patterns that were not possible before. Boicey uses a combination of MapReduce jobs, Hive, and Tableau to understand how care is influenced by the time of data, the combination of caregivers treating a person, medications delivered, and lab tests. What started as a curiosity went into production in January 2013. Boicey is continuing to experiment with other technologies, including MongoDB and Graph databases.

Universities can also be a great resource for innovation and for companies or BI teams to partner with to co-staff a BI lab. For example, Nielsen collects a lot of data on TV viewers and shoppers that is critical for marketers. They have to integrate data from over 800 different client databases. Wal-Mart alone accounted for 30 trillion new data points in 2012.[5] Gleaning insights out of such a treasure trove of data while also protecting consumer privacy is the ultimate big data challenge, explains Scott McKinley, executive vice president for product leadership and innovation at Nielsen. Social media and mobile have had profound impacts on how and where buyers are influenced. He established an Innovation Lab with the Stanford University Graduate School of Business in 2012 to collaborate on high-value opportunities, test and vet opportunities with academics, and do POCs with customers. Part of the impetus for the lab was in recognizing how much more quickly Nielsen's partners and customers are moving. "Facebook, Apple, and Google. These guys move at the speed of light. They are very, very nimble. They have a fail fast attitude. They have no problem with running down a road and if it is wrong, they stop, they back the truck up, and they go down a different path. That's an approach and a philosophy to product development that Nielsen wants to emulate."[6]

The opportunity to work in a BI lab can be inspiring and rewarding. However, in considering the most appropriate people to participate in such labs, leaders need to consider the right mix of skills for creativity, willingness to take risks, and visionary thinking. Some ideas may never come to fruition, and this can be frustrating and demotivating for more pragmatic workers. Some BI experts have expressed frustration that only certain team members get to work on all the cutting-edge technologies, while they get stuck with the mundane tasks of maintaining legacy BI. In this way, it may be useful to periodically rotate who works on innovation and in lab environments, both for motivational purposes and to ensure practical constraints are also considered.

Evangelizing and Promoting Your BI Capabilities

With business intelligence, there is sometimes the mindset of "build it and they will come." And yet, the *Field of Dreams* notion does not apply to business intelligence: You can build it, and users may not come. There are a number of reasons users won't automatically use the business intelligence application:

- Resistance to change
- Predominance of gut-feel decision-making
- Lack of relevance (see Chapter 9)

You never want "lack of awareness" to be one of the reasons, though, and to avoid this pitfall, you must proactively evangelize BI and promote your company's BI capabilities.

Users will go through an evolution as you promote your business intelligence solution (see Figure 13-3). During the funding and development stages of the project, you want to build *awareness* about what is coming and how it affects people. You want everyone—not just power users or initial users—to have heard of business intelligence and big data. Fortunately, with mainstream media now talking and writing about big data, your internal promotion efforts to build awareness are getting a nice boost from some outside resources. As you get closer to delivering

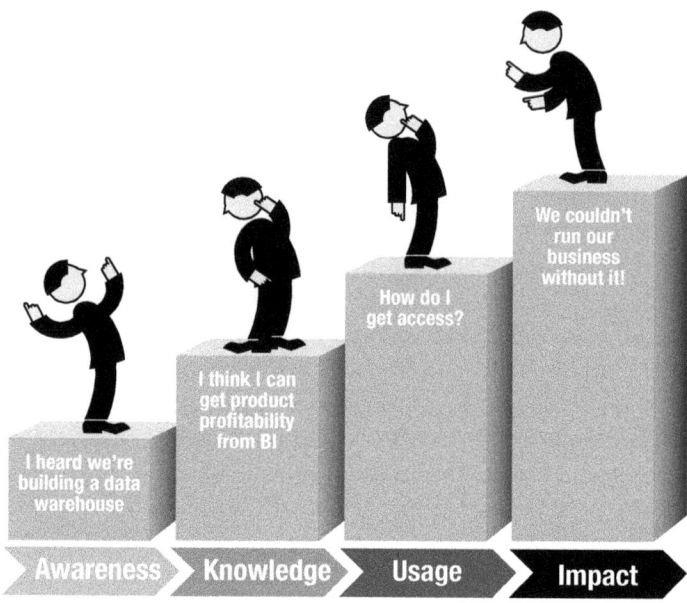

Figure 13-3 The phases of promoting business intelligence

capability for a particular group of users, you want to increase *knowledge* about BI and big data so that people will understand when and how to use them. The third phase of promotion is to increase *usage*, in which people within all levels of the organization are *aware* of business intelligence, *know* when to use it, and *use* it as an invaluable tool to achieve business goals. Effective and appropriate usage increases business impact. Use a variety of media to achieve these different promotional stages. Different user segments (see Chapter 12) will be at different stages simultaneously.

When to Promote

There is a comfort in waiting to promote your BI capabilities only when you are finished with the first phase of your project. If you wait until then, however, you are starting too late and it will take you longer to achieve any measurable benefits. Users must be aware of business intelligence long before they will request access to a system or sign up for a training class. Clearly, you need to manage user expectations and not promise more functionality than you can deliver. In early promotions, emphasize the high-level benefits, implementation waves, and broad time frames. Battered IT departments who have been criticized for being late in the past may truly cringe at this approach, preferring to keep a low profile until everything is done. However, to break down barriers and slowly build demand and excitement, you must promote early, well before you are ready for deployment.

Focus on Benefits

As you promote BI capabilities, focus as much as possible on the *benefits* your solution will deliver, not only on the technical *features* of the deployment. Consider some of the products you buy as a consumer. Particularly with business intelligence, a number of technical features will have little meaning to users. Restating the features in terms of the benefits is one of the hardest language barriers for the project team to overcome. Table 13-1 highlights some features that are better described to users in terms of the benefits they provide.

In a few instances, the feature and related benefit will be clear, but these instances are in the minority. For example, "24/7" (as in 24 hours a day, 7 days a week) is a feature of when the BI application may be available. As this phrase is repeated in so many contexts, users will immediately recognize the benefit as being access on demand, no matter the time of day, world time zone, or day of the week. Benefits may also be well understood when you refer to mobile BI.

A fun team-building exercise is to have the BI project team practice their elevator speech for real business users. The elevator speech is a

Feature	Benefit
Aggregate or summary tables	Fast queries.
Disconnected access	Ability to work with reports and dashboards while traveling or at a customer site.
Ad hoc queries	Explore the root cause of a problem without waiting for an IT report developer.
Exception-based reporting	Proactively manage the business when indicators fall below a certain threshold; fix a problem before it is out of control.
Mobile BI	Information at the touch of a finger on a lightweight device while traveling, at a customer site, remote locations.
Charts and graphs	Fast time to insight. Higher engagement and retention.

Table 13-1   **Emphasize Benefits, Not Features**

one-minute description of what the BI project team is developing, stated in terms of business benefits users can readily understand. It is a big departure from the technobabble that may be more familiar. It's also a useful way to ensure the team stays focused on the business value of BI rather than the cool technology!

Before—Technobabble	After—Business Benefits
"We're building a 10-terabyte data warehouse on an analytic appliance, quad-core processor. It's all in 3rd normal form, and we've custom-coded the ETL process. We're considering Hadoop for unstructured data."	"We're implementing software that allows you to explore information to reduce inventory holding costs and to deliver product faster to customers."

Key Messages

When you promote your BI solution, develop key messages or taglines that emphasize these benefits. The tagline you develop depends on the current situation and goals you have for deploying or enhancing your BI capabilities. For example, if users currently have to wait months to receive a custom report, a key message may be "information now." If one of the business goals is to retain customers, a BI tagline may be "helping you know our customers." In developing your BI taglines, look for inspiration from some of the most successful promotional campaigns, as shown in Table 13-2.

FlightStats, for example, initially used the tagline "FlightStats transforms information into travel intelligence." As summer 2007 became one of the worst on record for on-time performance and flight cancellations, they creatively promoted a new tagline: "When the travel gets tough, the tough fly smarter." EMBI uses "Stop chasing data. Spend more time managing patient risk and patient safety" as its tagline for promoting the BI solution to hospital administrators. A New Jersey school district uses the tagline "data drives instruction."

Naming Your BI Solution

In promoting your BI solution, you may refer to it by using the BI vendor tool name or with a unique name. The benefit of including the vendor-provided name is that you can leverage some of the vendor's marketing efforts, particularly as big data and BI seem to have entered mainstream media. Ten years ago, a business user would not have encountered such concepts or vendor references in newspapers such as the *Wall Street*

Product	Benefit & Key Message	Tagline
Dunkin' Donuts	Their coffee and snacks give you energy.	"America runs on Dunkin'"
MasterCard	Using MasterCard makes you happy and the costs are worth it.	"There are some things money can't buy; for everything else, there's MasterCard."
Milk, sponsored by the California Milk Processor Board	Drinking milk gives you strong bones and makes you healthier.	"Got Milk?"
Nike	Nice sports apparel will help you get there, but there is no excuse for getting started.	"Just Do It!"
M&Ms	Eat our chocolate candy to avoid a mess.	"Melts in your mouth. Not in your hands."

Table 13-2   Famous Taglines

Journal, *USA Today*, or the *Financial Times*. Instead, these concepts and vendors were only mentioned in tech industry journals.

The downside is if the vendor changes product names (a frequent event in the industry), then you may have to change your internal product name as well. If you are suffering from a stalled implementation or if there were negative impressions early in the implementation, change the name! When you develop your own BI product name, be sure to consider the acronym created. If it is a global deployment, take into account the cultural impact of acronyms.

Following are some other creative product names:

- **FlightStats**   Originally, the company name was Conducive Technologies and the BI application was FlightStats
- **OASIS**   Online Analysis Sales Information System
- **YODA**   Your On-line Data Access
- **PIMS**   Performance Information Management System, used by the Transportation Safety Administration (TSA)
- **Apollo**   Inspired from the Greek god of truth
- **SpendLINK**   UHC's (University HealthSystem Consortium) mobile app, developed by Novation, that provides member hospitals data on supply expenses

Promotional Media

In promoting your BI application, you must repeat your message often and use a variety of media. Remember, the goal with promotion is to move people from *awareness* of business intelligence to *usage*. It will take a number of repetitions, with different messages and media, to get there.

- **Road shows**   When companies first start developing a business intelligence solution, many have corresponding information sessions about what is coming, when phase 1 will be available, and who will be trained first. The most successful "road shows" include business success stories and user testimonials on how business intelligence has had a measurable impact.
- **Video clips and podcasts**   Some companies have created web videos and podcasts to explain their BI program and the benefits it delivers. Emergency Medical Associates, for example, has a web video on their home page describing the BI application. Podcasts allow people to listen to short sound bites and interviews over the Internet or via an iPod. Any of these media can be used in conjunction with a road show, and they are particularly useful if the executive sponsor states their vision for BI or if a business user gives a testimonial as to how BI has helped them. While a video or podcast may be difficult to produce at first, it helps reduce travel costs and logistic issues in always getting the right people together.
- **Company newsletters**   Company newsletters are an excellent medium for high-level messages to a broad audience. Given the readership of company newsletters, the primary purpose of these articles should be to build awareness, not necessarily usage. These articles should include information about the business goals and project milestones. Such broad newsletters are not an ideal medium for explaining detailed functionality.
- **Industry journals and events**   Some companies have a misconception that participation in user conferences and articles in industry journals help only the careers of the project staff and not necessarily the company. In fact, successful BI companies have said that the external media attention has helped motivate, attract, and retain top talent. There are a number of ways to get your project into an industry journal. You can author an article. You can volunteer to be interviewed by one of your BI vendors for a press release. Your company's public relations department can issue a press release either to technical journals such as *Computerworld, Information Management, InformationWeek,* and *CIO Insight,* or, if it has more of a business

slant, to industry journals. Finally, consider submitting an application for industry awards. In addition to taking time to reflect on your accomplishments, award winners enjoy additional exposure and speaking opportunities. Customers who participate in panels at industry events often further benefit by additional networking and complimentary education at the event.

- **Lunch and learns**   A lunch and learn is a casual information-sharing session in which participants bring a bagged lunch (or lunch may be provided) and discuss effective usage of business intelligence. Such sessions also may work as early morning breakfast or coffee round-tables ahead of the routine workday. Vendors may also participate in these sessions. A facilitator may start the lunch with a success story, tip, or project update. These provide a useful follow-up to training and another opportunity to raise awareness about best practices, success stories, and benefits.

- **Internal user conferences**   Just as BI vendors host periodic user conferences, do the same in your own company. Kick off the meeting with a review of the benefits, project milestones, and a key success story. Then ask users to share tips and techniques on both the how-to of BI tools and how it has helped them achieve business goals. When possible, include highlights of emerging trends and ideas from the BI lab to gauge interest and business value of POCs.

- **T-shirt days**   Many project teams give away T-shirts, sunglasses, mouse pads, thumb drives, and other promotional items to reward staff for their accomplishments. As both a motivational technique and a promotional opportunity, get the entire team to wear their give-away on milestone dates. This works particularly well if the T-shirt is brightly colored. Seeing 50 yellow T-shirts in the company cafeteria will generate interest and curiosity about what's new. One of Dow Chemical's early giveaways was silver dollars. Using the theme of the captain in *Moby Dick,* the project manager gave each team member a silver dollar for every 100 users trained. The goal was to ensure team members stayed focused on the user requirements and did not get distracted by what was then a new technology. (I still have my silver dollars.) An automotive company printed tips on mouse pads to promote usage and reduce help desk calls.

- **Portal**   The company portal or BI portal is useful for promoting to existing users and keeping them informed; however, it is a poor medium for new or potential users, who may not see these messages as they are not current users. You can best reach these potential users through staff meetings and company newsletters.

- **Routine staff meetings**   Most departments and business units have regularly scheduled staff meetings. Ask for a brief timeslot on the agenda each quarter to give an update on new deliverables, problem resolution, and how other departments are benefiting from business intelligence. A real sign of success is when the department invites you and increases your brief timeslot request to a lengthier discussion!

Training

A common theme with the successful BI case studies was the attention to training and that the training focused on the data and not only on the BI tools. Conversely, survey respondents who described their BI project as failing or only moderately successful cited lack of attention to training as an impediment to greater success. It seems to me that training is often the final leg of a BI marathon, an afterthought to a BI program that is often not budgeted or planned for.

> "Training and adoption [have] been longer and harder than expected."
>
> —IT director, state agency

Some of the promotional media, such as internal user groups, newsletters, and lunch and learns, are useful supplements to initial training mechanisms. Training should also be tailored to meet the needs of the various user segments (see Chapter 12). For example, executives may need only an introductory walkthrough (via phone or video), whereas knowledge workers who will become power users may need multiday classroom training.

At Emergency Medical Associates, this is where ease of use and web-based BI are also important. Explains Eric Bachenheimer, director of client account management, "You don't have to be a techy or a programmer to use WEBeMARS. It's self-serve and only takes a few clicks to call up a report. Nobody has to take a three-week training class. It uses a skill set they already have." In training hospital administrators to use WEBeMARS, EMA uses a combination of presentation and interactive demonstration that only lasts two hours.[7]

When there are cultural and political issues in sharing data more widely, training can provide a critical forum in addressing people's concerns. Ed McClellan, vice president of product development and client implementation at Learning Circle, explains the importance of this training: "Our challenge is providing the affordable manner to train our BI users or client base on how to take full advantage of our BI tool offering. Their data often reflects the reality of their struggling schools, but the culture is only slowly embracing the tenant that you must measure to improve. This cultural challenge is not systemic, but dictates a simple, consistent, and reliable BI presentation, and also a flexible and sensitive training program."

Following are some additional things to consider in developing a training approach:

- **Data vs. the tool** A BI tool delivers no value in itself; the value is in the ability to access *relevant* data via an appropriate interface. If you train users only on the BI tool with only sample databases, users may not be able to apply these skills against their own data. Generic software training is recommended only for IT professionals and power users. As you extend the reach of BI, a greater emphasis must be given to the specific data, business insights, and desired actions.

> Lunch and learns are a good way to supplement classroom or computer-based training on the tool with ongoing discussions about the data.

- **Internal vs. third-party** BI tool vendors and their training partners will train end users on the software. Some will customize the training material to include your specific business views, reports, dashboards, and data in the screen shots. You also may be able to buy the training material from vendors and incorporate your own screenshots.
- **Training method** While classroom-style training is the most traditional, it can pose a logistical challenge when users are at different sites, have busy schedules, and access different data sources. Some users may do quite well reading a book and then supplementing that with self-paced tutorials and webinars on their own schedule.

> Regardless of the formal training method, for a successful implementation, you must supplement scheduled training classes with other means to share tips, techniques, and uses on an ongoing basis.

Training will often receive consideration early in the BI process, but it seems to fall by the wayside as BI usage expands and as new capabilities are delivered. One of the successful BI case studies expressed concern: "Early on, we were committed to training, but then as the demands grew to build more capabilities, the BI team has gotten pulled into more development and less training." In this regard, recognize that training is an ongoing service and requirement that needs to be separated from the development team. The development team may still deliver initial training as part of a new capability, but at some point, consideration must be given to delivering ongoing training.

A Picture Is Worth a Thousand Numbers

Many of the successful BI case studies make much better use of visualizations than other companies I have worked with. This conclusion is not based on any statistical data; it's simply an observation. When I asked to see sample screenshots of how the case study companies were using business intelligence, rarely did I get a dense page of numbers. Instead, I would see reports and dashboards with charts, trend lines, arrow indicators, and greater use of conditional formatting (green to communicate good performance and red to indicate a problem).

Visualization expert Edward Tufte suggests that a tabular display of numbers is better when 20 numbers or fewer are involved. And yet, I continue to see reams and reams of reports, with dozens of pages of dense tables of numbers. In truth, sometimes you do need a precise number— you want the part number, the customer phone number, the charge on your credit card bill. But when you are trying to uncover patterns, anomalies, and opportunities, a dense page of numbers is useless. All too often, it seems report developers first try to re-create a report as it existed in a legacy system that may lack graphing capabilities. This approach may be a necessary first step to build confidence in the data coming from the BI solution, but it should not be the last. Instead, BI experts should better leverage the visualization capabilities within BI tools to more effectively communicate the data. All too often, longtime business query users will declare, "I never even knew the BI tool could create graphs!" Instead, data is either left as a dense page of numbers or routinely pulled into spreadsheets for graphing. This suggests that the problem lies in both inadequate training and lack of awareness on how best to communicate data.

A Harvard Business Review blog observed this trend from dense pages of numbers to graphics in several companies' annual reports, such as Starbucks.[8] In the 2000 annual report, investors were presented with the traditional income statement as shown in Figure 13-4.

Selected Financial Data
In thousands, except earnings per share and store operating data

The following selected financial data have been derived from the consolidated financial statements of the Company. The data set forth below should be read in conjunction with "Management's Discussion and Analysis of Financial Condition and Results of Operations" and the Company's consolidated financial statements and notes thereto.

As of and for the fiscal year ended (1)	Oct 1, 2000 (52 Wks)	Oct 3, 1999 (53 Wks)	Sept 27, 1998 (52 Wks)	Sept 28, 1997 (52 Wks)	Sept 29, 1996 (52 Wks)
RESULTS OF OPERATIONS DATA					
Net revenues:					
Retail	$ 1,823,607	$ 1,423,389	$ 1,102,574	$ 836,291	$ 601,458
Specialty	345,611	256,756	206,128	139,098	96,414
Total net revenues	2,169,218	1,680,145	1,308,702	975,389	697,872
Merger expenses (2)	-	-	8,930	-	-
Operating income	212,252	156,711	109,216	86,199	56,575
Internet-related investment losses (3)	58,792	-	-	-	-
Gain on sale of investment (4)	-	-	-	-	9,218
Net earnings	$ 94,564	$ 101,693	$ 68,372	$ 55,211	$ 41,710
Net earnings per common share -diluted (5)	$ 0.49	$ 0.54	$ 0.37	$ 0.33	$ 0.27
Cash dividends per share	-	-	-	-	-
BALANCE SHEET DATA					
Working capital	$ 146,568	$ 135,303	$ 157,805	$ 172,079	$ 239,365
Total assets	1,493,131	1,252,514	992,755	857,152	729,227
Long-term debt (including current portion)	7,168	7,691	1,803	168,832	167,980
Shareholders' equity	1,148,399	961,013	794,297	533,710	454,050
STORE OPERATING DATA					
Comparable store sales (6)	9%	6%	5%	5%	7%
Stores open at year-end:					
Continental North America:					
Company-operated stores	2,446	2,038	1,622	1,270	929
Licensed stores	530	179	133	94	75
International:					
Company-operated stores	173	97	66	31	9
Licensed stores	352	184	65	17	2
Total stores	3,501	2,498	1,886	1,412	1,015

Figure 13-4 Starbucks 2000 annual report, selected financial data[9]

In the 2012 annual report, the first page of the report included a much more impactful chart, as shown in Figure 13-5. Starbucks began using such simple charts as far back as 2001, but with less color and buried further in the report. Notice that in 2012, the most recent year is color-coded differently from previous years, making for a faster identification of the most important values.

The rise of visual data discovery tools is making the use of graphs more prevalent, but that is not to say they are always the most suitable displays. In fact, some companies may start out on this journey by adding so much color, complicated visualizations, and animated widgets that the dashboard looks like a bad pinball machine.

Stephen Few is an expert in BI and visualization and has authored a number of books and seminars on the best way to present data and design dashboards (refer to Recommended Resources in the appendix). Following are a few basic ideas from his work and others that are useful starting points to improving your report and dashboard design:

- Use color wisely and consistently. A bar chart that uses the same color for each bar is less distracting than a different color for each bar. The

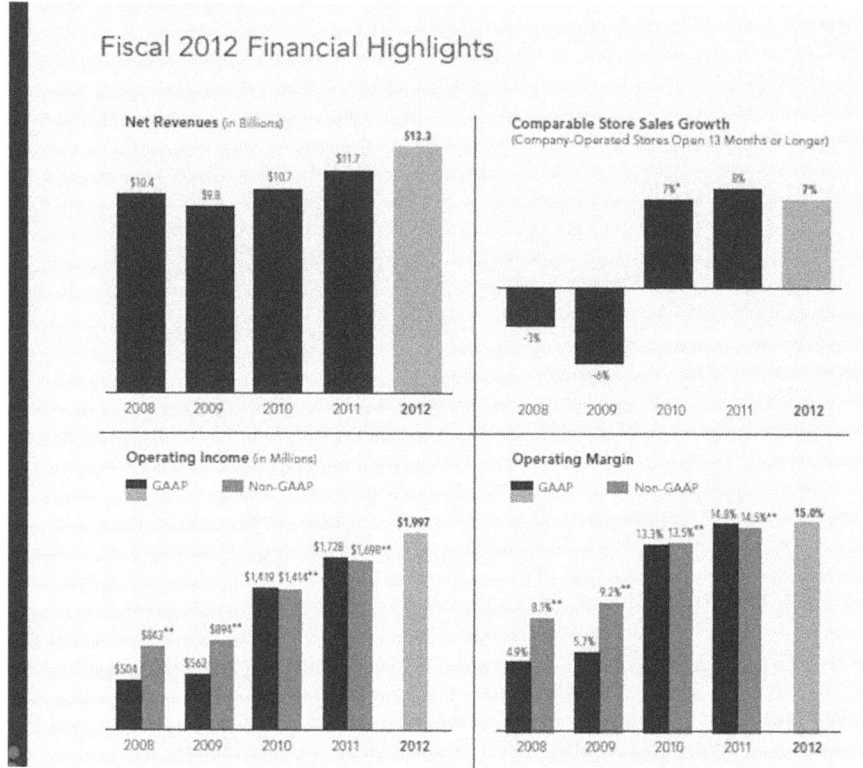

Figure 13-5   Starbucks 2012 annual report displays information graphically.[10]

colors of the bars should only change, for example, when there are multiple categories in the same chart (actual and budget, or salary by job type and gender).

- Don't use green and red alone, because an estimated 10 percent of the male population is color blind. Instead, combine texture with color to ensure all individuals can interpret a display.
- Maximize the use of space. A traditional speedometer gauge is an appealing and familiar display style. However, Few invented the concept of a bullet graph that many vendors now support out of the box that consumes less space. In polling my own class attendees on which style they prefer, new dashboard users prefer the speedometer, but more mature deployments and dashboard designers prefer the bullet graph.
- Balance appeal with insight. Visually appealing dashboards, reports, and infographics help with user adoption and engagement. At the same time, you want design considerations to speed the time to

insight. I've seen some very boring gray-color dashboards that will draw my attention to an anomaly, shaded in red. Time to insight was clearly high, but engagement and appeal were low. When engagement and interface appeal are low, casual users may be less likely to use a BI tool to investigate the anomaly. Instead, they may pass that part of the discovery process onto a power user.

- Be careful whom you emulate. I have read newspaper articles and other analyst reports and assumed they are more erudite than I because they use fancy charts like radar charts. I find radar charts hard to interpret. Early in my career, I assumed that I should use such constructs to appear more professional. The visualization community, meanwhile, is critical of a number of such conventions. Just because a software program allows you to create a particular chart type or dashboard style, that doesn't mean you should do so. A bar chart or small multiple might be a more effective chart than a radar chart. Also be careful about differences in online viewing and print viewing, and color versus black and white.

- Know your audience and design for that user segment. Different users will want different types of displays. An executive, for example, may want to see only a summary trend line of sales. Meanwhile, a salesperson may want the dense page of orders, by customer name, with a color-coded arrow to flag declines in this year's versus last year's sales.

- Continue to look for optimal designs. Visualization software tries to combine information from brain research with software design to optimize what we see and how we interpret what we see. Our understanding of the brain is continuing to evolve. What was considered an optimal design today may change in the future.

Best Practices for Successful Business Intelligence

You've built a perfectly architected BI solution and followed the other best practices in each of the preceding chapters, garnering executive support and fostering a strong business–IT partnership. And yet, your success may only be short lived unless you take into account the lasting effects of innovation, promotion, and training. To harvest the full and ongoing value of your BI efforts,

- Recognize that technology capabilities and user expectations change over time. Build innovation into your BI team to investigate new technologies and their business value.

- Promote business intelligence uses and success stories on an ongoing basis, using a variety of media.
- Deliver training that is tailored to user segments on an ongoing basis. Supplement formal classroom training with periodic web-based updates, internal user conferences, and lunch and learns. Train users on both the tool and the data they are accessing with their preferred tool.
- Leverage visualization capabilities in BI tools to more effectively present the data and communicate trends and exceptions.

Chapter 14

The Future of Business Intelligence

The future of business intelligence centers on making BI relevant for everyone, not only for information workers and internal employees, but also beyond corporate boundaries, to extend the reach of BI to customers and suppliers. As the Successful BI case studies have demonstrated, when best practices are applied, BI usage can expand beyond the paltry 24 percent of employees today to a much more prevalent business tool. It will take cultural shifts, new ways of thinking, and continued technical innovation. Business intelligence has the power to change people's way of working, to enable businesses to compete more effectively and efficiently, to help nonprofits stretch their dollars further, and to impact everyday life. All of this is possible based on insights available at the click of a mouse, push of a button, or touch of a screen.

As discussed throughout this book, much of the key to successful business intelligence has to do with the people, processes, and culture. Don't rely on technical innovation alone to solve the biggest barriers to BI success, but by all means, do get excited about the innovations that will make BI easier and more prevalent. BI as a technology has changed dramatically since its inception in the early 1990s. This chapter focuses on emerging innovations with examples of how customers are taking advantage of them. I also provide a maturity model so you can benchmark your current state and track your evolution by the factors that most enable big impact. In the final section, I leave you with some words of wisdom to inspire you to think about how your company can best unlock the full value of BI and big data.

Improvement and Innovation Priorities

As part of the Successful BI survey, respondents were asked to choose from a list of possible improvements and emerging technologies that they believe will help their companies achieve greater success. Figure 14-1 shows which items are considered most important in helping companies achieve greater impact. Dashboards were rated number one, an interesting priority given that 79 percent of companies already said they had successfully deployed them (see Chapter 12, Figure 12-6). However, many initial dashboard deployments were limited in scope and often based on custom-developed solutions. With new and improved dashboards now available from more BI platform vendors, the use of dashboards can be expanded well beyond just a handful of users and beyond just managers and executives. Self-service BI and mobile BI were the second most important priorities. As discussed in Chapter 3, self-service BI encompasses a spectrum of capabilities. Visual data discovery is just one module (but an important one) that delivers self-service BI. It was surprising to me that only 36 percent of companies cited

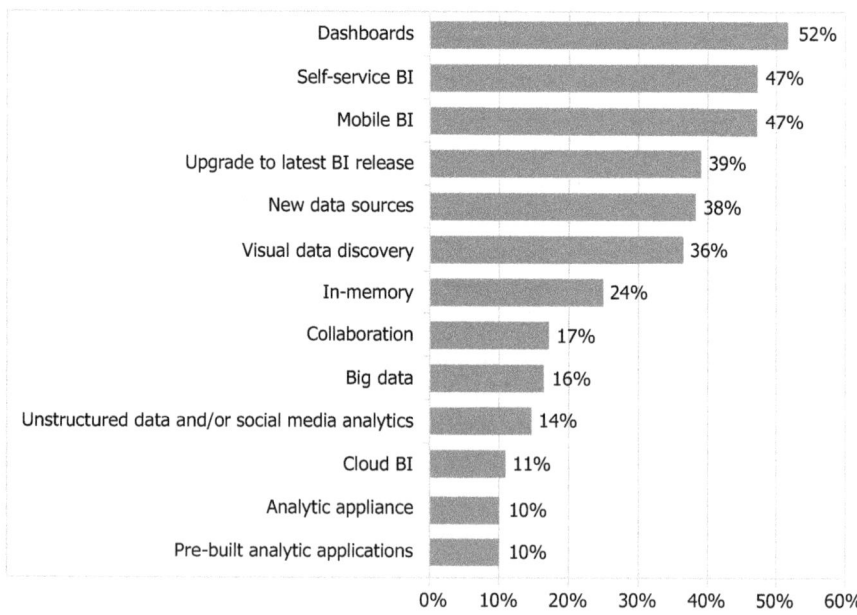

Figure 14-1 Dashboards, self-service BI, and mobile BI are top innovation priorities.

this as an improvement priority, suggesting that there is still a long way to go in educating people on the value and different uses cases for this module. Upgrading to the latest BI release and expanding to new data sources were rated third and fourth as priorities. Given that many BI teams do not have adequate resources, simply maintaining an existing environment and user base often trumps leveraging new innovations. As one BI director told me, "We are a victim of our own success."

If your BI deployment is successful, even on a small scale, demand can quickly outpace the BI team's ability to deliver.

These survey results show an interesting contrast: BI industry conferences and media headlines would suggest that big data and cloud should appear higher on the list of priorities. To a certain extent, the difference shows the hype around these technologies. More importantly, it shows that awareness and education precede widespread usage (similar to your own internal BI marketing efforts discussed in Chapter 13, Figure 13-3). Companies are still learning about these technologies, doing proofs of concepts, and assessing how best to use them. Also, when I think of the challenges of serving a large BI user base while simultaneously innovating, I recall a quote from a BI vendor working to deliver a major platform upgrade: "It's like retooling a jetliner mid-flight."

There is not an easy fix for this innovator's dilemma. However, I do think part of the solution has to be a continuing assessment of your BI organizational model and the business–IT partnership. As business users become more sophisticated in their technical skills, let those power users assume some of the responsibilities that once belonged only in the domain of the core BI team. This allows the core BI team to work on harder analytic problems and new innovations. Also, some of the technical innovations allow IT to do more with less:

- In-memory technology can free DBAs and other analysts from manual performance tuning.
- Cloud computing frees technologists from maintaining an on-premise infrastructure.
- Visual data discovery tools allow users to explore subsets of data without IT having to first extensively model a data source.

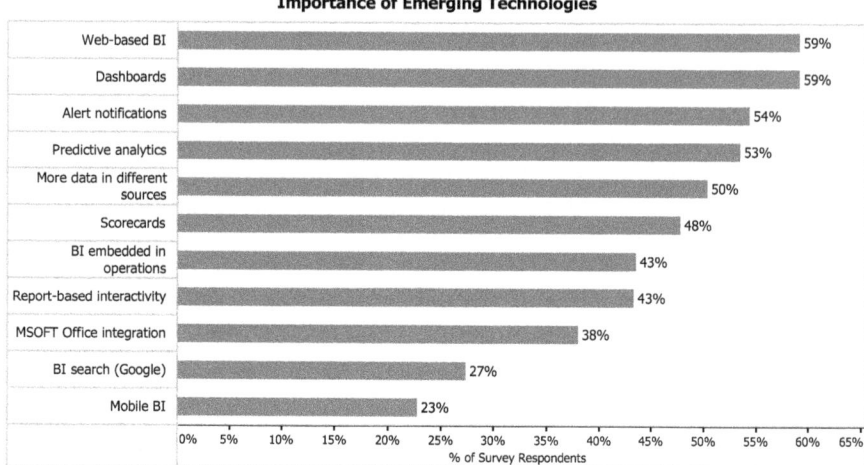

Figure 14-2   In 2007, web-based BI was the top innovation priority.

A Look Back: The Pace of Change

As I was re-reading the text from this chapter from the 2007 book, I was staggered to see that deploying web-based BI tools was the top innovation priority back then. Really? I had forgotten that only six years ago, most BI tools were predominantly desktop based. Their web-based counterparts were still rudimentary. This web-versus-desktop debate is recurring with visual data discovery tools. And mobile BI was rated last for priorities. So for the sake of posterity, and to show just how quickly technology changes, I thought you might find it informative to compare priorities from 2007, as shown in Figure 14-2.

A Framework for Prioritizing Innovations

In teaching my "Cool BI" classes at The Data Warehousing Institute (TDWI) conferences, I use the concept of MVP to help companies assess their innovation priority:

- **M for Maturity**   Consider the maturity of the technology or the maturity of your solution provider's capabilities for the technology. Less mature solutions may have more risk and disruption. However, there also can be benefits in terms of first-mover advantage to pursue less mature innovations.

- **V for Value**   Some innovations provide value in terms of big insights or lower cost to serve.
- **P for Positioning or Pervasive BI**   Consider if the innovation solves a problem for a small segment of users, such as power users, or helps BI become more pervasive to the outer spectrum of more casual BI users

Figure 14-3 provides a framework for evaluating changes in BI technology to determine which new and emerging capabilities will prove most valuable to your company, how mature they are, and when to monitor them or when to embrace and actively deploy them (adapted from TDWI's Technology Evaluation Framework). The X axis provides an indication of how mature the technology is, and the Y axis gives an indication of which technology will make BI pervasive. Recall from Chapter 4 that the average usage of BI within a company is currently at 24 percent, and even if the budget were available and the deployment were wildly successful, survey respondents felt the use rate would extend only to 54 percent of employees. The Y axis, then, indicates the degree to which an enabling technology will take BI's reach closer to

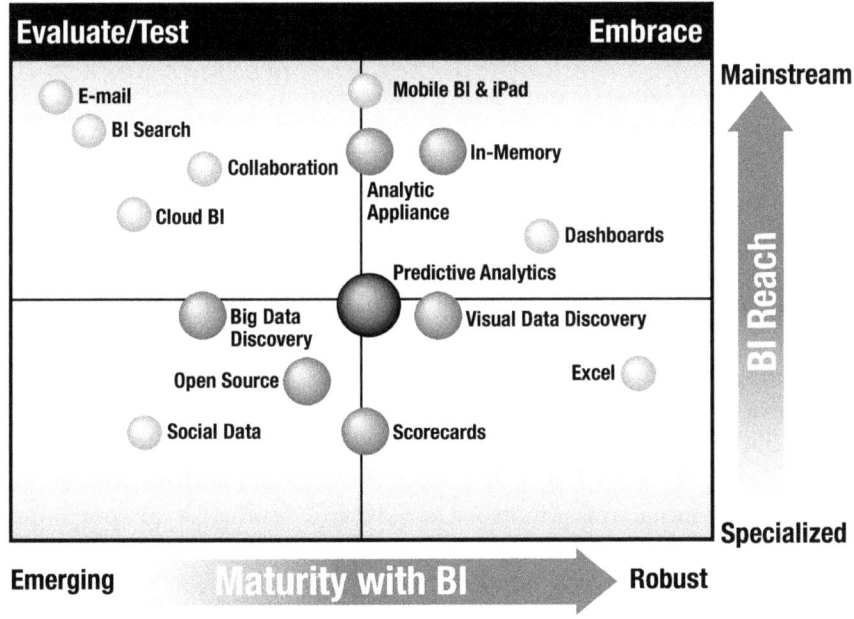

Size & Color of Bubble = Value to Single User or Decision

Figure 14-3   BI technology evaluation

100 percent of employees. Business impact and BI prevalence are not linearly correlated, however. One enabling technology, such as predictive analytics, may yield a big value for a single decision—say, a $4 million savings by better marketing campaign management. Another enabling technology, such as BI embedded in operational processes, may affect thousands of users, each of whom makes dozens of decisions on a daily basis; the monetary value of these individual decisions may be small when measured in isolation, but enormous when taken in aggregate. The size and shading of the bubbles in Figure 14-3 give an indication of which items have a bigger value from a single application or insight. The bigger the bubble and darker the shading, the bigger the impact on a single decision or person.

For each innovation, consider both the technical maturity and the business impact when deciding how to proceed:

- **Embrace** Items in the upper-right quadrant show innovations that are mature and that should be embraced, as they will help speed user adoption across multiple user segments.
- **Adopt Where Appropriate** Items in the lower-right quadrant show innovations that are mature but that may serve only specific segments of users. Excel integration with BI is an example of this; the technology is more mature than BI integrated with e-mail, for example, but benefits only power users who use spreadsheets as part of their daily work.
- **Test** Items in the upper-left quadrant are relatively new but will have a profound impact on user adoption. BI Search (a Google-like interface, discussed in the next section) is a good example of this. The technology is not well understood or widely supported across the industry. A number of usability and performance issues still need to be worked out, but the potential impact on user adoption is enormous. You may build some prototypes and conduct proofs of concepts with business users to validate the value of these innovations.
- **Evaluate** Items in the lower-left quadrant are so new that they may be riskier investments. Items here are less proven and have less market adoption. You may have to invest in solutions from start-up companies. For some of these technologies, you may simply monitor industry trends and case studies of early adopters. For others, and if you have an innovation lab as discussed in Chapter 13, you may do some prototyping and adopt for particular use cases.

Figure 14-3 portrays the broad industry maturity of these capabilities and the degree to which most vendors offer the capabilities. For clarity, I have selected only certain innovations; it is not meant to be an exhaustive list of all things going on in the industry. I consider the items in the context of integration with business intelligence. So while advanced and predictive analytics is certainly a mature concept and technology, the integration of it with business intelligence is still a work in progress. Similarly, the use of social networking is mature, but analyzing that data using traditional BI tools for business decisions is immature. Instead, most of the social analytics rely on stand-alone Hadoop deployments that are not integrated with a larger information analytic environment.

The subsequent sections describe these capabilities that have not otherwise been addressed in Chapters 2 and 3.

BI Search & Text Analytics

The concept of BI Search offers a number of promising benefits to business intelligence and big data:

- Simple user interface.
- A more complete set of information to support decision-making, with the integration of structured (quantitative) and unstructured content (textual). Structured data refers to the numerical values typically captured in the operational systems and subsequently stored in a data warehouse. Unstructured content refers to information stored in textual comment fields, documents, annual reports, websites, social media, and so on. Some people will refer to this as semi-structured information.
- Users can find what they need through search, rather than through navigating a long list of reports.

Text analytics is closely related to search in that unstructured information or text can be transformed into quantitative data. For example, it allows for the searching of information in a comment field to see how many times a customer praised a particular product. Text analytics is the numerical analysis of textual information.

Despite all the improvements in data warehousing and BI front-end tools, users continue to feel overwhelmed with reports, yet undersatisfied with meaningful information. They don't know what's available or where. Similar reports are created over and over because users don't know which reports already exist or how, for example, the report "Product Sales" differs from "Product Sales YTD." In addition, consider how at Medtronic some of the most valuable information is hidden in textual comment fields that were not readily accessible in the past. Similarly, BI initiatives at Constant Contact may have started in marketing and in statistics around e-mail campaign effectiveness (such as open and click rates), but they are evolving to include looking at the content within those emails to determine which messaging is more effective.

A BI Search interface promises to change the way users access information. Picture a Google interface to BI. Without any training in a BI tool, users can enter a phrase such as "Recent sales for customer A" and then be presented with either a list of predefined reports or, in some cases, a newly generated query. The added benefit is that in addition to displaying reports coming from the BI server, the search engine will list textual information that may be relevant—a customer letter, sales call notes, or headline news. When search capabilities are combined with text analytics, a report may include numerical data based on a scan of comment fields to compare the number of complaints with the number of positive comments. Never before has such unstructured data been so nicely accessible with structured or quantitative data.

If the integration of search and BI is successful, it is yet another innovation that will make BI accessible and usable by every employee in an organization. According to Tony Byrne, founder/president of The Real Story Group, a technology evaluation firm focusing on enterprise search and content management systems, search as a technology has existed for close to 60 years.[1] *Consumer* search (Google and Yahoo!, for example) as a technology emerged with the Internet in the mid-1990s. In many respects, the success of consumer search has helped spur interest around *enterprise* search, in which companies deploy search technology internally to search myriad document repositories. Text analytics has existed for more than 30 years but with usage in limited sectors, particularly, the government. The convergence of search with business intelligence first emerged in 2006. Google is not the only enterprise search solution that BI vendors support, but it is one that has the most consumer recognition and thus has helped business users to understand the possibilities. As open source has gained traction, a number of BI vendors are leveraging the open-source search engine Lucene.

The incorporation of text analytics with traditional business intelligence is still in its infancy. I place BI Search along the left side of the quadrant in Figure 14-3 because it is less mature than other innovations. Again, both technologies, independent of BI, have existed for decades; it is that convergence with BI that is new. While the convergence is still relatively immature, the promise it brings for BI to reach more users and in the value of incorporating textual data is enormous, and that is why I position BI Search near the top of the quadrant.

The number of organizations taking advantage of the BI Search and text analytics integration is a small portion of BI deployments. BlueCross BlueShield (BCBS) of Tennessee (TN) is an early adopter of these capabilities.[2] BCBS of TN is a not-for-profit provider of health insurance. In 2006, it paid $17 billion in benefits for its 2 million commercial members.[3] Managing claims and negotiating rates with providers is critical in ensuring BCBS can meet its obligations to the members it insures. While the insurer has had a mature business intelligence deployment since the late 1990s,[4] Frank Brooks, the senior manager of data resource management and chief data architect, recognized that there was value in bringing the text data stored in comment fields from call center notes together with information in the data warehouse.[5] Given how new the technology is, Brooks asked their BI vendor, Cognos, along with IBM (who produces the search solution OmniFind) and SAS (who offers text analytics solution Text Miner) to work together to develop several prototypes and show the business users the concept of bringing BI, enterprise search, and text analytics together. With this capability, a business user can enter the keyword "diabetes" in the OmniFind search box and be presented with a ranked list of things, such as

- Cognos reports and Online Analytical Processing (OLAP) cubes that show claims paid for diabetic treatments
- Call center notes that involve diabetes
- New research on improving care for diabetes patients

The business was enthusiastic. There has been a high degree of collaboration between BCBS of TN and its information technology partners to understand the new capabilities, develop the right infrastructure, and optimize the indexes to provide the best search performance.

Consistent with the evaluation framework in Figure 14-3, understanding new technologies requires a significant amount of evaluation and testing. BCBS of TN evaluated the capabilities for more than a year before developing plans for implementing this in production.

Text analytics is part of the SAP Hana platform and was a key reason Medtronic selected this technology despite its newness.[6] Prior to this, users would download long comment fields and search through text manually. Hana includes a simple Google-like interface so users can enter a keyword such as "Stent" and it will yield results from all comment fields. Hana can use natural language processing to determine if the context of the reference was positive or negative, as well as provide occurrence counts.

Collaboration

The rise of social networking has offered another source of data to be analyzed and explored. It also is having an influence on the way people want to share and interact with data. For most large BI vendors, initial attempts at collaboration have centered on adding comments to particular fields in a tabular display, a database, or a point in a chart. However, more forward-thinking vendors are trying to bring a Facebook-like or Twitter-like feel to the BI platform. There is a concept of "following" people who are the experts in the company. With this model, a central IT organization does not grant access to the data. Instead, the knowledge owner grants access. This degree of flexibility can be unnerving with certain data types and in certain industries. However, assuming privacy and security rules allow the collaboration, imagine how much more quickly decision-makers could find the data and the people with the insights.

Panorama Software in Israel has been doing some interesting work in this space. Panorama Software is a privately held company that sold the OLAP technology to Microsoft in the mid-1990s that later became Microsoft Analysis Services. Their BI platform that includes collaboration is referred to as Necto and is shown in Figure 14-4. Notice across the top the people to follow. Comments around the visualizations appear in the pane on the left. And just as social networking sites such Facebook and LinkedIn will recommend connections, Panorama Necto will look at a user's usage pattern and recommend other data sets or experts to follow.

A few other vendors have been applying the concepts of social and collaboration in the BI tools and platforms, but adoption has been limited and a preferred approach continues to be debated. Should the collaboration occur in the report or dashboard or should it occur in an overarching product such as a company portal? In some cases, the vendor initiatives seem to be just checkboxes of features ("yes, we do

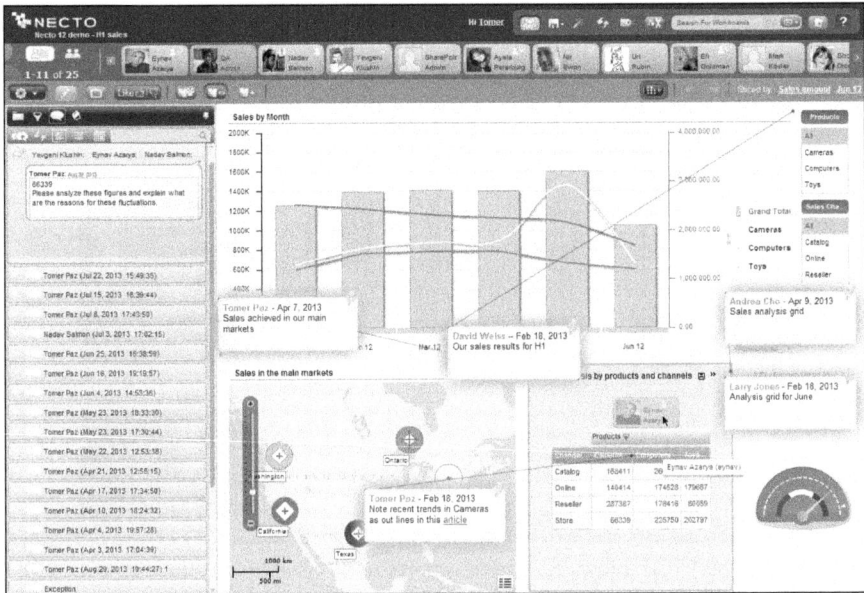

Figure 14-4   Panorama Software brings concepts of social networking to BI.

collaboration"), rather than getting at the heart of how decisions are made and how information is shared. To be sure, collaboration in BI has the potential to be revolutionary, but only if there is a strong culture for openly sharing data.

E-mail and Microsoft Office Integration

Integration of BI with Microsoft Office Excel is a mature product category, and spreadsheets may be the preferred interface for business analysts. But moving beyond the inner spectrum of potential BI users (refer to Figure 12-4 in Chapter 12), an interface more widely used than spreadsheets is e-mail. If you think about how much time you spend in e-mail versus other office tools, e-mail probably accounts for the largest portion of time. E-mail and text messages are natural interfaces for sending an alert when there is an exception. But imagine if e-mail was the primary interface to all your BI reports and dashboards, not just the ones with alert notifications. SAS is currently one of the few vendors that use the Microsoft Outlook client as a BI interface. Notice in Figure 14-5 how folders of reports from the BI server appear as e-mail folders. Critical key performance indicators (KPIs) can be displayed in a gadget

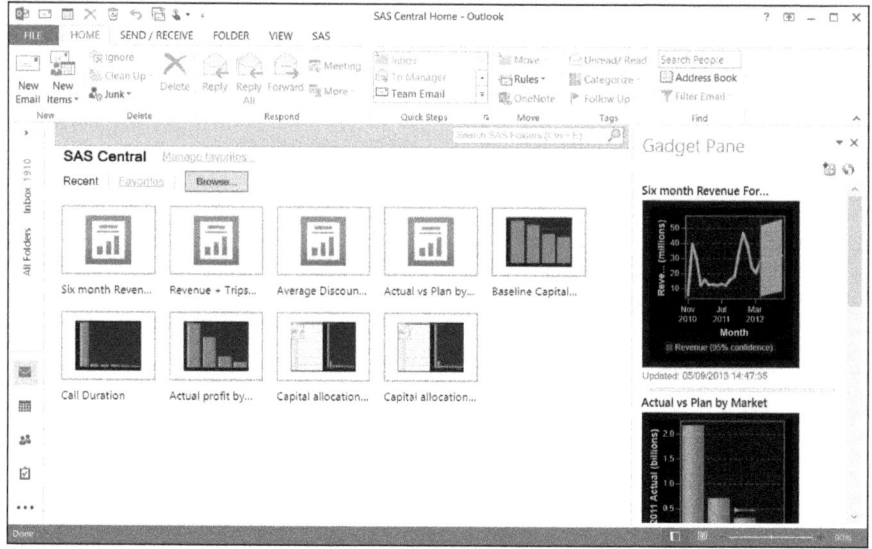

Figure 14-5   SAS BI allows KPIs and reports to be navigated from within e-mail.

pane along the right. In this way, the e-mail interface becomes the main access point for BI content, bringing BI into a user's daily workflow.

In addition to e-mail integration, some vendors are improving the integration with PowerPoint. PowerPoint is typically used for presentations, and data from a BI tool may often be embedded in or replicated within a presentation. As the concept of story telling with data grows, vendors may leverage PowerPoint or other means of presenting data in a guided way.

Will Hadoop Kill the Data Warehouse?

As discussed in Chapter 2, two of the biggest differences between Hadoop and data warehousing are software cost and the degree to which data must first be modeled before it can be analyzed. With these things in mind, some Hadoop experts have predicted the demise of the data warehouse. On the other side of the information divide, data warehouse experts think such claims are premature and fueled only by industry hype. Is each camp being myopic and vested only in furthering their own interests?

At this point, it's too early in Hadoop's lifespan to say if it will continue to complement or eventually fully replace the traditional data warehouse. Industry experts have complained that Hadoop lacks some of the system monitoring, auditing, and maintenance tools that more mature databases have. We are beginning to see commercial versions of Hadoop address these shortcomings. As a number of examples throughout the book have illustrated, Hadoop has a sweet spot for certain unstructured data (Constant Contact), streaming data (Netflix), and low-cost storage (University of California Irvine). As data scientists try to access and analyze that data, they currently will write their own programs, a sophisticated skill that most BI experts lack. Relevant data may be loaded into an optimized engine (whether a BI tool's in-memory layer as King.Com or Macy's do) or into the data warehouse or analytic appliance to allow for faster, broader, and deeper analysis. In this regard, independent analyst Richard Winter of Winter Corporation, who specializes in data warehousing scalability, published a report that compares the total cost of ownership of Hadoop and the traditional data warehouse using parallel processing.[7] The difference in cost was mostly driven by the type of analytics performed. For example, in his first scenario, both types of technologies were used in what he calls a "data refining" application in which 500TB of data with rapid throughput of sensor data were required. In the data refining example, Hadoop had a lower cost of ownership. The second use case is for a range of users and query complexity in a financial services industry, also comprising 500TB of data. In the financial analytic scenario, the traditional data warehouse had a much lower total cost of ownership than Hadoop. Beyond Winter's research, I think it is telling that early Hadoop adopters such as Facebook have also added traditional data warehousing into their analytic ecosystem.

Beyond the considerations of storage, cost, computing, and analytic workload that drive the debates of when to use Hadoop or data warehousing, there is also the issue of data cleansing. Some of the same conceptual differences in purposes for an operational system and an analytic system described in Chapter 2, Table 2-1, also apply to the Hadoop versus data warehouse debate.

The bottom line: In the near term, I don't see Hadoop replacing traditional data warehouse technologies and analytic databases. I continue to see it as complementary and just one potential part of that analytic ecosystem.

Privacy in the Age of Big Data

In the era of big data comes an enormous responsibility for anyone who generates, captures, stores, and explores data. Use the data wisely, and your efforts will be rewarded. Use the data recklessly, and there will be a backlash on data integrity, privacy, and viability.

The case of National Security Agency (NSA) worker Edward Snowden has shown how privacy in the age of big data is a work in progress. Snowden revealed that the NSA has been spying on U.S. citizens and other countries by monitoring phone calls made abroad. The project, named PRISM, is intended to protect the United States against terrorist attacks. While there has been a certain level of masking of individual phone calls, most experts say that the degree of granularity and scope of phone calls tracked were excessive. No matter where your opinion falls in this debate, most would agree that our digital footprints are larger than ever before. Even analytically savvy companies are collecting more data than they, as of yet, know what they will do with.

For retail customers, a loyalty card transaction, past purchase, or a "like" on a Facebook page may generate a personalized coupon. Some retailers are beginning to use the built-in global positioning system (GPS) on a smartphone to generate the coupon when that customer enters a store, or even a region of a store. Shopping in the candy aisle? How about a discount on that nice big bar of chocolate? Perhaps this is a generational thing, but I find this degree of personalization creepy. My teen children assume such coupons are spam. My husband, on the other hand, thinks such personalization is cool, particularly if the coupon were to appear in the steak aisle at Costco. But he's a technical neophyte and doesn't seem to get those deals. A friend of mine who also works in IT routinely deletes his browser cookies and never, ever turns on location awareness on his phone. Lucky for him he's never lost his phone! I'm careful about sharing too much data, and despite that, I still get the creepy text messages on a cell phone number that I use only for personal calls. Someone, somewhere probably didn't protect my cell phone number as carefully as they should have.

It worries me too, that in talking about data and privacy with a medical doctor, he said he hesitates to put some patient information in an electronic medical record because such data gets shared more rapidly than paper files once did. If people—whether doctors, teachers, or business people—intentionally omit data that may be relevant to a diagnosis or a decision out of fear of how that data will eventually be used, there is an enormous downside. In everything, the benefit of providing or omitting the data has to be weighed against the risk, and the likelihood that the data would be lost, stolen, or used inappropriately. This same doctor suggested the U.S. government needs a new cabinet position, that of a chief data officer, to help organizations more safely store and share data. It's an interesting thought—agriculture and transportation have some oversight but not the data that fuels the new economy. The flip side, of course, is fear that such a government involvement might stifle, rather than foster, innovation in this area.

This range of views shows that privacy concerns will vary by age, knowledge of what's happening, and the value provided to the customer. If customers and business partners are willing to provide you with private information, you need to protect that data and treat it as a limited resource, the "new oil," as it were.

Evolving Your Capabilities

Technical innovation is only one aspect that will help increase BI's prevalence. In discussing future plans with many of the case study companies, much of their concern was not about technology, but rather, in finding new ways to use BI to address common business problems. For the more large-scale deployments, some expressed concern about managing the risk of making any kind of major change to such a business-critical, complex application. With success, of course, come greater demands on the systems and the people. Ensuring an effective way of prioritizing competing requests warrants constant attention. One business leader expressed frustration at his department's inability to make wise investments, while witnessing other departments working in more unison and getting more value from business intelligence. Yet he remains optimistic that his business will get there and that BI will be the first thing people look at, even before e-mail. "To have one screen I can get to with a single click that shows sales, margin, price, opportunities in graphical form, with drill-down—that would be magic!" His comments remind me that the technology is sometimes the easy part; getting the organization aligned is harder. Even the most successful BI companies, then, continue to have their battles.

Industries, companies, and individual departments and business units will evolve their BI capabilities at different paces. No matter where you are on your BI journey, you have to evolve the people, treatment of data, processes, and technology. It's easy to fix the technology. It's much harder to change the people and culture. Use the model in Figure 14-6 to assess where you are today and to develop a roadmap for your future BI capabilities.

BI Maturity Model

People, Culture & Organization	• Gut-feel decision making	• Individual departments dabbling with BI • Executives and managers do not allow data to be shared until fully vetted • BI used only by power users • Fact-based decision making valued but hindered by poor data access	• Executives support broader BI initiatives • BI teams struggle to keep pace with demand, conflicting priorities • Reactive Data Governance	• BICC with business alignment and cross-staffed teams • Proactive Data Governance • Executives use BI as well as frontline workers • Hypotheses backed by facts; alternative views encouraged • Business uses self-service BI; IT handles complex requests. • KPIs provide organizational alignment
Process	• Reports provided by operational systems	• BI needs considered in application design • First-in, first-out prioritization • Backlog of reporting requests • Waterfall development	• Transparent process for new and enhancement requests • Project oriented • BI productivity measured • Agile development	• Proactive alignment of BI to business goals • BI experts involved in business problem solving • Program approach • Value-based prioritization
Data	• Data quality unknown • Data captured but not used beyond operational process	• Poor data quality • Inconsistent master data • Data quality considered an IT problem • Silo'd data marts	• Good data quality • Uni-directional MDM for some reference data • Data standards and common business definitions being developed • Centralized data warehouse with dependent and independent data marts	• Data validated at source • Bi-directional MDM • External and internal data considered strategic assets • Business glossary and data lineage accessible
Technology	• Multiple ERP systems • Reporting only within operational system • Overreliance on spreadsheets	• Standardized ERP system per functional area, business unit, or region • Custom, hand-coded ETL • Business query and production reporting tools from multiple vendors deployed	• Commercial ETL tools • Standardized BI platform • Standardized metadata platform • Variable query performance	• Consistent ERP approach • Analytic eco system that includes EDW, analytic database, Big Data as needed • Fast query performance • Right tool for right user with BI platform complemented with specialty tools to include self-service, dashboards, predictive, visual discovery, and mobile BI

Figure 14-6   A model to benchmark your BI maturity

Words of Wisdom

I hope this book will inspire you to ensure BI and data have a profound impact on your organization. I'd like to see the techniques and insights shared by the most successful BI companies and the innovations from leading and niche vendors help move the industry beyond the current average of 24 percent adoption, 24 percent very successful, and 34 percent significant impact to much higher rates. Business intelligence is all encompassing in its ability to improve an organization's efficiency, competitiveness, and opportunities. Through the process of writing and researching this book, these business intelligence visionaries have assured me that this way of thinking is not just analyst-speak or vendor hype; it can be a reality. Following are some words of wisdom that I hope will inspire and guide you as you strive to make business intelligence a wild success in your company.

"Slicing and dicing the data has to be easier—easier than picking up a piece of paper. Even then, there is an education that needs to happen—getting people to *think* business intelligence."

—Dr. Ray Iannaconne, vice president of operations,
Emergency Medical Associates

"Make your first BI solution embarrassingly small in scope and build to the biggest pain point."

—Mike Masciandaro, business intelligence director,
The Dow Chemical Company

"Strong management and a cultural change have most contributed to our success. The CEO got Norway Post to be more business oriented, and the CFO drove the management system. In adopting this cultural change to one of accountability, sometimes we had to change the people."

—Dag Vidar Olsen, former manager Business Intelligence
Competency Center, Norway Post

"To our surprise, the applications and markets we serve are much larger than we envisioned and we are now an integral part of the global transportation market. As we retool our platform to take full advantage of new technology such as NoSQL, cloud-based processing and distribution, and big-data analytics, we believe we will continue to grow the market by supporting even more use cases."

—Jeff Kennedy, CEO, FlightStats

"Our business intelligence initiative has been a terrific success in the way we can optimize our team and the greater sense of control of the business. We are always tweaking things. Before, too many decisions were based on assumptions, generality, anecdotal, off the gut. It's made us more agile as a company."

—*Dave Walker, vice president of operations, 1-800 CONTACTS*

"Data should not be a substitute for business decision-making, but rather a torch to help illuminate which business actions are likely best."[8]

—*Jesse Harris, chief analytics officer, Constant Contact*

"Start small and prototype. Data is where it's all about, not the technology. The outcomes of the data drive the decisions and the growth. Establish clear data governance and usability. Get the top people in this space. Consider both the soft and hard skills."

—*Mike Hedges, chief information officer, Medtronic*

Appendix A

Successful BI Survey Demographics

The Successful BI survey was conducted from June through September 2012, with 634 qualified respondents. Questions that involved ranking of items used a survey feature to randomize the order of the displayed options so that results were not skewed by the order of the possible selections. The survey was promoted through The Data Warehousing Institute (TDWI) newsletters and articles, *Information Week* newsletters, BI Scorecard newsletters, and social media. The survey is run periodically, either annually or every 18 months. If you wish to take the survey, please register via the BI Scorecard website to be notified when the survey is open. Survey respondents are provided a complimentary copy of the summary findings. Figure A-1 provides survey demographics by company revenues. Figure A-2 provides survey graphics according to the respondent's geographic location. Figure A-3 shows survey demographics by user role within the organization. Figure A-4 shows survey demographics by industry.

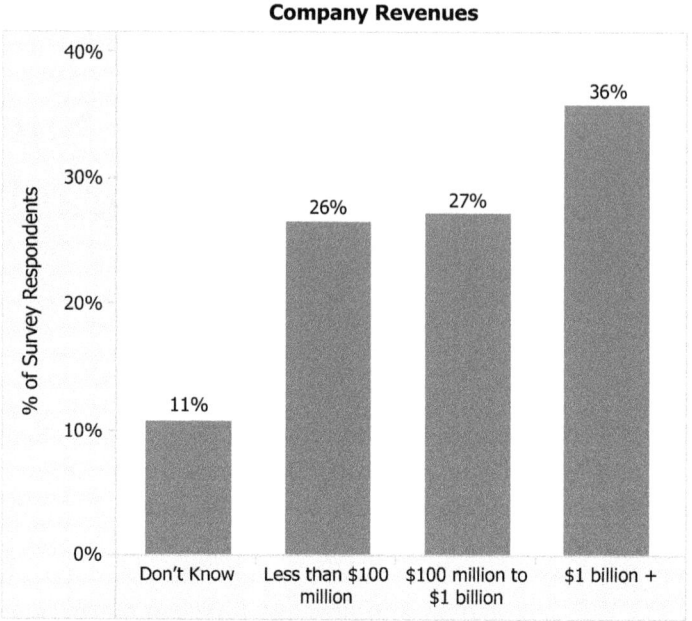

Figure A-1 Survey demographics by company revenues

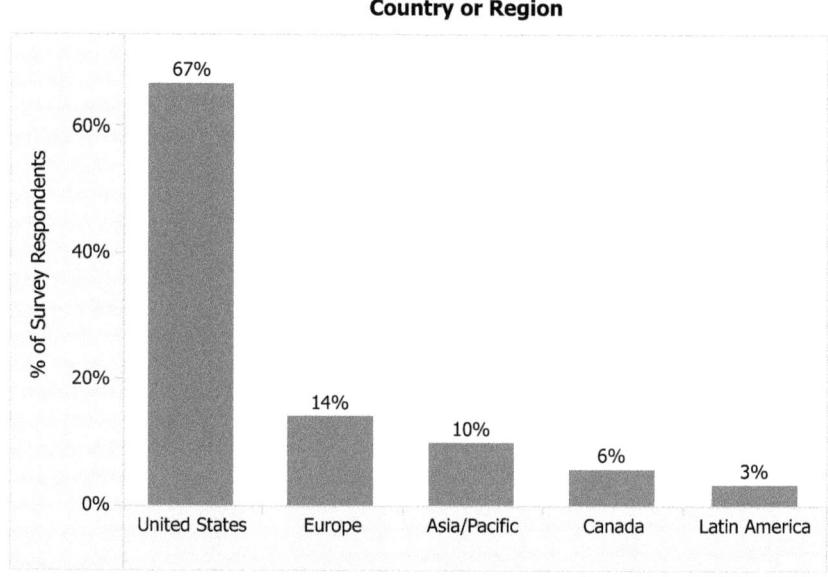

Figure A-2 Survey demographics by world region

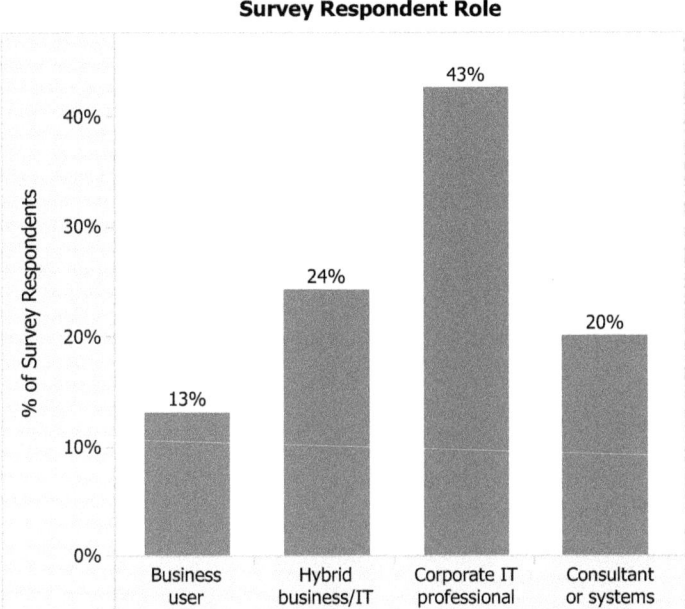

Figure A-3   Survey demographics by functional expertise and role

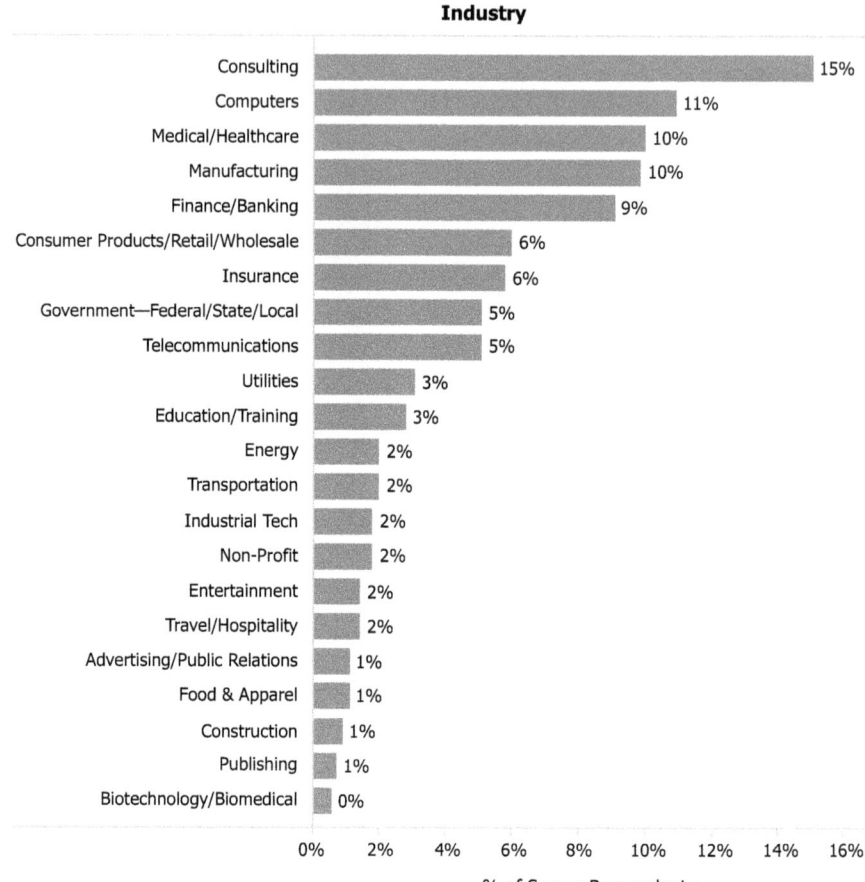

Figure A-4   Survey demographics by industry

Recommended Resources

There are dozens of excellent resources on data warehousing, business intelligence, and big data. Some are relevant to a specific vendor's solution, and some are more conceptual in nature.

Following are a few recommended reads:

Agile Data Warehousing Project Management: Business Intelligence Systems Using Scrum by Ralph Hughes (Morgan Kaufmann, 2012)

Big Data for Dummies by Judith Hurwitz, Alan Nugent, Dr. Fern Halper, and Marcia Kaufman (For Dummies, 2013)

Building the Data Warehouse by William Inmon (Wiley, 2005)

Business Intelligence: The Savvy Manager's Guide by David Loshin (Morgan Kaufmann, 2003)

Business Intelligence Roadmap: The Complete Project Lifecycle for Decision-Support Applications by Larissa Moss and Shaku Atre (Addison-Wesley Professional, 2003)

Competing on Analytics (Harvard Business School Press, 2007) and *Analytics at Work* (Harvard Business Review Press, 2010) by Thomas Davenport and Jeanne Harris

Customer Data Integration: Reaching a Single Version of the Truth by Jill Dyche and Evan Levy (Wiley, 2006)

Data Modeling Made Simple: A Practical Guide for Business and Information Technology Professionals by Steve Hoberman (Take IT With You Series, 2009)

The Data Warehouse Toolkit: The Complete Guide to Dimensional Modeling by Ralph Kimball and Margy Ross (Wiley, 2013)

Information Dashboard Design: The Effective Visual Communication of Data (O'Reilly Media, 2006) and *Show Me the Numbers* (Analytics Press, 2012) by Stephen Few

A Manager's Guide to Data Warehousing by Laura Reeves (Wiley, 2009)

Performance Dashboards (Wiley, 2010) and *Secrets of Analytical Leaders* (Technics Publications, LLC, 2012) by Wayne Eckerson

Predictive Analytics: The Power to Predict Who Will Click, Lie, or Die by Eric Siegel (Wiley, 2013)

Smart Enough Systems: How to Deliver Competitive Advantage by Automating Hidden Decisions by James Taylor and Neil Raden (Prentice Hall, 2007)

Following are a few media resources that focus on business intelligence and big data:

Information Management (www.information-management.com)

Information Week, either the Software Business Intelligence channel or Big Data channel (www.informationweek.com/software/business-intelligence)

The Data Warehousing Institute (www.tdwi.org)—Sign up for *BI This Week* newsletter

Notes

Chapter 1

1. Lohr, Steve, "The Origins of 'Big Data': An Etymological Detective Story," *New York Times*, February 1, 2013.
2. Laney, Doug,"Deja VVVu: Others Claiming Gartner's Construct for Big Data," Gartner Blog, January 2012.
3. Davenport, Thomas, *Competing on Analytics,* HBS, 2007, p. 45.
4. *Outperforming in a data-rich, hyper-connected world,* IBM Center for Applied Insights study conducted in cooperation with the Economist Intelligence Unit and the IBM Institute of Business Value, 2012.
5. Collins, Jim, *Good to Great: Why Some Companies Make the Leap... and Others Don't,* 2001, p. 79.
6. Walt Disney World presentation, Business Objects User Conference, 2005.
7. Arbiter, Brandon, Fresh Direct presentation, SAP Influencer Summit, December 2011.
8. Vandevanter, Kay, and McDaniel, Mark A., Boeing, Gartner Summit presentation, March 2013.
9. *Computerworld* Technology Briefing, "The Business Value of Analytics."
10. Nugent, Karen, software engineer, Continental Airlines, interview notes, April 2005.
11. Dempsey, Andrew, Netflix interview, February 13, 2013.
12. Information Builders press release, March 19, 2007.
13. Cody, Crystal, systems and application manager, Charlotte Police Department, Information Builders Summit conference, June 2011.
14. Thomas, Kim, "Humberside Police Updates Criminal Intelligence Databases," *Computing,* March 15, 2007.
15. Cleveland Clinic, interview notes, April 2012.
16. Howson, Cindi, "Ease of Use and Interface Appeal in BI Tools," B-EYE Network, 2010.
17. DeFord, Drex, CIO, Seattle Children's Hospital, TDWI presentation, May 2012.
18. Gray, Elizabeth, acting assistant director, Austin Fire Department, TDWI presentation, May 2012.
19. ASUG User Conference presentation, September 2012.

20. Teichman, Steve, Medtronic, SAP Tech Ed presentation, October, 2011.
21. McGregor, Carolyn, "Big Data & Analytics Client Use Cases," IBM Analyst Summit, June 2013.
22. Wimmer, Hermann, "Measure What Can Be Measured– Footballonomics and Today's Decision Makers," Teradata blog, April 17, 2013.
23. Wikipedia.
24. Wagner, Kurt, "Nate Silver: What Big Data Can't Predict," Forbes, April 26, 2013
25. Vesset, et al., "Worldwide Business Analytics Software 2013–2017 Forecast and 2012 Vendor Shares," IDC, July 2013.
26. Pew Research Center, "Internet and American Life Survey," February 2013.
27. IDC Digital Universe study, "Big Data, Bigger Digital Shadows, and Biggest Growth in the Far East," December 2012.
28. Gens, Frank, "IDC Predictions 2012: Competing for 2020," 2011.
29. McGee, M. "Managers Have Too Much Information, Do Too Little Sharing," *InformationWeek,* January 8, 2007.
30. Graham, Fiona, "Pretty Pictures: Can Images Stop Data Overload?," BBC News, April 16, 2012.
31. Acohido, Byron, "Microsoft's New World View," USA Today, April 15, 2013.
32. Wikipedia.

Chapter 2

1. Russom, Philip, "Next Generation Master Data Management," TDWI Research, Q2 2012.
2. Watson, Hugh, "Which Data Warehouse Architecture Is Most Successful," *Business Intelligence Journal,* Q1 2006.
3. TDWI, *What Works,* November 2006, "Enhancing the Customer Experience and Improving Retention Using Powerful Data Warehousing Appliances," November 2006.
4. Madsen, Mark, "Evaluating New Database Technologies for Data Warehousing and Analytics," TDWI Class, November 2012.
5. Monash, Curt, interview notes, May 2013
6. Dow Chemical, interview notes, March 10, 2013.
7. Constant Contact customer presentation, New England Netezza User Group, April 2013.
8. Ferguson, Mike, and Howson, Cindi, "Cloud-Based BI: A Market Study," February 2012.

9. Krishnan, Sriram, and Tse, Eva, "Data Science & Engineering, Hadoop Platform as a Service in the Cloud," Netflix Technical blog, January 10, 2013.
10. FlightStats, interview notes, March 12, 2013.
11. Menzie, Dean, Huntington Bank presentation at MicroStrategy World and webcast, January 2013.
12. McClellan, Ed, The Learning Circle, interview notes, February 2012.
13. Groff, James, and Weinberg, Paul, *SQL: The Complete Reference*: McGraw-Hill/Osborne, 2002, p. 4.
14. www.noSQL-database.org.
15. Hurwitz, Judith, et al., *Big Data for Dummies*, Wiley, 2013.
16. Datanami, "Six Super-Scale Hadoop Deployments," April 26, 2012.
17. FlightStats, interview notes, March 12, 2013.
18. Russom, Phillip, "Integrating Hadoop into BI and DW," TDWI research report, April 2013.
19. Macys.com, interview notes, March 20, 2013.

Chapter 3

1. Few, Stephen, *Information Dashboard Design*, Analytics Press, 2013, p. 26.
2. Eckerson, Wayne, *Performance Dashboards: Measuring, Monitoring, and Managing Your Business*, Wiley, 2010.
3. Schiff, Craig, "Performance Management Gap: Goals versus Reality," *Business Intelligence Network*, August 23, 2012.
4. Morris, Henry, "Trends in Analytic Applications," *DM Review*, April 2001.
5. Davenport, Thomas, "Data Scientist: The Sexiest Job of the 21st Century," *Harvard Business Review*, October 2012.

Chapter 4

1. Atre, Shaku, "The Top 10 Critical Challenges for Business Intelligence Success," *Computerworld*, June 30, 2003.
2. Learning Circle, interview notes, February 2013.
3. Nationwide presentation, Information Builders Summit, June 2009.
4. Netflix, interview notes, February 2013.
5. "Netflix Long-Term View," www.ir.netflix.com, April 25, 2013.
6. www.ir.Netflix.com.
7. Cohan, Peter, "How Netflix Reinvented Itself," Forbes.com, April 23, 2013.
8. Netflix Quarterly Earnings, July 22, 2013.

9. Boulon, Jerome, "Using Big Data at Netflix to Grow Our Business," Cloud Connect presentation, February 2012.
10. Wong, Albert, Netflix, *MicroStrategy World,* January 2013.
11. S. Paul Wright, John T. White, William L. Sanders, and June C. Rivers, "SAS EVAAS Statistical Models," March 25, 2010.
12. Constant Contact, interview notes, July 2013.
13. Constant Contact, New England Netezza User's Group presentation, April 2013.
14. Morris, Henry, et al., "The Financial Impact of Business Analytics, an IDC ROI Study," December 2002.
15. Lipsitz, Jonathan W., "The Total Economic Impact of Oracle Business Intelligence Applications," October 2012.
16. Novation, interview notes, September 2012,
17. Customer presentation, Oracle Open World 2012,
18. Gray, Elizabeth, Austin Fire Department presentation, TDWI, April 2012.
19. IBM Cognos Analyst Summit, June 2013.
20. Klein, Allen, *Up Words for Down Days,* Gramercy Books, 1998.

Chapter 5

1. WorldofQuotes.com.
2. Computerworld Honors Program 2005.
3. Richardson, Karen, "Keeping Accounting Close to Home," *The Wall Street Journal,* October 29, 2006.
4. FlightStats, interview notes, April 2007.
5. DOT, Bureau of Transportation Statistics website (http://usgovinfo.about.com/gi/dynamic/offsite.htm?site=http://www.dot.gov/airconsumer).
6. FlightStats, interview notes, April 2007.
7. FlightStats website (www.flightstats.com).
8. FlightStats, interview notes, March 2013.
9. Emergency Medical Associates, interview notes, April 2007.
10. EMA, website video.
11. EBMI, interview notes and company brochure, June 2013.
12. EMA, interview notes, July 2013.
13. Tullo, Alex, "Dow Will Cut Workforce by 8%," *Chemical & Engineering News,* May 7, 2001.
14. The Dow Chemical Company, interview notes, May 2007.
15. Dow, interview notes, June 2013.
16. Macy's, interview notes, March 2013.
17. National Retail Federation & U.S. Department of Commerce, "NRF Forecasts 3.4% Increase in Retail Sales for 2013," press release, January 28, 2013.

18. Macy's annual report and five-year performance.
19. www.wikipedia.org/wiki/Macy's.
20. Macysinc.com, Press Room, Macy's History.
21. 1-800 CONTACTS website, company profile.
22. 1-800 CONTACTS, interview notes, May 2007.
23. http://dealbook.nytimes.com/2012/06/04/wellpoint-acquires-1-800-contacts/?_r=0.
24. SAS Customer Story, "Macy's.com Sees What's in Store for Customers with SAS Business Analytics."
25. Gayathri, Amrutha, "U.S. 17th in Global Education Ranking; Finland, South Korea Claim Top Spots," *International Business Times,* November 27, 2012.
26. Ohio Department of Education, Graduation Rates Report Card.
27. Learning Circle, interview notes, February 2013.
28. Columbus City Dispatch, "Counting Kids Out" video: http://www.dispatch.com/content/topic/special-reports/2012/counting-kids-out.html.
29. The Forums Institute for Public Policy, "An Overview of Charity Care in NJ—Past, Present and Future," September 29, 2004.
30. New Jersey Hospital Association, "What Will Happen to My Hospital?" 2007.
31. Joint Commission website (www.jointcommission.org).
32. EMA web site.
33. http://www.evancarmichael.com/Famous-Entrepreneurs/5338/Reed-Hastings-Quotes.html.
34. Medtronic, interview notes, May 2013.
35. http://newsroom.medtronic.com/phoenix.zhtml?c=251324&p=irol-overview.
36. www.medtronic.com/aboutus.

Chapter 6

1. Eric Lundquist, "CIO Role in 2013: Four-Headed Monster?" August 14, 2012.
2. Julian Goldsmith, "CIOs Dismissed as Techies Without Business Savvy by CEOs." *ComputerWorld UK,* April 18, 2012.
3. "Business Intelligence Strategy: A Practical Guide for Achieving BI Excellence," IBM, 2010, p. 38.
4. Constant Contact, interview notes, July 2013.
5. Lutchen, Mark, *Managing IT as a Business,* Wiley, 2004, p. 33.
6. Constant Contact, interview notes, July 2013.
7. "Business Intelligence Strategy: A Practical Guide for Achieving BI Excellence," IBM, 2010, p. 45.
8. Murphy, Chris, "P&G CEO Shares 3 Steps to Analytics-Driven Business," *Information Week,* February 7, 2013.

9. Netflix, interview notes, February 2013.
10. Collins, Jim, *Good to Great,* HarperCollins, 2001, p. 70.
11. Dow, interview notes, February 2013.
12. Emergency Medical Associates, interview notes, April 2007.
13. Hammond et al., "The Hidden Traps in Decision Making," *Harvard Business Review,* 1998.
14. Gladwell, Malcolm, "The Formula: Enron, Intelligence, and the Perils of Too Much Information," *New Yorker,* January 8, 2007.
15. Hammond et al., "The Hidden Traps in Decision Making," *Harvard Business Review,* 1998.

Chapter 7

1. Wikipedia.
2. 168 Feng Shui Advisors, Yin and Yang Theory (website)
3. Martin, Charles, Ph.D., *Looking at Type and Careers,* Center for Applications of Psychological Type, 1995.
4. Ibid, p. 19.
5. Martin, Charles, *Your Career: Looking at Type,* CAPT, 2009.
6. Ibid, p. 42 and 50.
7. Ibid.
8. Rudin, Ken, "Facebook," TDWI Presentation, May 2013.
9. Netflix, interview notes, February 2013.
10. Kaplan, Robert, and Norton, David, *Alignment,* Harvard Business School Press, 2006, p. 3.
11. Dr. Jacknis, Dr. Norman, "Beyond Typical Business Intelligence," *Network Computing,* November 9, 2006.
12. Dow Chemical, interview notes, May 2007.
13. Dow, interview notes, February 2013,
14. FlightStats, interview notes, March 2013.

Chapter 8

1. English, Larry, "Do We Need a Clean Information Quality Act?" *Business Intelligence Network,* May 9, 2007.
2. English, Larry, "Plain English about Information Quality: Information Quality Tipping Point," *DM Review,* January 2007.
3. www.dataladder.com/blog/2011/09/20/dirty-data-debacle-a-3-1-trillion-problem/.
4. Friedman, Ted, Gartner, Information Builders Summit presentation, June 2013.
5. Dyche, Jill, and Levy, Evan, *Customer Data Integration,* Wiley, 2006, p. 145.
6. 1-800 CONTACT, Interview notes, April 2013.

7. Costa, Mike, board of directors, Central Michigan University Research Corporation, interview notes, May 2007.
8. Harry, Mikel, and Schroeder, Richard, *Six Sigma: The Breakthrough Management Strategy Revolutionizing the World's Top Corporations*, Doubleday, 2000.
9. Ibid, p 14.
10. Department of Transportation, "Airline On-Time Performance Slips, Cancellations and Mishandled Bags Up in June," August 6, 2007.
11. Dow, interview notes, February 2013.
12. www.dow.com/investers/jointventures.
13. Medtronic, interview notes, May 2013.
14. Norway Post, interview notes, May 2007.
15. Norway Post, Annual Report, 2008.
16. *Deutsche Welle*, "EU Backs Plans to Liberalize Mail Delivery Market from 2011," July 11, 2007.
17. Norway Post presentation, Hyperion user conference, April 2006.
18. Ariyachandra, Thilini, and Watson, Hugh, "Which Data Warehouse Architecture is Most Successful," *Business Intelligence Journal*, First Quarter 2006.
19. King.com, user interview, QlikTech presentation, November 2011.
20. Whyte, Jim, corporate data architect, The Dow Chemical Company, "Dow's Master Data Management Business Processes," Chemical Industry SAP User Group, April 2006.
21. Dow, user interview, February 2013.
22. Medtronic, user interview, May 2013.
23. White, Colin, "Building the Real-Time Enterprise," *TDWI Report Series*, November 2003.
24. 1-800 CONTACTS, interview notes, May 2007.
25. Hackathorn, Richard, "The BI Watch: Real-Time to Real-Value," *DM Review*, January 2004.
26. FlightStats, interview notes, April 2007.

Chapter 9

1. 1-800 CONTACTS, interview notes, July 2006.
2. Frankel, Glenn, "Britain: U.S. Told of Vaccine Shortage," *Washington Post*, October 9, 2004.
3. Whiting, Rick, "BI Tracks Disease Outbreaks," *Intelligent Enterprise*, November 2005.
4. Emergency Medical Associates, interview notes, April 2007.
5. Costello, Tom, "Hospitals Work to Improve ER Wait Times," *NBC News*, November 20, 2006.
6. GAO-09-347 Emergency Department Crowding, April 2009.
7. Emergency Medical Associates, interview notes, April 2007.

8. Robb, Drew, "EMA: Measuring the Emergency Room's Pulse," *Computerworld,* September 18, 2006.
9. Learning Circle, user interview, April 2013.
10. Levitt, Steven, and Dubner, Stephen, *Freakonomics: A Rogue Economist Explores the Hidden Side of Everything,* HarperCollins Publishers, 2005, p 7.
11. Welsh, Patrick, "Don't Judge Teachers' Test Scores," *USA Today,* June 5, 2013.
12. Raden, Neil, "Toppling the BI Pyramid," *DM Review,* January 2007.
13. Netflix company website, Long-Term View, April 25, 2013. http://ir.netflix.com/long-term-view.cfm.
14. Kaye, Kate, "At Starbucks, Data Pours In. But What to Do With It?" *Ad Age,* March 22, 2013.
15. Constant Contact, interview notes, July 2013.
16. Lundin, Barbara, "UK Smart Meter Plan Could Be Too Ambitious," *FierceEnergy,* July 3, 2013.
17. http://stopsmartmeters.org.uk/.

Chapter 10

1. Heldman, Kim, *Project Management Professional Study Guide,* Sybex: 2013.
2. http://www.agilemanifesto.org/history.html.
3. http://www.ambysoft.com/surveys/agileMarch2007.html.
4. Ambler, Scott, "Results from Scott Ambler's July 2010 State of the IT Union Survey, " posted at www.agilemodeling.com/surveys/
5. Schwaber, Ken and Sutherland, Jeff, *The Scrum Guide,* October 2011.
6. Hughes, Ralph, *Agile Data Warehousing,* iUniverse, 2008.
7. Hughes, Ralph, interview notes, June 2013.
8. http://www.infoq.com/articles/hiranabe-lean-agile-kanban.
9. http://agile.techwell.com/articles/weekly/what-best-scrum-or-kanban.
10. http://en.wikipedia.org/wiki/Kanban_(development).
11. Watson, Hugh, "Are Data Warehouses Prone to Failure?" *TDWI Journal,* Fall 2005, 454 respondents.
12. Netflix presentation on culture, http://jobs.netflix.com/jobs.html.
13. http://www.evancarmichael.com/Famous-Entrepreneurs/5338/Reed-Hastings-Quotes.html.
14. Netflix press release, October 10, 2011.
15. Netflix, Interview notes, February 2013.
16. Tseitlin, Ariel, et al, "Announcing Ice Cloud Spend and Usage Analytics," Netflix Technical Blog, June 2013.
17. Medtronic, interview notes, May 2013.
18. 1-800 CONTACTS, interview notes, May 2007.

Chapter 11

1. www.modelt.org/tquotes.html.
2. Wikipedia.
3. Eckerson, Wayne, and Howson, Cindi, "Enterprise Business Intelligence," *TDWI Report Series*, August 2005.
4. 1-800 CONTACTS, interview notes and e-mails, April 2007 and September 2007.
5. Miller et al., *Business Intelligence Competency Centers*, Wiley, 2006.
6. Netflix, interview notes, February 2013.
7. Rudin, Ken, Facebook, TDWI Keynote, May 2013.
8. www.ni.com/case-studies.
9. National Instruments, interview notes, April 2012.
10. Cognos Analyst Summit, customer presentation, September 2007.
11. Kanter, Rosabeth, *e-volve! Succeeding in the Digital Culture of Tomorrow*, Harvard Business School Press, 2001, p. 205.
12. Collins, Jim, *Good to Great*, p. 21.
13. 1-800 CONTACTS, interview notes, April 2007.

Chapter 12

1. Microsoft User Conference, May 2007.
2. Taylor, James, and Raden, Neil, *Smart Enough Systems*, Prentice Hall: 2007, p. 15.
3. Jim Jelter, "Kodak Restates, Adds $9 Million to Loss," *MarketWatch*, Nov. 9, 2005.
4. "RedEnvelope Cuts Outlook, Shares Fall, CFO Eric Wong Resigns Amid Budget Errors," Associated Press, March 29, 2005.
5. Schenker, Lisa, "Utah Education Officials Make $25m School Funding Mistake," *The Salt Lake Tribune*, April 11, 2012.
6. Coy, Peter, "FAQ: Reinhart, Rogoff, and the Excel Error That Changed History," *Bloomberg BusinessWeek*, April 18, 2013.

Chapter 13

1. King, Julia, "No 1 Place to Work in IT: USAA," *Computerworld*, June 21, 2010.
2. Burks, Ricky, and Thomas, Charles, "USAA: The Analytics Advantage: Converting Big Data to Business Growth," Computerworld presentation, September 2012.
3. Kaplan, Rachel, "CIO Michael Hedges: Medtronic," *Minneapolis St. Paul Business Journal*, September 2011.
4. Boicey, Charles, interview notes, June 2013.

5. McKinley, Scott, "Nielsen," IBM Business Analytics presentation, June 2013.
6. Innovate1st.com, "Conversations on the Cutting Edge, Interview with Scott McKinley," February 2013.
7. Emergency Medical Associates, interview notes, April 2007.

Chapter 14

1. Byrne, Tony, CMSWatch, interview notes, August 2007.
2. BlueCross BlueShield of Tennessee, interview notes, April 4, 2007.
3. BlueCross BlueShield BCBS of Tennessee, 2006 Annual Report.
4. Morris, Henry, "Bridging the Structured/Unstructured Data Gap at BCBS of TN," *IDC Opinion*, December 2006.
5. BlueCross BlueShield of Tennessee, interview notes, April 4, 2007.
6. Medtronic, interview notes, May 2013.
7. Winter, Richard, Gilbert, Rick, and Davis, Judith, R. "Big Data: What Does It Really Cost? A WinterCorp Special Report," August 2013.
8. Isson, Jean-Paul, and Harris, Jesse, *Win with Advanced Business Analytics*, Wiley & SAS Press, 2013, p. 88.

Index

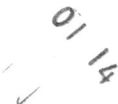

Milton Keynes UK
Ingram Content Group UK Ltd.
UKHW021959300923
429691UK00009B/126

9 781265 943042